WHOLE
TRUTH

So Help Me God

the
WHOLE
TRUTH

So Help Me God

An Enlightened Testimony
from Inside ENRON'S Executive Offices

Published by Tate Publishing & Enterprises, LLC
127 E. Trade Center Terrace | Mustang, Oklahoma 73064 USA
1.888.361.9473 | www.tatepublishing.com

Tate Publishing is committed to excellence in the publishing industry. The company reflects the philosophy established by the founders, based on Psalm 68:11,
"The Lord gave the word and great was the company of those who published it."

Book design copyright © 2007 by Tate Publishing, LLC. All rights reserved.
Cover design by Leah LeFlore
Interior design by Kandi evans

Published in the United States of America
ISBN: 978-1-60247-905-0
1. Business: Business Ethics
2. Corporate Finance
08.02.25

Dedication

In loving memory of my friend and mentor, Ken Lay, who believed in me; a little five-year-old boy, Jake Nieto, who saved me; and my two-year-old Great Pyrenees, who loved me unconditionally.

Acknowledgments

First and foremost I am thankful to God for providing me the life experiences that I not only write about in this book, but that have made me who I am today. I thank him for bringing many wonderful people into my life: the friends who have helped me write this book, the people I worked with at Enron, my family, and my wonderful husband.

This book would not have happened had it not been for those who encouraged me to tell my story. Joe Nieto, a friend of many years, was the first person to plant the seed of this book. Sarah Davis, another good friend with whom I worked for many years at Enron, also encouraged me to write. In addition, both of these people have been a significant part of my walk of faith.

There have been countless people who have helped edit, rewrite and remember things that I had forgotten. These people include, but are not limited to, Terrie James, Beth Tilney, Patrick Stupeck, Howard Jefferson, Kelly Kimberly, Lynn Brewer, Bob Sparger, Sherron Watkins, Amber Alexander, Elyse Kalmans, Rick Causey, Kevin Hannon and Liz Lay Vittor. I appreciate all the help and suggestions these people have taken the time to give me, but most of all I appreciate their friendship.

Of course I could never have conceived of this book had it not been for the unbelievable experiences that

Enron provided me. I lived a fairy-tale career and had the opportunity to know and work for one of the most wonderful men anyone could hope to know—Ken Lay. I am also thankful for the countless other creative and outstanding people I had the opportunity to work with at Enron.

Thanks to all of my family. My mother, my dad, my sister and brother are all priceless. They each played a positive and significant role in my growing up and becoming who I am today. Every one of them offered me crucial support in the wake of the Enron collapse. Their love has empowered me to share this story.

Finally, I thank my wonderful husband, Grady. My hope is that we will have many more years together growing stronger in our faith, raising our "kids with fur," and learning to enjoy and love each other more and more each day that we have on this earth together.

Table of Contents

Author's Note

As I was finishing the editing process on this book an article appeared in *USA Today* featuring Lynn Brewer. I had previously asked her to write the foreword for my book because she alerted me in 2002 of an attempt by a member of Congress to set me up for perjury during the congressional hearings, shortly after Enron had filed for bankruptcy. I felt, as I do today, that this set the stage for the basis for my book, *The Whole Truth…So Help Me God.* I have realized, through this enlightening experience we all went through at Enron, how so often the whole truth does not get told and thus errors in judgment get made by those on the outside based upon the media's slant on the truth, hurting people trying to do the right thing.

Although I never met Lynn while she was at Enron, long after she had left the company she contacted me to organize a Day of Healing for the ex-employees immediately after the company filed for bankruptcy and laid off nearly four thousand workers. Unfortunately, we both got shut down as there were very few people in Houston interested in helping anyone from Enron.

The *USA Today* article focused on the fact that she had written a book, which Lynn told me about in February 2002 when she flew to Houston to discuss the Day of Healing. The article highlighted that Lynn was calling herself an Enron executive, when in fact she was a senior specialist. Although I have no personal knowledge of the level of work that she did while at Enron, I thought that she might have been tempted to sensationalize her actual title for her book. The article also confirmed that she was calling herself a "whistleblower", creating a possible confusion between her and Sherron Watkins.

My personal knowledge of Lynn's effort to help her former colleagues in late 2001 and her attempt to "blow the whistle" on a member of Congress to me in 2002 was not motivated by anything other than her effort to help others.

She and I got back in touch with one another after she got my contact information from Ken Lay, who she met with a few weeks before his death in 2006. We talked about what a great man he was during those conversations and I realized that Lynn did understand something that not everyone got—Ken Lay was a wonderful person who was truly saddened by all that had happened. She was right about Ken and the tape she had sent me was certainly the "truth." (An audio recording of the actual conversation is posted on my website at www.cindykay-olson.com.)

I had numerous people call me and tell me they thought I should take this foreword out of my book because of what the recent article said about Lynn. For a moment I actually considered doing just that and then my heart told me that I personally knew everything in the foreword she had written was the "truth." If I chose to remove her foreword I would, in fact, be treating her like I had been treated by so many people that I write about in this book. Only telling a partial truth was what all of us were forced to do. At the end of the day I decided that I had to be true to one of the messages I was sending in my story. I decided to tell *The Whole Truth...So Help Me God*.

The following is the foreword Lynn Brewer wrote, and I am proud to have it as a part of my story.

Foreword

Life for most of us has an element of predictability—the sun rises in the east and sets in the west unless something has gone terribly wrong. For those of us who worked at Enron, one minute we were on top of the world and the next we felt lost at sea. Many of us had risen to the top believing we were in charge of our own destinies, yet those of us who were able to grow through the experience were reminded that even the predictable can become unpredictable. We are the beneficiaries of grace, who have learned that ultimately the only sustainable thing we have is our faith in God.

I have also learned that the need to have every question answered may circumvent faith. Perhaps two roads do diverge in a wood—or perhaps in retrospect they are really the same path, momentarily divided, only to be joined again beyond the horizon. Perhaps it is only on the backside of our lives that we are able to see the picture created from these finely woven paths we take. At times we believe we know our way. At times we believe we are lost. Ultimately, I believe we must all realize that it is only in letting go of the need to control our direction that we will find our way.

As a former mid-level employee, and one of the first to call an outside party about what I saw happening at Enron, I relied on one scripture. Proverbs 3:5–6 proclaims, "Trust in the Lord with all your heart and lean not on your own understanding; in all your ways acknowledge Him and He will make your paths straight." It was at the time I was relying on this scripture, a time of great chaos and uncertainty, that by the Grace of God, my life would intersect with Cindy Olson's.

I had watched Cindy from afar, quite frankly often finding myself envious of her position within the company. The "truth" as I saw it was that Cindy had gotten "lucky." It had never occurred to me that maybe she had actually worked hard during her time at Enron; that perhaps at times she had sacrificed her own happiness for the greater good of the corporation. In hindsight, I believe Cindy Olson is perhaps responsible in some way or another for every (and I do mean every) great experience I and others had at Enron. Although I had never personally met Cindy until after I had left Enron, there were two things about her that impressed me during my time there: her constant, infectious smile, and her love for the company and its role in the community—the very thing that had made Enron great.

It was Cindy's dedication to Enron and its employees that led me to turn to her for help in the aftermath of Enron's bankruptcy. I was not seeking assistance for myself. My concern was for the employees, many of whom had lost everything. Cindy did not disappoint. She immediately stepped up to help with a Day of Healing, brokering a deal that would provide Enron Field as a venue for Christopher Reeve to talk to the employees about facing adversity. For the next two months, I worked with Cindy to try to create programs to help the employees of Enron. We worked until it was obvious that no one in Houston was interested in constructive discussion of either Enron or Ken Lay. In the end, the same city politicians who had benefited from Enron's generosity proved viciously unwilling to help the company's employees. One reporter even stated, "These employees are not victims." Never mind the fact that they had just been put out in the street. The city that had gladly taken millions of dollars of Enron's support was now unwilling to even provide a food bank.

Cindy wanted desperately to help the employees—I could see it in her eyes and felt it in her heart. I suddenly realized I had been wrong about Cindy Olson; she had gotten where she was inside Enron because she was determined and passionate about the employees.

I did not speak to Cindy Olson again until I realized she was being set up/framed within the halls of Congress. I suddenly realized this was not about "justice," this was about a pack of wolves looking for a carcass upon which they could feed. They weren't interested in the "whole truth;" Congress and the media were interested in "ratings" among their constituents and viewers.

On Monday, February 17, 2002, I listened intently via the Internet to Sherron Watkins' testimony in the Congressional Hearings to determine just what she knew. I was trying to get an overview on the complex set of circumstances that caused Enron to fall so far so fast. I certainly had my theories, but I was hoping Sherron might add to them. The audio streamed over my computer and at one hour, thirty-eight minutes and six seconds into the testimony, a recess began. As the testimony came to an end, there was a lull and I continued to work at my desk while the audio played in the background. A few moments into the recess, I heard the Chairman of the

Subcommittee, James C. Greenwood (R-Pennsylvania) say, "Do you know how Olson knew that Fastow...'cause you know that that's how Watkins learned that Fastow wanted her fired...from Cindy Olson? Do we know how Olson learned that?"

He obviously didn't realize the audio was still streaming out over the Internet for whoever wanted to listen. Or record it. I grabbed my recorder and hit the record button. "Right...but then how do we think Olson learned that Fastow...?"

Greenwood's voice was followed by inaudible dialogue from an unidentified person.

Greenwood: "Fastow told Olson?...but...I represent the workers..."

Now I was intrigued. Greenwood seemed to be planning a strategy for the next round of questions.

"And, umm, no one has asked, no one's brought this out? I'm hoping that somebody can bring this out."

Greenwood was looking for a mouthpiece.

"Cindy Olson is also a trustee....Is somebody ready to ask these questions? Because Cindy Olson may have perjured herself last week when she denied talking to anybody other than Jeff McMahon."

Now it was making sense. Greenwood seemed interested in setting up Cindy Olson for perjury over her testimony the previous week. Greenwood struggled with the words to form his plan."Other than...but she, on her duty...she knows that Fast...she knows that Sherron Watkins has given all this information to Lay."

There were a few inaudible exchanges between Greenwood and the unidentified person then Greenwood laid his cards on the table, "Olson betrays the workers this way…she knows that Watkins has all these detailed allegations. Second, the end of August somehow she knows directly or indirectly that Fastow wants Olson to fire her. Fastow wants Watkins fired. He's going to stoop…stoop to the level of skullduggery to have her…very few Congressmen have gotten it. Is somebody going to get into this?"

Someone interrupts and he continues, "Look, it's the whole case for the workers. Nobody's talked about the workers yet today. Cindy Olson knew all of the information she needed to shut down the company stock fund and start selling off the company stock. Who's sharp enough to ask that question? I don't think a lot of congressmen understand."

Cindy Olson's fiduciary responsibilities as trustee of Enron's 401(k) made her the guardian angel of the employees' retirement fund. Because of the issues raised by Watkins, Greenwood wanted to hang Cindy Olson for not reading the handwriting on the wall and shutting down the 401(k). What Greenwood failed to acknowledge was that the responsibility for protecting a 401(k) lay primarily with the individual who owned it. As one who lost retirement money, I'd be the first to admit that.

Greenwood: "How did Olson say that she knew that Fastow wanted her [Watkins] fired?"

Greenwood, and whomever he was speaking with, began parsing Cindy Olson's testimony to determine how she found out Fastow wanted Watkins fired. When Fastow learned that, at the suggestion of Cindy Olson, Sherron Watkins visited Ken Lay to voice her concerns over the accounting treatments, Fastow schemed to rid himself of Watkins, and, in typical Enron fashion, demanded that her computer be seized. In the end it was Fastow, not Watkins, who got the boot. Greenwood's attack centered on who knew what and when, and who told who.

Greenwood: "She [Olson] totally withholds; she withheld all this information. She played dumb."

A brief, inaudible discussion ensues.

Greenwood: "Like I said, she has exposure problems. She [Olson] said the only people she spoke with about this, about Watkins' concerns, were Jeff McMahon, which she barely admitted, and Ken Lay, about it. So the more that comes out about Cindy...see it's very bizarre, and then what happens is that Watkins goes and sees Olson, and Olson suggests...and the only thing that follows is that Olson encouraged Watkins to talk with Lay. And she set up the meeting. What would be great for the workers is to establish a breach of duty from Olson because she was the trustee...would be to elicit that Lay, that Watkins spoke further with Olson, but further get in some details about how Olson knew that Fastow wanted her fired, communicated it to Ms. Watkins, but try to find out how did Olson know that. All that came out right here—very quickly she says."

Although his excitable, almost stream-of-consciousness rhetoric barely indicates it, Greenwood assumed that Fastow found out Sherron Watkins had been to visit Lay because Cindy Olson must have tipped him off. Cindy testified she spoke only with Lay and McMahon regarding the matter. Hadn't Greenwood considered the possibility that Lay or McMahon told Fastow about Watkins? Regardless, Greenwood was not going to abandon his attempt to nail Olson.

"Who do I want to ask the question?" asked the chairman, searching for someone to do his dirty work. Then in the tape there was an inaudible question to which he responded, "I don't know. Anybody who is good. Is there a lawyer who still has questions?"

But a lawyer would not be enough. This also had to look like a partisan issue.

"No, I mean is there a lawyer on the Democratic side who can understand the two hat thing? Is Markey a lawyer?" (referring to Congressman Edward Markey, D-Massachusetts). "I mean I could brief somebody really quickly."

There's a discussion and someone else speaks, "I'll go get him." Greenwood sizes up Watkins as a pawn.

"Okay, just let me say a quick thing in terms of pitching it...it's like Watkins didn't know at the time that Olson wore two hats. All she knew is that [Olson] was an HR person. Watkins didn't know [Olson] was a trustee. This cost Watkins money."

It's apparent, Greenwood is working hard to sell his concept. I hear him getting frustrated in his attempts to convince the other guy of the importance of getting Olson.

"No trustee! Trustee! She's a fiduciary. She should have shut down the company stock fund."

An unidentified female responds, "Well, I don't know about that."

Greenwood: "Well, I do. I'm a pension lawyer." Then he laughs. "This is like our only chance to get this out from Watkins. Olson had two hats. Because, she's friends with Lay, trying to get back on the executive committee. In her rush, the workers were betrayed. Watkins...

but Watkins didn't know at the time of her Olson's other role."

Here, he coaches his interrogator.

"'How do you feel now, Ms. Watkins? When you find out that Cindy Olson had control over the stock fund?' I'm telling you it's a great question—it's a great question. She [Olson] had control over the stock fund. Right then you can ask Ms. Watkins, 'If you were a trustee of the stock fund wouldn't you have prevented people from buying more stock? Provided that the stock was inflated. Cindy Olson knew everything you were saying. Cindy Olson knew that Fastow wanted you fired, was going to seize your computer, which is an admission by conduct that everything you were saying was true. If you were a trustee of the stock fund…that is draped with Enron stock wouldn't you have started selling or at least stopped buying more stock? How do you feel Ms., now that you know Cindy Olson [was the Trustee]?'"

I still couldn't determine who Greenwood was talking to but it was obvious his "assassin" was finally on board. "Yeah, Yeah."

Greenwood: "The other thing is, Cindy Olson testified that Watkins was tentative—this *isn't* a tentative woman."

I had remembered my criminal lawyer's words, "Someone's going to jail." It appeared Greenwood wanted that person to be Cindy Olson.

"But here's the point—this is the problem. Olson was the one who told Watkins that Fastow wants her fired and seizes her computer. Shouldn't that Ms. Watkins have told Ms. Olson that everything you were saying was true? Basically, use the burning building analogy. There's a burning building and she was a trustee, she should have run in and saved these peoples' retirement, but she covered it up."

"And Olson knew?" At last I heard the voice of the person Greenwood nominated to go after Olson.

"Olson knew, in August, everything. Fastow was trying to fire Watkins." Greenwood laughs. "Is that the response of a responsible CFO? Somebody who raises accounting questions—you fire her and seize her computer? It's the equivalent of shredding. And Olson had all of the information; she could have literally saved people hundreds of millions of dollars. As trustee of the 401(k) plan. Trustee of the 401(k) plan. Meanwhile she jets around in the company jet with uh, Linda Lay. That's interesting and everybody knows that. They're really buddy-buddy with Mrs. Lay, letting her personal, her personal interests...She's tight with Mrs. Lay...flies around on the company jet— get that out. They'd go to Aspen together—that was common knowledge in the company. Trying to get back with the top echelon of the company 'cause Skilling kicked her out and he was gone. She betrayed the workers."

Greenwood concludes: "Here, let me give you the dates: 8/14 Skilling resigns; 8/16 Watkins memo number one; and then Watkins goes to Olson; 8/22 Watkins meets with Lay, and then 8/30 Olson tells Watkins that Fastow wants her fired and wants her computer seized. *This is the point.* Why isn't Olson selling the stock? [inaudible] Because she knows the whole thing is a house of cards. She betrays the employees." Then Greenwood goes in for the close. "Somehow Olson finds out that Fastow wants Watkins fired. You're the man—the perfect guy to ask this."

It was my first up close and personal view of a conspiracy. Twenty-eight minutes in all, I wondered who
Greenwood had gotten to do his dirty work. I listened
as he explained the circumstances to some unidentified
member of Congress, a man he had recruited to go for
Cindy Olson's jugular. I was curious about which Democratic hit man Greenwood was proselytizing.

It turned out to be Congressman Bobby Rush, a
Democrat from Illinois. Rush was given the floor and he
directed his question to Sherron Watkins.

"I want to thank you, Mr. Chairman and Mrs. Watkins. It is certainly very pleasing that you are here and
your testimony has been forthright and I would say
without any kind of a value—in terms of Ms. Temple's
testimony [in-house counsel at Arthur Andersen]—it is
diametrically opposed to the kind of testimony that Ms.
Temple presented to this committee and it's certainly
appreciative by the committee, at least with one member
of the committee, and I believe that it's appreciative, that
your testimony is appreciative, is appreciated [corrects
himself] by the American public. On what date did you
first speak with Cindy Olson or communicate with her in
any way about your concerns about the financial condition of Enron?"

I could almost hear Greenwood doing a slow burn as
Rush botched the attack. But if Greenwood didn't have
a pretty good sense he was grasping at straws then I suppose it was a good idea to make someone from the oppo-
sition look like a dummy. Rush stepped valiantly into
that role. In his zeal to put some scalps on his belt to
satisfy the bloodlust against Enron, it's sad Greenwood
went after one of the small fish. I suppose he was as afraid

of the Skillings and Lays and Fastows as much anyone in Congress who understands the power of their money and friends.

I picked up the phone and called Cindy Olson. As the greeting on Cindy's voicemail began I remembered it was President's Day, which meant Enron was closed, but then so were government offices—or were they? I left her a message to call me immediately, omitting any details until I could speak with her personally. I ran into town to buy a better tape recorder. The first recording I made was slightly muffled and I wanted the clearest evidence possible. I would re-record the conversation with Greenwood off the Web site when I got home. As I neared my home my cell phone rang. It was Cindy.

"What's going on? Your message scared the hell out of me."

"Cindy, I hate to tell you this, but you're being set up." I explained what I had heard, and told her of my intention to tape it again before someone realized what had gotten out over the Internet.

"I'll forward the tape to you tomorrow via FedEx."

When I got back to my office, after being gone no more than thirty minutes, the very Web site I had recorded was down. At least I had the initial tape. I left a message on Cindy's voicemail telling her that someone had taken the site down between the time I had left my house and returned. The next morning at approximately 10:00 a.m., the Web site finally came up when I logged on. I navigated to the Congressional hearing and searched for the incriminating recording of Congressman Greenwood. It was there, but now ten minutes were missing from the conversation I had heard the day before.

It was then that I realized that Greenwood wasn't interested in the "whole truth"—he made Cindy Olson out to be a monster that didn't have the slightest care for the employees, that somehow she blindly robbed the 401(k) plan of its riches. That was not the "whole truth" that was the "truth" Greenwood wanted the world to see. That's "spin"—not "truth."

The "truth" is woven in the paths we take through life, but the whole "truth" is never likely to be seen except through the eyes of God. Perhaps the attestation "the whole truth…so help me God" is not about God's wrath upon us if we fail to tell the truth as we know it, but a plea for God's help in lending His truth.

I would not realize the importance of the "whole truth" until Ken Lay was convicted. Ken Lay never knew the "whole truth." I know because I kept it from him to protect myself. It just never occurred to me he might go to prison because of my failure to tell the "whole truth." Just two weeks before his death, I met with Ken Lay for the first time and finally saw what the court of public opinion with its half truths will do to a man. Ken Lay gave me the greatest gift that day—his forgiveness for failing him as an employee, as part of his legal staff, and as a human being. Ken was persecuted for my sins. It was that day that I realized I had been right—Cindy Olson had gotten lucky in her career at Enron. She had worked beside one of the great leaders who lead the company by a deep faith in the goodness of others, those who would ultimately betray him.

God has answered our pleas for the "whole truth" with Cindy Olson's beautiful and heartfelt story. If we choose to hear the truth, Cindy Olson will be recognized for having the courage to tell such a personal story and for giving us a deeper understanding of the power of God's ultimate forgiveness and plan for our lives.

Lynn Brewer
Author of *Confessions of an Enron Executive:
A Whistleblower's Story*
Former Enron Employee and Founder and CEO of
The Integrity Institute

Preface

As I have looked back on my life in the process of writing this book, it has become clear to me the one thing you can expect is that life will change. Those things that often define who you are change. Your profession changes. Your friends change. Your family changes. Your focus changes. Your home changes. What you believe and how you behave changes.

The years following the collapse of Enron brought about a windfall of such changes in my own life. Some were positive, others painful. Yet, in retrospect, I can see that these are the events God used to bring me closer to the truth of who I am and the purpose He has for me. My life was turned inside out by the United States Justice Department, the United States Labor Department, the FBI and the press, though ultimately they found no reason to indict me. Nevertheless, I did not escape being tried and convicted in the court of public opinion. In the process, however, I was able to reexamine and come to terms with my life.

I was, in fact, guilty. I was guilty of loving Enron so much that I couldn't let myself believe that something bad could happen to it. I was guilty in believing equally in all the people at Enron and that they were inherently good. I was guilty of making Enron my whole life. I was guilty of getting caught up in the money I earned and the success I experienced. I was guilty of letting my role at Enron define me. I was guilty of treating some people badly and thinking less of others who did not have the same sense of urgency that I did. Finally, I was guilty of thinking that I was so great that my success was only the result of my own efforts.

I believed for years that you could plan out your whole life and it would be perfect. That it was all up to you to create just the life you wanted, and that I was totally in control of what happened to me. Fortunately or unfortunately, however you look at it, we are all destined to realize that ultimately someone else is in charge. That the tragedies and joys we face depend upon our own attitude. There is a plan for our lives. I am more attune now to those who also struggle with their own identities, who wonder what God's plan for them might be.

With Enron's collapse, my identity could not remain unchanged. I went from high-powered executive to just another resident of Western Colorado. It has taken me some time to be okay with that. I was so proud of being at Enron. To this day I am still extremely proud of what we accomplished and the company we all built, even though many people don't see it the same way I do.

My family changed how they interacted with me. My mother used to feel bad about calling me because I was always too busy with my own things to just chat. I got irritated with people who bothered me just to say "hello" or to find out what was going on in our lives. Now I am probably the one "bothering" my family. I love to call them just to see how their day is going.

Some of our long-time friends are no longer our friends. Many of them were at Enron. Sadly, the majority of those people are not part of our lives today. The Enron investigation forced many of them to cut off all communication with us for several years.

The priorities in my life have definitely changed. I don't spend all my waking hours working. I don't get up at 5:00 a.m. and run six miles before I head off to the office for at least a ten-hour day. My husband, Grady, and I linger in bed and cuddle with our dogs in the morning. I actually cook breakfast and drink coffee at home with my husband.

I don't check my voicemail or get on my Blackberry every few minutes like I did when I was at Enron. In fact, I don't even own a Blackberry today. My job was my entire life and the number one most important thing. It didn't bother me that while others were enjoying their time off I was making sure I didn't miss a single email or voice message without sending off an immediate response.

I don't start thinking about the work week on Sundays. I know a lot of people that still keep in touch with me via email do that very thing because I get messages on Sunday afternoons. That's exactly what I used to do. Now, my Sundays are reserved for going to church and spending time as a family or with friends.

We don't fly to destinations much anymore. We take our time and drive so we can take in the beautiful scenery across this fantastic country. We set our own schedule instead of having it set for us by an airline or the companies for which we work.

Don't misunderstand—it's not that I don't want to work again, or thanks to Enron I am set financially and don't need to work. In fact, anyone who knew me could attest that I have always been pretty energetic, so idling away time has never suited my personality. After being labeled an Enron insider, however, work was impossible to find. Interestingly, many former Enron employees, including myself, have chosen to build our own businesses and find ourselves networking with other former Enron people. It makes me so proud to see the entrepreneurial spirit that was so prevalent at Enron is still alive and well in the people who worked there.

I don't yell at people or make ridiculous demands like I used to. I believe now I would make an even more effective leader because of what I have learned. Oh, don't get me wrong. I am definitely not perfect and I still give my husband an occasional "look" or comment that I wish I could take back. I am much more relaxed, however, and I get things accomplished without making life miserable for everyone around me.

The money I made while at Enron allowed me to have a lot of stuff. I became addicted to money and things, and to be honest, I still miss that at times. But I realize now that to be a Christian means acknowledging those weaknesses. I understand that success isn't only about the house or the car that you own, but it is more accurately measured by how truly happy and content you are and how much joy you bring to the life of others.

The Enron bankruptcy and collapse was the worst thing that had ever happened to me, but it was also the best thing in many ways. It was good because the loss of my job forced me to slow down and determine what was really important to me. The loss of the money and the status associated with my position at Enron helped me understand that those things can be taken away from anyone at any time. Only faith in the Lord provides true security and a certain future for all of us.

Jeff Skilling, former Enron CEO, demoted me and it was hurtful, but it turned out to be a blessing. Stan Horton, who I worked for at Enron, challenged me, but his harsh words gave me the strength to handle what was to come later in my life. What happened to my husband's business was devastating, but now we both can enjoy life together with our little family of dogs and focus on building a business together. Finally, the death of a little five-year-old boy was horrible, but in the end, he saved us.

Through this book I describe the journey through my life, including the twenty-three years I spent at Enron. I talk about the successes, the fears, the hurt, the anger, the disappointments, the people and finally the forgiveness, understanding, and ultimate faith and surrender.

So many things are not what they first seem. I believe now that everything works together for the good. My story isn't finished, but with the faith I now have I know the ending. I just don't know what will happen between now and then.

A friend told me recently to look at how the trees grow in the mountains. I didn't understand exactly what he was saying. So, he pointed out that trees grow in the valleys not on the top of the mountains. People are like that too. They grow when they are in their lowest places. I know it's true because it happened to me.

Introduction

I was the first Enron executive to testify in front of the United States House and Senate in February of 2002. I had to raise my hand twice that week and promise to "tell the truth, the whole truth, nothing but the truth...so help me God." When I did that for the first time in 2002 I sincerely thought that was what everyone wanted—to get to the bottom of what really happened at Enron. I naively believed that the truth would come out, the few culprits would be identified and prosecuted, and all of this chaos would pass.

When I testified for Ken Lay, former Enron Chairman and CEO, at his trial in April of 2006, more than four years later, I again had to raise my hand on the witness stand and promise to tell the truth. By that point however, it had become clear to me that the truth didn't matter. The only voices being heard were those that supported the belief that Enron was an evil company, a house of cards, and Ken Lay and Jeff Skilling and all the other executives in fact were guilty. The only thing I know Ken and Jeff were guilty of for sure is that they trusted people to do the right thing and they had been betrayed.

When the book *The Smartest Guys in the Room* was published in 2003, I remember thinking two things. First, I had to know what they'd said about me and if it was the truth. There have been so many things portrayed in the books and movies that were simply not true. I went to Barnes and Noble, sat on a couch and perused the appendix to find the pages where my name was mentioned. I concluded it was a book written by outsiders who didn't really know Enron. Secondly, I remember thinking that the title was arrogant, and yet that was what everyone had done to us all. They twisted our success into arrogance and this book was echoing that same story. It wasn't until much later I was told that "the smartest guys in the room" was in fact the phrase Cliff Baxter, my former colleague who committed suicide, used to refer to all of us at Enron.

I suppose we were somewhat arrogant. Enron was, for a time, a remarkably successful company. It was named the most innovative company by *Fortune* magazine six years in a row. In addition, *Fortune* ranked our management second, employee talent fourth, and quality of products and services fifth. We were the seventh largest company of the Fortune 500 companies, the eighteenth most admired, the twenty-fourth best company to work for and the twenty-ninth fastest growing company. There were a lot of achievements to brag about and we weren't the only ones bragging. There were countless articles written about our successes.

In 2000, when I was a member of Enron's executive committee and a 16B insider, the executive team held an offsite meeting to determine a new vision for the company. Our old vision had been to become "The World's Leading Energy Company." We had achieved that vision and we were ready to define a new vision for the future. Ken Lay always laid out a vision for the company since the early years of Enron. I remember the very first vision we had was to become the "World's First Natural Gas Major." Ken liked to go on and clarify that vision by explaining that he wanted us to become a major, but not like Exxon. He wanted Enron to become more nimble and creative than Exxon was perceived.

This time Ken wanted our new vision to be the "Most Respected Company in the World." This of course, was telling of Ken's character. Others in that room wanted our future vision to be "The Coolest Company on the Planet." Several of the members of the executive committee even suggested that we place a big pair of sunglasses on the top of the Enron building. We were looking for something edgy and innovative that would be consistent with the culture we had created.

Kevin Hannon, who was then COO of Broadband, got a huge laugh from the group when he quoted a line in the movie *The Sixth Sense,* "We see dead companies, but they don't know they are dead." Sadly, no one present at that meeting could foresee that our own death would come in less than two years.

By that point I was caught up in my own success. I didn't think for a minute there was any reason to thank someone else for the achievements I experienced. I truly believed that the people at Enron were, in fact, the smartest people anywhere, and that included me.

In my mind I had become so successful with Enron that I really didn't need anything else, or so I thought. I had everything I could possibly imagine. We owned a big expensive house in the suburbs, a townhouse near downtown Houston, and a third home near Aspen, Colorado. Grady and I drove exotic cars, I wore expensive jewelry and I, like many other Enron employees, attended some of the most prestigious events around the world. It was only after the fall of Enron, the devastation of my husband's company and the death of a friend's five-year-old son, all in the course of a couple of years, that I finally realized that success can be defined by things other than a lot of money and a lot of stuff.

Jeff Skilling used to put people down by saying they just didn't "get it." He was definitely the brightest person most of us had ever been around and the driver of Enron's innovative culture, but I am not sure what he seemed to get that others didn't. I don't think he got that he was not in control. I don't think he understood that success and who you are is not defined by a successful business model or moving up the corporate ladder. I know I was definitely guilty of that kind of thinking as well.

Ken Lay was different. He did get it. He loved the employees. He treated everyone, and I do mean everyone, the way he would want to be treated. I am not sure when I realized the depth of Ken's faith. I don't think you can see that in someone unless you yourself understand your own faith. Ken was truly a humble man of God. He simply trusted some people that were not trustworthy. When he came back as Enron's CEO four months before its bankruptcy, he did what any other CEO in this country would have done. He went to work to do everything in his power to save the company. I know, because I witnessed it firsthand. The most important thing about Ken was that he really did care, and he did love Enron's employees. He also understood that there was someone more powerful than himself ultimately in control.

This is the first book written by a true 16B Enron insider whose peers included the highest level executives.

Oh, there have been countless books written so far, but no one has had the twenty-three year history with Enron, and the personal access to Ken Lay and other executives like I did. *I was with Enron before it was Enron.* I was there as Enron grew to be the seventh largest company in the world, and became known as the most innovative company for six years in a row. I helped Enron reach the twenty-fourth spot on the 100 best companies to work for. Sherron Watkins, best known now as Enron's whistleblower, brought me her now infamous letter before it went to anyone else. I was the first executive to testify in front of the U.S. Senate and the U.S. House. I was the one the world would watch enthusiastically answer an employee question about investing in Enron's 401(k). I was referred to as "Enron's cheerleader" because everyone knew I loved working for Enron and Ken Lay.

Enron had nearly 200,000 resumes in our database from people who wanted to work there. We employed close to 25,000 people worldwide, and we had hired some of the best and brightest people anywhere. Our employees were incredible. We had created an employee benefits package that included on-site childcare, a computer at home, a concierge on staff, take out meals, a Starbucks in our lobby and a state of the art fitness center in our building. All of these things helped create the culture that incubated innovation. Nearly everyone in Houston wanted to work for Enron. We had become the model for corporate community support in Houston, and our culture, and for that matter our accounting, were being emulated by major corporations all over the country. Enron was one of the most admired companies in America.

In this book I reveal my own personal experiences with

those whose names we heard nonstop once everything began to unfold: Ken Lay, Jeff Skilling, Rick Causey, Mark Koenig, Kevin Hannon, Andy Fastow and Sherron Watkins, to name a few. I talk about the experience of being the first Enron executive to testify in front of Joe Lieberman's United States Senate committee, and John Boehner's United States House of Representative committee within that same week.

I discuss how the FBI, the Justice Department and the U.S. Department of Labor investigated every aspect of my life. How they all had one goal in mind—to prove we were all guilty of something. It is interesting to me now, that we raise our hand in the name of God when innocent until proven guilty means nothing.

I talk about how the fall of Enron impacted my family, friends, and my own identity. Finally, I reflect on how a tragedy such as Enron did in fact help me understand there is a higher power in control of my life.

This book also contrasts our country's justice system with the justice system of God, and exposes how the media was so instrumental as the judge, jury and assassin. It reveals the depth of personal tragedy suffered by Enron employees; a tragedy amplified because there were so many celebrating our demise. Finally, I show how the "truth" was never what the government or the media actually wanted to hear, even though so many of us were longing for the "truth" to be told.

I suggest that Enron became a scapegoat for "sins" of which many other companies were also culpable. Human nature always tempts us to point the finger away from ourselves. I believe that the very people who cried "Greedy," were often in fact greedy themselves. There were so many other companies that were using the same kind of accounting practices and paying their employees generously based on stock price. Banks were lining up to loan us money for their own gain. Vendors were screaming to do business with us because they wanted a piece of the large amount of business Enron generated. It was easy to avoid identifying and dealing with these all-too-common faults by projecting them on Enron.

Enron was a tragedy in so many ways. Many lives were impacted or destroyed. The real tragedy, however, is that things might have turned out very differently if only the truth was honored, valued and allowed to be told.

This book reveals insight into the true Ken Lay. I worked side by side with him for many years and out of my own personal experiences I describe the wonderful man he was. Ken Lay not only talked about his faith—he lived it each and every day. I was with him many times and I never saw him treat anyone badly. He always did things with Enron and its employees in his heart. He would never have intentionally jeopardized what he had created. His death is tragic and many people miss him, but we also are relieved that God took him home so he would be free of the persecution he endured for so many years.

This is a book written about my life growing up and my career. I describe what I experienced at Enron as a woman and as an executive. This is my story but *I* am not what this book is truly about. It is about achieving success in corporate America. It is about an incredible company that allowed so many of us to achieve things we never dreamed we could, and the incredible man that made that happen. Most importantly it is a book about God, who was working in my life all along, and how He finally brought me to understand how much I need Him.

My mother told me not too long ago, "God puts people in their places." Maybe many people feel the same way, but I believe that God gets your attention in whatever way He can and He brings you to Him because that is what we were all made to do—glorify and worship Him. It's not punishment; it's simply His love for you. Through His grace and with His help we are lucky enough to figure it out.

My hope for this book is that the sharing of my own experiences will help others to see God's work in their own lives and their own need for him. This hope is especially for those who believe they already have all they could possibly need or want just as I did.

Sadly, it is often only under pressure that faith is forced into the open and shows its true colors. Adversity produces maturity that can't be achieved any other way. I am forever thankful for all of the life experiences God has dealt me, the grace and mercy He has given me and for the wonderful people He has brought into my life. This book is about the truth—so help me God.

I Had Finally "Arrived"

I had worked for Enron for twenty years and had just gotten my twenty-year service award. It was a classy pen and pencil set I selected from a number of choices offered in a nicely-done catalog put out by HR. The gift came with a personal note from Ken Lay thanking me for everything I had done to help make Enron the company that it was today. Ken always wrote personal notes to people, and Enron was good at honoring tenure at the company. In fact, if you were with the company for twenty-five years you could choose a grandfather clock for your anniversary gift. Twenty years passed quickly, it seemed. There were some great memories, and like with any company, a few I could just as soon forget, but I loved Enron and I loved my job.

Like a lot of women in the business world, I had sacrificed to get there. I had postponed having children and then when I finally thought I could handle it, I couldn't get pregnant. It's something I think many women struggle with. They become so focused on their success that they look around one day and they have forgotten to have kids. Then, when they think they are ready for them, they can't seem to get pregnant. I have often wondered why God did not bless me with children, but obviously it was in His plan for me to have "kids with fur."

I missed seeing my sister's and brother's children grow

up by not being around so I could be involved in their soccer games, graduations and birthdays. My husband, Grady, and I even missed out on some things as a couple because of the demands of the corporate world, but we didn't complain because we loved what we were doing, had a comfortable life and enjoyed a lot of nice things. My drive to keep climbing the Enron corporate ladder just wouldn't stop.

It was late in 1999 when I finally reached that sought after position at Enron—a seat on Enron's executive committee. I was now one of the top twenty people in the seventh largest corporation in the country. I had a potential earnings target of $3 million a year in salary, bonus and stock options. I was very proud of where I was and where I had come from. I was from Kansas and like many of us at Enron, had not attended an Ivy League college. We all talked about how Enron allowed us to become more than we had ever imagined.

I had been on the "executive committee" before, but this time it was different. This time it was "Jeff Skillings' executive committee." It was well known that Jeff was soon to take over as CEO for Ken Lay. Ken was starting to spend his time outside of Enron, primarily helping Houston become a "world-class city" so that corporations such as Enron could attract world-class talent into their work forces.

Jeff was putting together his management team, and unfortunately I hadn't originally made the cut. I was in charge of a corporate function that wasn't considered important enough to warrant a place on the executive committee. I was in charge of community relations, which I believe Jeff and others thought didn't provide real bottom line value to Enron.

Shortly after Jeff took over as CEO, the Alley Theatre, a strong nonprofit in Houston, wanted to honor Enron for its contribution to its success. Our community relations team thought it would be a great time to expose Jeff to the nonprofit world, and ask him to accept the award for Enron.

The Alley presented the award to Jeff during an intermission of one of their performances. The executive director of the Alley thanked Jeff and Enron for our participation in their success, and shared with the audience the total amount of the contributions we had made during the past several years. I don't remember the exact amount, but it was in the million dollar range. Jeff's expression said it all. His face showed utter surprise, and you could almost see him thinking, *things are going to change.* It was our first indication that we were going to have to work on Jeff for him to see the value our function did provide to the company.

I had also just received the responsibility for "diversity" at Enron, which consisted of encouraging the promotion of more women and minorities to management positions, and purchasing more products and services from minority businesses. Ken Lay was focused on both of these areas and understood the value they created. Because of that, he had many friends in the minority and nonprofit communities of Houston. Even with Ken's support it was still difficult to get everyone at Enron on board with what he wanted Enron to achieve in these areas. If Jeff didn't focus on them as CEO it would be even more difficult to continue Enron's commitment.

I watched as my good friend and mentor, Beth Tilney, was moved out of the corporate function of marketing and advertising a few months earlier and into the Enron Energy Services operating group. This happened, I believe, because Jeff didn't see the value in what she was doing with Enron's brand. The brand was another priority of Ken Lay's and he was passionate that Enron would become a well-known company that was community minded. Beth's move was actually good for me as I would report directly to the office of the chairman instead of through her. Mark Palmer, who had also worked for Beth, was promoted to the corporate public relations role and reported to the office of the chairman through Steve Kean, Enron chief of staff.

I thought a lot of Beth and I liked reporting to her. I had learned a lot from her. Ken Lay brought her into the company sometime in 1997 when he started focusing on building the brand and what he wanted Enron to be known for. Beth had a background with Ogilvy and Mather, an advertising firm in New York, and Ken quickly trusted her.

When she moved to Enron Energy Services (EES) she worked for Lou Pai doing the same thing for EES that she did in corporate. Because the consumer was more important in the EES business model than in other operating groups, her talents were welcomed.

Lou Pai was the CEO of Enron Energy Services, but was a part of the Enron Capital and Trade management team in the early to mid 1990s. He was brilliant like a lot of the other people Jeff brought in to build Enron's new businesses. I didn't really know Lou that well, but I knew he was a key player in building the original trading organization, and he helped Beth, and because of those things I personally appreciated him.

During her time in EES, Beth and I continued to work together. I kept her involved in the corporate environment and everything we were doing in my areas of responsibilities. I knew she wanted Enron to be known as the best employer, best energy provider and the best corporate citizen. She definitely believed in what we were doing in community relations because she understood what it contributed to those goals and Enron's overall image.

I missed her at the corporate level. In fact, everyone in my group missed her. She was not only good at what she did she was kind and always nice to everyone. Sometimes as I think back on our relationship, I wonder how I got so lucky to have such a good mentor and friend. Most women didn't help each other get ahead in the corporate environment. I don't think that was unique to Enron. The corporate world was tough for women and you learned to take care of yourself. I was very lucky to have such a good friend in Beth Tilney. In retrospect I am sure her friendship was a gift from God.

I always suspected the same fate that Beth had experienced with Jeff awaited me eventually, but I still wanted to be on the sought-after executive committee. Besides, I rationalized, it sent a strong signal to women in the organization that you could, in fact, be a woman and be one of the top executives of a Fortune 10 company. Because I was in charge of diversity, I had done a lot of research that showed Enron was not necessarily doing all that it could to promote women and minorities. Of course a lot of companies were in that same condition.

In August of 1999, Grady and I went to Colorado for the weekend. We had built a log home near Aspen in 1996, which was our getaway from the stress of Houston. We enjoyed our time there as we escaped from the day to day pressures of both of our jobs surrounded by spectacular scenery. The house was built with mammoth logs and faced Mt. Sopris, a nearly 13,000 foot peak, like it was a painting in our living area. We were located a good five miles off of the main highway, and once we got there we both wanted to just relax and enjoy the incredible views.

I loved running in the morning through the vast ranch lands surrounding our house regardless of the time of the year. Just being in that place you felt more in touch with everything. As wonderful as our home was, I really never left Enron very far behind when we were there. I couldn't. My job required that I stay in touch with what was going on back in Houston. We had email at the house and we had voicemail that I checked hourly. Rosalie Fleming, Ken Lay's assistant, had become a very good friend of mine. She knew how to get hold of me and would track me down if "Mr. Lay" needed to talk to me.

During the course of that particular visit in the summer of 1999, Ken actually did call me. Rosie always placed the call and asked me to hold for Mr. Lay. Rosie was friendly and soft spoken. She was kind to everyone and Ken knew he had a jewel in her. Ken's previous assistant had left Enron in 1997 and her departure was actually why I was asked to take over the corporate community relations role that year.

Nancy McNeil had taken on the community role in addition to running Ken's office. Prior to her departure, it was rumored that she had been involved in a relationship with Rich Kinder, who was the COO (chief operating officer) of Enron at the time. He was in line to become CEO when Ken retired. Rich and Ken had been good friends for many years and both had originally come from the Florida Gas organization.

I was never exactly sure of the circumstances surrounding her departure, but I could sense the tension between Nancy and Ken. In addition, Rich Kinder, who had always seemed to be a supporter of mine, stopped speaking to me. Luckily for me, Ken continued to be the CEO of Enron and Rich eventually left. Thankfully, I didn't have to deal with that particular issue very long.

I thoroughly enjoyed getting calls from Ken Lay. He was the best person in the world to work for because he really cared about what you thought. He treated everyone with respect and you could tell he actually listened to what you had to say. Ken's management style was always inclusive and he looked for different opinions and points of view. I think that is one of the reasons he was such a strong supporter of Jeff Skilling. Jeff and Ken definitely had different management styles and focuses.

I worked for other managers in the past, both at Enron and other companies, who were not as easy to work with as Ken Lay. Just the thought of getting a call from them made me half sick at my stomach. In fact, to this day, I can still remember one of my old Enron boss' internal phone numbers. I worked for him in the early 1990s, and thinking about his phone number today still makes me nervous. Anyway, when I answered the phone that particular day in 1999, Rosie asked if I could speak to Mr. Lay and she put me on hold for him to pick up.

"Cindy, this is Ken Lay." He always started our conversations this way and consistently used his last name as if I didn't know who he was. He asked me how the weather was in Colorado and we talked about how much we both loved Aspen. "Cindy, I called to let you know about some organization changes that we are in the process of making," he told me. He went on to explain that they would be making some changes to the executive committee and I was not going to be on it going forward. The executive committee consisted of the top twenty executives, and was responsible for defining Enron's strategy. Finally, he told me that I was going to report to Steve Kean instead of reporting directly to the office of the chairman.

He asked me if that was okay. I remember thinking for a minute, *No, its not okay, how could you do this to me with the issue of diversity so critical at Enron,* but instead of voicing my thoughts I told him that if that was what he wanted, I was fine with it. He probably thought that would be the end of that conversation and I would do what he asked me to do. I was tired of fighting for everything. It seemed to me at the time that since Jeff had started taking over the company as the future CEO I had to fight for a lot of things. It wasn't until years later that I finally realized that Jeff simply had a different focus on the areas that I was responsible for.

When I hung up the phone after talking to Ken, I called my friend Beth Tilney and left her a message about the conversation I'd just had. It finally happened. I was going to have the same fate as she had. In less than an hour I heard back from her. She told me that she would not let me say it was okay to be taken off of the executive committee. She was adamant that if I wasn't going to fight to stay on the committee she was going to fight for me.

I can't say enough about how much I admired Beth, not only because of how she treated me but how she treated everyone. Not many women at Enron, or for that matter any major corporation, helped other women like Beth did. Beth was definitely an exception. She was fighting right along with me just like it was for her. I am sure she coached me on the things I needed to say to Ken, but I was thinking of my own speech by that point and don't remember exactly what she told me. The important thing was I was now ready to tell Ken what I wanted. I realized that the worst thing that could happen to me would be that he would say "no", and I would be in the same position I was in at that moment—off the executive committee.

When I called Ken back to tell him I had reconsidered my response to him he was in a meeting and I had to leave a voice message for him. I told him that I actually didn't think it was okay I was going to be taken off the executive committee and not report to the office of the chairman going forward. I chose to leave him a voice message since I did a lot of that and I knew he listened to them. I had evidence of it even though I am not sure I would have listened to some of the long-winded messages I left him.

This time in my message I simply told him I was not comfortable with our previous conversation and pleaded my case to continue to be on the executive committee from a diversity argument. In other words, I used the reasoning that there were not enough women at the top of the organization. At the time I believe there was only one other woman on that committee of twenty executives. We still had a ways to go at Enron to show the employees that we truly supported promoting women and minorities. A move to take women off of that committee without adding any sent the wrong message to the employees, I reasoned.

I also asked Ken to let me know what I had done to potentially jeopardize my spot on the committee and what I needed to do for them to consider letting me stay on the top management team. I reminded him of all the accomplishments I achieved during the past year. I learned early in my career to discuss my value statistically, so it was easy to analyze my worth to the organization. I finally asked him if there was something in my performance review that I needed to know so I could correct it going forward.

We exchanged several voice messages over the weekend and by Monday, when I returned to Houston, I was in Ken's office with a suggestion. The final message he left me was to get creative. That wasn't hard for me; I was pretty good at thinking of innovative solutions for everything. I told him that based on his feedback, it seemed that there was absolutely nothing wrong with my performance. I felt that the only reason that I was not being considered a top officer was because I was responsible for areas that were considered "fluff," or just were not that important to the bottom line of the organization.

I came to that conclusion because I had gotten excellent performance reviews and there was nothing that Ken could tell me that I needed to do differently in my current role. I think he was a little hesitant to tell me that the areas he valued so highly were not valued as highly by everyone within the organization.

I also knew that Ken was not happy with the current head of Human Resources. He didn't trust him, and to be honest, Ken was justified in thinking that. I had some personal experiences with him that made me question his motives. In addition, I didn't feel he was truly an advocate for the employees, which I believed was critical for this role.

So, on that next Monday, when I went to the 50th floor to meet with Ken, I suggested that in addition to my current responsibilities of community relations and diversity I would like to take on the corporate Human Resources function. With that additional responsibility, I argued, I should be considered to be part of the executive committee. He listened to me like he always did and told me that he would have to discuss it with Jeff Skilling and Joe Sutton who were both part of the "office of the chairman" with Ken.

Since all three were now an equal part of "office of the chairman," all decisions had to be supported by the three of them. I left Ken's office confident that at least I would know where I stood with the two people that would take Ken's place eventually as CEO.

It took nearly a week for a decision to be made. Ken called me to his office to give me the news. Joe and Jeff agreed that I would become executive vice president of global Human Resources, report directly to the office of the chairman and be a member of the executive committee. He told me that Jeff wanted me to give up my community relations role, but I told Ken I thought I could do both. We were starting to use employee participation

in our community programs and support higher education initiatives, and I felt there was a synergy between the
functions. Ken left that decision up to me and told me
that I would receive a raise in compensation, which Joe
Sutton would discuss with me.

I was already making a lot of money, I thought, and
wasn't sure I needed anymore base salary. The compensation package was so generous with respect to stock
options. I remember feeling mixed emotions of happiness
and a little fear. I knew that the current head of Human
Resources reported to my good friend, Rick Causey, and
I was hopeful that Rick would not be unhappy with me
because of what I had done.

When I met with Joe Sutton about my compensation,
I told him that I felt I already made enough money and
didn't need another increase in my base salary. I think
Joe was shocked, and he told me that it was a first for
someone to tell him they already made enough money.
We compromised and I ended up agreeing to a smaller
increase than he was originally offering.

Now don't get me wrong. By that time in my career
I was into making a lot of money, but something told
me that large increase just didn't feel right. After all, I
reasoned, I had been promoted less than a year ago and
received a substantial salary bump. I had actually taken
on the diversity function and gotten compensated for it
after I proved myself. I was much more comfortable with
salary increases when I proved I deserved it.

As far as making it right with Rick Causey, I was never
really sure how all of that worked out. Rick told me that
Jeff met with him and Jeff asked him to give up Human
Resources so I could lead it. He must have agreed because

he didn't seem to be upset with me and we continued to be friends. On the other hand, the previous head of Human Resources who had previously reported to Rick now worked for me and eventually left Enron. Actually, I asked Rick for his help as I made decisions later on about the analyst and associate program that I became responsible for with my new Human Resources role.

I was now in charge of Human Resources globally for Enron, community relations and diversity. My compensation was in the seven-figure range, I was on the executive committee of a Fortune 10 company, and reported directly to the office of the chairman. I asked for a promotion and I had received it. I didn't have a thought about giving credit for this achievement to anyone or anything but myself and Ken Lay. In retrospect, I am sure all of these things were blessings from God and part of His plan for my life.

The "Absolutely" Infamous Video

The first Enron all-employee meeting, since my promotion to the head of Human Resources and to the executive committee, was scheduled in late 1999. The Human Resources team knew that many of the questions that would be asked at the meeting would be regarding our employee benefits.

As with any major corporation, we wanted the executives prepared and informed when they dealt with employees. It made our Human Resource jobs much easier if the executives answering the employee questions knew the details of what was going on. We drafted a list of potential questions and answers for the three men that made up Enron's office of the chairman: Ken Lay, Jeff Skilling and Joe Sutton. I also made sure I knew the answers to those questions myself, just in case they needed a prompt from the front row where I knew I would be sitting.

As I walked from the Enron building to the downtown Hyatt hotel that morning to attend the employee meeting, I was reviewing the list of questions the Human Resources team had prepared. I felt good about knowing the answers to the questions. When I walked into the large ballroom it was a good twenty minutes before the meeting was to start. There were rows and rows of chairs, and many of the employees were already streaming in to find their seats.

There was a lot of laughter and chatter and the atmosphere was upbeat. It just felt like it was going to be a good meeting. When everyone was seated, there were probably close to 3,000 people in that gigantic room at the Hyatt. If you didn't look up, you probably wouldn't notice the huge crystal chandelier hanging in the center of the room glistening in the lights.

Every employee meeting we had in the last few years was in that ballroom, a short two block walk from the Enron building. Large screens were displayed on each side of the stage so everyone had a good view of Ken Lay, Jeff Skilling and Joe Sutton. There was a podium positioned in the center of the stage between the two large screens. On the front of the podium a large, now infamous, Enron "E" was displayed proudly.

I made my way up to the front row where I planned to sit so I could help the three guys answer questions if they needed it. As I walked to the front of the room, through the employees who were selecting their own seats, I greeted many of them. I knew a lot of people since I had been with Enron more than twenty years. It was especially fun for me to walk through the room of employees that morning. There had been an all company announcement of my new job and promotion, and today many employees gave me their personal congratulations. I had received nearly two hundred emails from people in the company that acknowledged my promotion, and I was happy that my new position was well received by most employees.

As I look back on that day and the days following that promotion, I was much more arrogant and prideful of my accomplishments than I should have been. I was becoming addicted to the success and recognition I was receiving. I didn't realize, at the time, how I was changing into someone I didn't really like a whole lot. Even though many employees never really saw that side of me, I knew it existed and I regret feeling that way. I understand now that even God uses our feelings about ourselves to bring us close to Him.

At these meetings, most of the executives usually sat on the first couple of rows. As I was deciding where to sit, I saw Beth Tilney and moved quickly to be next to her. Several of my Human Resource team members sat behind me. The room was filling up quickly with some people actually standing in the back along the wall. There was definitely a constant roar in the room as many employees were carrying on conversations of their own.

Ken Lay kicked the meeting off as he usually did. He always wished everyone a huge "Good morning," and wanted that response back from them. That usually got everyone's attention and quieted the crowd. He spoke generally about our stock price which was at an all time high, up to that point, of close to $40 per share, and he shared with everyone that he expected it to go higher. Jeff reviewed the financials and spoke of the huge potential Enron had in its future new businesses. Joe talked about the importance of managing our human capital and the diversity of our workforce.

The meeting usually lasted a little over an hour and today was no exception. After their presentations, all three gentlemen came back up on stage to field questions from the employees. Because the meeting had an upbeat feel, the questions were most likely going to be fun for them to answer. I was a little nervous because of my new role, but I had Mikie Rath and Cynthia Barrow, who reported to me in the benefits department, seated in close proximity, so they could help if I needed it.

Ken answered a lot of questions and then handed several to Jeff for him to answer. Just before Jeff said it, I knew he was going to ask me to come on stage. I didn't feel I had his support even though he had agreed to my promotion. It was just one of those feelings that nagged at me. That may have been more about my own insecurity than reality, but regardless I didn't feel good about his support.

Sure enough, he said it, "Cindy, would you come up here and answer a couple of questions." He was still answering a question about the analysts and associates being invited to the business unit Christmas parties as he handed me the card with the question that he wanted me to answer. It was an easy one. "What and when will we know the program that will replace the current ESOP?" someone had written on the card. ESOP stood for Enron Stock Ownership Plan and the six-year plan was about to expire.

The ESOP was a brilliant idea. It was basically our retirement account, and anyone who had been in the current program long enough saw their money triple in just a few years because it was in Enron stock. I read the question and quickly answered it with a matter of fact answer that we would know the details of the new program by the first quarter of 2000. I went on to explain that we would release information about it then. Great! I was finished, *That was a snap,* I thought.

But not so quick; Jeff handed me another card. This one was hard to read and I had gradually been losing my ability to read without glasses. That happens to most of us over forty. One day you can read, the next day you have to hold whatever you are reading a little farther from your face than the day before.

I didn't have my glasses with me so Jeff helped me determine what it said, "Should we invest all of our money in our 401(k) in Enron stock?" was the question on the card and I repeated it to the audience. Then, in a very cheerleader-type way I answered it, "Absolutely…right, guys?" and I turned around and gave Ken, Jeff and Joe a chance to add anything to the answer I had just given.

The audience broke out in laughter at the answer and the reaction from the three standing behind me. Then the three guys on stage all started handing me the cards they had in their hand and told the audience, "She's doing such a good job we are going to let her answer all the rest of the questions."

As I exited the stage I was happy with the way that had gone. The audience thought it was funny and so did my three bosses. *Good job,* I thought. Then when I sat down next to Beth she confirmed it—I had done well!

Never in a million years did I imagine that the answer to that last question would change my life. The video of that moment of me on stage saying "Absolutely!" would end up on national television, in numerous Senate hearings, in a movie (twice) and in the federal courtroom of the corporate fraud trial of the century. An off the cuff remark would be the reason for me to be a target of several federal investigations. Yes, the changes that were about to take place within the next three years were the farthest thing from my mind as I sat down and relished my performance on stage.

Growing Up in Kansas

I grew up in Kansas, just like Dorothy in the *Wizard of Oz*. In fact, a good friend of mine gave me a wonderful poster in the mid 1980s that simply stated in black and white "Toto.....I don't think we are in Kansas anymore." I kept that framed message in each office I was moved to throughout my career. I even have it hanging in my house today. I always smile when my eyes are drawn to that saying.

It actually held a double meaning for me. Physically I wasn't in Kansas anymore, which is how it could be read literally since I grew up there. Most importantly, however, my simple Kansas life was a long ago memory. Now I was in Houston, Texas, in a Fortune 10 company, as one of its senior executives. That saying simply stated the obvious, and it helped remind me where I had been both physically and emotionally.

I was actually born in Omaha, Nebraska, in July 1952. I don't remember my first year in Omaha as I was much too small to remember anything at all. I always found it interesting that I would return to Omaha more than twenty-five years later to start my career with the company that I would spend the majority of my life working for.

The earliest childhood memories I have were in Coffeyville, Kansas. At the time, Coffeyville was not much

bigger than a spot in the road. I vividly remember living on a dirt road with a huge corn field across from our
house. I don't have that many memories of Coffeyville,
but for some reason, when I think of Coffeyville, the first
memory that comes to my mind was the Sunday I ran
home from church.

I believed my family had left church without me. I
can still see myself running down that dirt road crying
as clearly as it was yesterday. I wonder what God was
thinking as He saw me running from church. Maybe He
was thinking" Well, at least she knows her way home."
Later in life that would become appropriate, as finally at
the age of fifty-two I did find my way back home to the
church and to God.

We moved to Wichita, Kansas, in 1957. Actually, we
moved to Park City, a suburb of Wichita. I have many
memories growing up in that little house. I had a younger
brother and sister and the house was only nine hundred
square feet. The house had one small bathroom that all
five of us used, but we didn't care or ever think that was
bad at the time.

That small house would become famous in 2005 when
the Wichita police finally identified Dennis Rader as the
BTK killer. BTK stood for "bind, torture and kill," which
is what he did to his victims. The BTK killer stalked
Wichita for more than twenty-five years, and he was living in our old house all of that time. My parents had sold
that house to him and his wife, Paula, sometime in 1976.

In 2005, when my parents found out Dennis was to
be arrested, they started getting media calls from reporters who wanted any kind of information they could get
their hands on about the suspect. I remember telling my

mother that whatever they did, don't mention to any of the media that they also had a daughter that had worked for Enron. I thought that if the media picked up on that bit of information as well, my parents might have to answer a lot of other kinds of questions. I didn't want them to have to deal with both issues.

We have a close family and all three of us kids felt a lot of love growing up. I was the oldest of the three and we were spaced in age two years apart. We were always told we could do anything we wanted to do and I believed it.

We didn't really talk about "bad stuff" a lot. In fact I don't think I ever saw my mom and dad fight. That would be a problem later in my life as I was married and started having disagreements with my husband, Grady. Because I had never seen my parents fight, I thought it wasn't normal to argue with your husband.

My mother was nice to everyone. I don't remember ever seeing any kind of confrontation involving my mother, or for that matter, I don't think she ever said anything bad about anyone. Unfortunately, I think because of that, I was always trying to please people. I wanted everyone to like me no matter what. That would prove to be one of my biggest management weaknesses. You can't please everyone all of the time and be an effective manager. That was something I had to continually work on throughout my career.

My mother is a worrier. She worries about all of us kids constantly, and I think she can even sense at times when we are having a bad day. I am not sure exactly how my dad feels about a lot of things. Like many men, he has a hard time expressing his feelings, but I know he loves us.

I never heard my dad say a harsh word to anyone or about anyone either. I love for him to come to our house to help Grady build things. Grady blows up when something isn't going just right. My dad on the other hand, stays calm and just figures if out. I don't think I have ever heard him say a swear word. My parents married in Wichita, Kansas, in 1949 and except for the brief move to Omaha and Coffeyville stayed there all of their lives.

My dad was the youngest of three children and my mother was the next-to-the-youngest of five. I have always felt fortunate that I grew up in a home with all of the love and encouragement my parents gave us. They led a simple life in Kansas and couldn't relate to the Enron world I was living in. It wasn't until that world of mine fell apart as an adult that I realized neither of my parents were equipped to help me through the toughest thing I would ever go through.

I was very close to my maternal grandmother. She loved to come and visit Grady and I wherever we lived, and she helped me make curtains or pillows or what ever we needed for our early houses. I still miss her. She never sat idle. She was always busy with her hands making something for someone else. I was fortunate to inherit a bracelet of hers that I had a jeweler refurbish, and I feel like she is with me when I wear it.

My mother's father was an executive with Texaco. He only had an eighth-grade education, but advanced to the level he did because everyone liked him so much. He died before he saw my success with Enron. In fact, he, my grandmother, and Ken Lay died the exact same way—massive heart attacks. My grandparents were married for more than sixty years, and the extended family they are responsible for numbers almost sixty people. Thanks to their love, our family is close and pretty darn normal as families go.

My dad's mother was hard to get to know and consequently I was never very close to her. She didn't want me to marry Grady because he had not gotten a college degree. My dad's father was successful in Amway, but he died when I was still in high school. I really did not know him that well either. My dad's side of the family rarely sees each other, which is too bad because I would love to know them.

My mother's side of the family gets together for almost every holiday and all weddings. We have a great time when we are together, and its so much fun to see all of the grandkids and great-grandkids growing up. Unfortunately, I became so arrogant about my success with Enron that I wouldn't be surprised if some of my family actually thought I deserved what happened to me.

Growing up in Park City, which was a relatively small community, we lived close to the grade school. We could walk to school, come home for lunch, and there was never any worry about being abducted like there is today. I was chubby when I attended grade school. In fact, I recall I was the third heaviest in the third grade class, right behind two boys. One day the teacher had posted our weights on the chalkboard and there I was. I was right up there with those two fat boys weighing in over one hundred pounds.

I guess that is when I started feeling embarrassed about my weight. Mother always made our clothes, so I really didn't focus on my size until later in life. My sister wasn't heavy growing up, in fact she was voted the

Heights High School Homecoming Queen her senior year of high school. I have always had a negative feeling about my weight and I felt like I had a fat body. Even at my smallest weight, which was a size four, I felt I was too fat.

I graduated sixteenth in my high school graduating class of almost six hundred, but still felt like I wasn't smart enough. My memories of high school focus on the times when my grade point fell below the 4.0 mark. Everyone that held a 4.0 grade point had a pass that allowed them to leave the campus periodically for lunch out, or for an afternoon personal outing. I had my honors pass taken away several times when my grade point dropped below 4.0.

I was in the pep club and on the debate team. I was never crowned a queen. I was up for the prom queen my senior year, but the student vote ended up in a tie between me and another girl. We flipped a coin in the vice principal's office to determine the winner and she won the toss. I have always kicked myself because if I had voted for myself instead of her I would have won fair and square.

Growing up we attended a small church a mile or so away from our house in Park City. We went to Sunday school every Sunday, and I was baptized sometime in the third grade. We learned all of the Bible stories but honestly, I don't recall studying bible scripture.

As I study scripture now, I have realized that there are so many things I have yet to learn. Thanks to my parents we at least got a good Christian foundation and I am thankful for that. I always knew it was right to treat people like you wanted to be treated, and I knew what Christmas and Easter really meant. I only wish I would have known enough to turn my life over to God at an earlier age. I could have avoided a lot of worrying and anxiety over issues that, in the scheme of things, just didn't matter.

I don't have many memories of boys that really stand out in my mind until the summer of 1967. That was the summer that I started to notice them, boys that is. My mother worked at the community swimming pool and I spent everyday during the summer swimming at the pool. That was the summer that I could dive, head first off of the ten-foot board. Something I would never think about doing today.

I am sure everyone has memories of their first love and of all of the songs that were popular at the time you fell in love. My first love was Steve Rogers and he was popular with a lot of the girls that also hung out at the swimming pool that summer. "To Sir with Love" was our song, and we would sit in the park near the pool and talk for hours. He was a great guy, but would not have been the right person for me to marry and spend the rest of my life with.

My best friend was Naomi Hall. Naomi was tall, thin and popular and married a guy that went to West Point. After they married, they stayed in Wichita, Kansas, all of their lives and had a son and daughter. We lived two houses apart growing up and we spent most of our teenage lives together. Naomi still remembers my birthday and our anniversary and I get a card from her like clockwork. She even writes a note in every card, which I find amazing, and I always vow when I get one of those cards to do better about keeping in touch with friends. Her parents and mine have continued to do things socially together all of these years. It is amazing to me how a friend like that can stay in your life for so long. We rarely see each other, but we still know what is going on with each others' lives.

I thought I had found the guy that I would spend the rest of my life with in Steve Rogers. I can still remember him coming to pick me up for dates in his 1955 Chevy and all of the fun memories we shared going to proms, homecomings and the drive-in theatre. I think we, along with a lot of other people in our lives, thought that we would get married and have a whole lot of kids and live happily ever after. As I look back on those years I am so thankful that we didn't marry. I truly found the love of my life after Steve.

In the summer of 1970, after I graduated from high school, I met that love. A TG&Y Family Center was being built right across the highway from the drive-in theatre where I worked during the summer. Most people don't remember TG&Y's. The initials stood for Thomlinson, Gosselin and Young, who were the founders, but a lot of people thought the initials stood for Turtles, Girdles and Yoyo's! When Wal-Mart eventually came into the market many people were hired away from TG&Y, and the competition caused TG&Y to go out of business in the 1980s.

That summer in 1970, I decided to apply for a part time job at the new TG&Y on 61st and Broadway in Park City. I was hired in the Ladies' Apparel Department and was later promoted to work in customer service. Within a few weeks, I started noticing the guy that would eventually steal my heart for the rest of my life.

Grady Olson was one of the co-managers of the large

family center. He was tall, blonde and great looking. In fact, many people have told me he looks like the younger, thinner version of Nick Nolte. I had a great time flirting with him when we worked together even though he was my boss. He tells me he actually asked me out twice before I finally agreed to go out with him, but I don't remember that. I was still with Steve.

Finally, I told Steve that I felt like I should at least date other guys. He reluctantly agreed. To make a long story short, the date with Grady went well, and soon it was over with Steve. Grady and I were together—forever.

Grady was also raised in a good Midwest family, went to church, and had two sisters and a brother. His parents loved him, but his dad never told him that he did, and his mother was not happy in their marriage. They both gave the kids all the necessities in life, including a solid moral and ethical foundation.

Grady was funny and made me laugh. Oh, we had our fights and I think that was why my dad wasn't that thrilled we were together when we first started dating. Little did my dad know, Grady would be the best thing that ever happened to me.

It seemed to me and everyone else that we dated forever. Finally though, on October 18, 1975, we were married in the church Grady grew up in. The minister who married us cautioned us that our marriage would not last. During our pre-marital counseling, he picked up on something that led him to believe that we were not exactly right for each other. I'm not sure my dad was all that happy either as I was told he cried as he walked me down the aisle. I never have asked him why, and I don't think I even noticed.

I was so happy that day and all I could see walking up the aisle toward the altar was Grady. It was like we were alone in that church. He told me I was beautiful as we walked back down the aisle together. As I look back now I know God was there smiling because he knew we would grow more and more in love with each other. Even more than we thought we did on that day.

Through all of the trials He had in store for us we would eventually become each others' true friend, each others' supporter, and still be head over heels in love. God knew what He was doing. Perhaps this was my first indication that God knows the whole truth. Grady would be the person who would eventually give me the right kind of support when I needed it later in my life. When I thought my world was falling apart, Grady would be the example that showed me patience and kindness and the kind of understanding I needed when I would be at the very lowest point in my life.

The Beginning of My Career

I attended Wichita State University in Wichita, Kansas, and joined Delta Gamma sorority after I graduated from high school. I started at Wichita State in the fall of 1970, which was the year the university's football team was killed in a plane crash near the Eisenhower Tunnel in Colorado. I can still remember where I was that afternoon. We were putting the finishing touches on a Delta Gamma float for the homecoming parade scheduled for the next weekend.

I was a sorority legacy, which means my mother had been a Delta Gamma, so it was assumed I would pledge DG. All of my friends from Heights High School, where I attended high school, pledged Tri Delta. So, I was on my own and became friends with many girls from all over the city of Wichita. I enjoyed the Greek life, even though Wichita State was a commuter college and the sorority houses were not live-in houses. It gave me an opportunity to be involved in the school and make some very close friends.

While in college I worked part time at a small advertising agency every afternoon after classes. I was originally hired as the receptionist, but I really couldn't type very well and after awhile it was clear that I was much better at numbers than typing. So, I was promoted to be the bookkeeper. I later learned that I was hired because one of the owners thought I reminded her of her own daughter.

One day, early in my tenure with the company, we were getting a mailing ready to go out to all of the banks in Kansas. I happened to notice that the dates on the flyer announcing the bank event were not correct. I quickly called the error to the owner's attention and we immediately stopped the mailing and had to rerun the flyer. They were so appreciative of my initiative and went on to share with me that I could not only handle people effectively, but I also had a strong attention to detail. I would hear that same compliment many times in my career at Enron.

I didn't see much of the two people who I worked for at the advertising agency because by the time that I came into work after classes they had gone to lunch and they took very long lunches. I was a self-starter so that didn't bother me much. When I graduated, I thought it would be nice to continue to work there, but my boss told me that she saw much more potential in me than that and encouraged me to find a better job.

So, in 1975, after I graduated from college I went to work at Koch Oil Company. Many graduates of Wichita State went to work for either Koch or Pizza Hut there in Wichita. Koch was a great company and I was lucky that they considered graduates from Wichita State and didn't get too concerned with GPAs. College was not as easy for me as high school, and my GPA was only 2.9. I felt fortunate that I was offered a job as an accountant in the crude oil division at Koch. I enjoyed working for Koch as it was so close to where I lived, and I was learning about the energy business.

During the three years that I worked for Koch, Grady and I got married and we moved to Winfield, Kansas, where he was a co-manager of the TG&Y in town. Winfield was a town of approximately 15,000 people and I drove nearly fifty miles to work in Wichita every single day after we were married.

Kansas is famous for tornados. I was terrified of them, not because of ever being in one, but just hearing the stories. I remember there were many afternoons, when the sky was threatening, I would make the fifty-mile drive between Wichita and Winfield and worry the entire way that I would encounter a tornado in route. I think I had identified a number of possible ditches that I could take cover in should the need arise.

It wasn't until I worked for Enron in downtown Houston many years later that I actually encountered a tornado. I was on the 37th floor of the Enron building, which was all glass, and a tornado hit the building, breaking windows and throwing debris on the floors. I guess because of my early fear of those things I was on the ground floor in sixty seconds! That had to be some kind of record as I was wearing heels and literally running down the stairwell.

After three years of driving back and forth between Wichita and Winfield I was tired of the drive, and I was becoming dissatisfied with my first job. It was pretty clear during those three years that to progress within Koch, it helped if you were a guy. There were several things that happened to convince me of that. Not only were there no women in mid-level management positions, there were not that many even at the lower levels where I was. When my office partner, a guy who started at the company after

I did, was given his own private office, I decided it was time to leave. I remember feeling so hurt that I had not been considered for that office. So, I answered a newspaper ad for an auditor with Pizza Hut, and was hired in the fall of 1978.

Pizza Hut was also a great company in Wichita. The Carney brothers, who were from Wichita, had started their business in a small brick building on Bluff Street, right around the corner from where my mother grew up. I accepted the job as an internal auditor, which would prove to be valuable as I progressed within Enron. The job with Pizza Hut was both challenging and a lot of fun. It was a very young company and had just been acquired by PepsiCo. The average age at the time of the employees who worked there was thirty-five and I felt right at home.

The job involved a lot of travel all over the country. I got to see many places I otherwise would not have had the opportunity go to. The travel also gave me confidence that I could be on my own anywhere. I spent much of my time, on the road, visiting the actual restaurants and performing audits of their operations by myself. I was so glad that Pizza Huts had red roofs, as I had trouble locating them at times and the red roofs stood out and made them easier to spot. Of course the navigation systems of today would have made that job a whole lot easier!

After nine months on my new job at Pizza Hut, Grady had an offer that we both felt we could not refuse. He was still working in retail for TG&Y as a manager of one of the family centers but he was now in Wichita. A couple of prominent Wichita businessmen approached him about becoming the operational manager of several pizza chain restaurants they were opening in Omaha, Nebraska. They offered him an equity stake in the operation as part of his compensation.

This was the first time either of us thought about leaving Wichita, but it really wasn't hard. We both liked the idea of owning a piece of something. That possibility was exciting, along with the change it brought into our lives. I believe that was the first time I realized how much I liked change. It always presented new opportunities and those opportunities always seemed to work out well for us.

Grady went to Omaha in the fall of 1979. I stayed in Wichita and got us ready to move. I gave my notice at Pizza Hut with mixed emotions. I was happy for our move, but thought I was leaving the best company that I would ever work for. I had no clue that I would ultimately be wrong about that assumption as I sent out many resumes to companies that had a major presence in Omaha.

After we moved into the very first "new" house we ever had, I went to work for General Electric. We moved from an older, small, two-bedroom brick "starter" house we had purchased on Wichita's west side to this new house, a simple tri-level in a new subdivision of Omaha. It had been a builder's model home so it had a lot of extras. We lived in a small cul-de-sac and got to know most of our neighbors very well. It was a fairly young neighborhood except for the couple that lived next door to us.

They had a son, Joe Nieto, who also lived in the same subdivision several blocks away. He was married to a girl, also named Cindy, and we four became very good friends. We water skied together and went on river trips on Cindy's father's boat. Joe ran his father-in-law's restaurant.

It was a fantastic Mexican restaurant that we all loved to go to on Friday nights. They had great margaritas and cheese dip, which are still my weaknesses. Joe and Cindy went on vacations with us and Joe eventually ran one of Grady's pizza restaurants. Unfortunately, after a couple of years the restaurant closed, and Joe and Cindy moved to Houston. We all got involved in life and lost touch. Joe would come to play a significant part in my life later on, however.

After a couple of months at General Electric I realized that it was not the company I was looking for. It was like working in a factory. Everyone sat out in the open in rows of desks. The employees were older than I had been used to at Pizza Hut, much older in fact, and it just didn't seem progressive enough to suit my ambition.

Luckily I received a call from Northern Natural Gas which was a subsidiary of InterNorth. I was asked to come in for an interview with their company. I had submitted my resume to several companies in Omaha, but I thought that my experience with Koch Oil made me a natural for the job with InterNorth.

I was hired by Northern Natural Gas in general accounting in the spring of 1979. I remember when I first started; I sat next to a couple of guys that didn't have a lot of ambition. Richard was from Amarillo, Texas, and complained about the women in Omaha. He compared them to the more attractive Texas women he was used to. He said that Omaha women were not good looking enough for his taste. In fact he was almost obsessed with that, and I don't think he stayed in Omaha very long.

Warren was on a joy ride and spent most of his day plugging the parking meter and playing card and board games with his friends. He was a nice guy and I got along great with him, but I really never saw him accomplish a thing.

I buckled down and learned as much as I could about the company and the area in which I was working. Quickly I felt there was, unlike Koch, the potential for a woman to advance in this company. There was actually a woman who was in a supervisory role on my floor that I got to know fairly well. I remember sharing with her that I was proud that a woman could advance that far.

Not too long after I started in accounting I was promoted to the Internal Audit Department. I have always thought that my experience with Pizza Hut helped me with that first promotion. Regardless, it was a great move for me, and gave me the opportunity to see a lot more of the company.

Once in the Internal Audit Department, I learned how to quantify the amount of money that we recovered from our audit work. That gave me a firm foundation of how to quantify my worth to the corporation. We performed what I referred to as operational audits of the wells where Northern purchased gas from producers in Oklahoma and Texas. It was a lot of fun, and it came easy for me to determine if and how much we were being overcharged for the gas we purchased.

It was a fluke that allowed me to take responsibility for the Northern Natural Gas producer auditing. Another woman wanted the job and was set to travel to the first audit, but she became ill and could not go. I took the lead on the audit after she became ill and luckily the audit was very successful.

The experiences I had with previous companies and

within the InterNorth organization were critical to my career growth at Enron. During my internal audit experience I identified several million dollars in overcharges we paid to a particular producer due to misallocation of the wellhead production. Wellhead production is the gas taken directly from the ground at the well. With that success I was insured the lead in several major audits after that, and I was very good at identifying the issues. As I look back now and see the entire chain of events in my career growth, it is clear God was working in my life. The early success I had in the Northern Natural audit role was key as I progressed up the Enron corporate ladder.

I learned a lot in the couple of years that I worked in the audit department of Northern Natural. The energy industry was changing and wellhead pricing was based on the date the well was drilled. Actually it was fairly complicated and you had to know the rules to do an effective job auditing the production.

I enjoyed traveling to Oklahoma and Texas. The people in Texas were friendly and I felt like I was right at home there. I always prided myself on my personality and the way I treated other people. These people in Texas actually smiled at you and seemed to care about where you came from and what you were doing. I would be told in one of my performance reviews while in Omaha that I tended to be overly "friendly" to people.

These women from Texas also dressed fashionably and wore "big hair" even though they were in management positions. I started to feel right at home when I traveled to Texas.

My observation was that a lot of Omaha women were overly conservative. I was even coached by my managers in Omaha to dress more conservatively myself. They told me to wear less jewelry and wear my hair differently. I thought that was strange, but I tried to comply. Actually my boss in the audit department gave me the feedback that other executives were suggesting that I should dress more professionally. He told me, however, to be my own person and dress and wear my hair the way I wanted to. I would remain good friends with that particular manager for many years after that.

I thoroughly enjoyed my time in the audit department because of the travel, the ability to quantify my worth to the organization, and the things about the company I was learning. In addition, the people I worked with were lots of fun. After a couple of years in that group, a job opening as the manager of the Northern Natural Gas Accounting Department was posted. The job posting process was something I was not familiar with in my previous jobs.

If you were interested in a particular job you could apply for it. In most other companies you were only considered for promotions when management identified you for a particular job. For some reason, I felt an urge to apply for this particular position. I can remember that it came down to me and a guy that was very well thought of in the company. He had already previously worked in the gas accounting area.

He was a shoe-in for the position, I thought. But, I was chosen for the job. I was surprised and very, very happy. I had now been promoted twice within two years, and I started to think that I might be able to achieve success in this company. For the next couple of years I did just that within the gas accounting organization. I kept asking for more and more responsibility, and soon I was known as one of "Chuck Radda's favorites." Chuck was the head of the Finance Group for the Northern Natural Gas subsidiary of InterNorth. I was never a direct report of Chuck Radda's, but he was keeping track of my career.

It was early in 1980 that Grady's business partner in the pizza restaurants introduced us to Aspen. He took us skiing there several years in a row and we fell in love with it. After that first trip we would never go anywhere else in Colorado to ski. We became hooked on the glamour and life style of Aspen, Colorado, which I think, looking back, played a role in my drive for success, no matter the cost.

I was not only doing well in my position in Gas Accounting, I had also been asked to participate in a group that looked at the merger strategy of the large energy players. It was a time in the energy industry that many companies were merging to take advantage of the economies of scale that the combination of the two companies created. It probably wasn't a coincidence again that one of the players we focused on was Ken Lay and what he was doing with Houston Natural Gas and Transwestern Pipeline. I remember we all thought he had a brilliant strategy combining Houston Pipeline and Florida Gas.

Looking back, I recall being very interested in what Ken Lay was doing. Even more than would have been normal as a member of the task force. Something told me that he was a person to keep track of. I was also taking several leadership classes, was being asked to take leadership tests and being considered for upper management positions.

Years later, a very good friend I had known since the early 1980s told me that one of the InterNorth officers had asked her what women at InterNorth had management potential. She told him that she would include me on that list.

She also loves to tell the story about a deposition that a production company asked I give in regard to Inter-North's wellhead gas purchases from them. She remembers that the producer representatives thought they were going to be deposing a typical accountant, and the way she describes it, were surprised when I walked into the room and I was a good looking blonde. She tells me that I was so nervous that I didn't even hear them ask for my name and address several times before one of the other attorneys asked if they were trying to, in fact, get my phone number!

I was getting more and more wrapped up in my job, myself and the possibility of future promotions. Because of that, I believe, Grady and I started having issues in our marriage. Unfortunately, the pizza restaurants weren't doing well, and I think Grady saw me progressing in my job but he didn't know where he was going with his.

Even then I was starting to get a little arrogant about my success. I have seen this happen to other women who have been close to me. They became more successful monetarily than their husbands and ultimately ended up divorcing. I was lucky that I married someone who hung in there with me even though I was probably becoming pretty hard to live with.

Grady eventually went to work for a truck line in Omaha. He was hired as a salesman for the company and started to learn the trucking business. He worked with a couple of women I didn't care for. One afternoon Grady and I attended a party hosted by one of these women. She deliberately introduced Grady to a former Miss Nebraska without acknowledging me standing right next to him. They all did a lot of traveling together and I was jealous when I took the time away from my work to think about it.

It was a Sunday afternoon in early 1984. I had gone into the office to catch up on some things I had not gotten to during the week. With no one else in the office I thought I would be able to make a lot of progress that afternoon. It was that day, however, that Casey Olson showed up in my office. Casey was a vice president in the rate department. He told me he had some mail delivered to him that belonged to me. Because our initials were the same, (C. Olson), that happened a lot.

He was charming, good looking, and he was definitely flirting with me. After that Sunday he came to my floor to see me frequently or called me when he traveled just to say hello. It felt good getting that kind of attention from an executive within the company. We spent a lot of lunch hours going to some of the best places in Omaha together and gradually our relationship developed into something more than friends. I started thinking that maybe he was the person that I should have in my life instead of Grady. I even went home to Wichita and discussed it with my family.

Casey said all of the right things and seemed totally in love with me until one night he was suppose to meet me at a restaurant in Omaha and he didn't show up. He had started showing an interest in one of the waitresses we had gotten to know at one of our favorite restaurants. Soon after that I realized he was married and his wife had found out about us through a mutual friend of mine.

It was clear that he was a smooth-talking womanizer that knew how to charm women who were vulnerable.

We stopped seeing each other in 1985. I don't think I had ever really recovered from my suspicions a few years before about Grady and a woman that worked near his pizza restaurant in Omaha. Maybe in the back of my mind I was actually getting involved with Casey to show Grady and myself that I was still desirable. That was probably God in my life testing me and unfortunately, I failed miserably. Not only had I not really forgiven Grady for what I thought he had done, I had gotten involved with Casey.

One evening, years later, when I lived alone in my apartment in Houston I answered a knock at the door. It was Casey. He had gotten a divorce and his ex-wife and I had become good friends. She was living in the same apartment complex that I was in and Casey had been over at her apartment helping her move in. I didn't let him in my apartment. We stood at the door and made small talk. Finally, I told him that knowing him had really made me appreciate my husband. With that, he left and I don't think I ever saw him again.

After the Enron collapse, I can't count the number of people who wanted to know if I had been involved with Ken Lay. Even the Justice Department investigated the possibility that I had been involved with Ken. I guess it's too bad that the perception exists that you have to be involved with the CEO to rise to the level I was at Enron. I was with Ken Lay a lot and not once did I ever feel anything other than total respect from him.

Casey taught me a valuable lesson. He made me appreciate my husband and what I had. Oh, Grady and I would still have challenges to deal with, but I knew that I loved Grady and I wanted to be with him. Grady, in contrast to Casey, loved me more than anything. He was honest, and even though we had our struggles it was really never about us loving each other. I would figure out years later that our conflicts came from Grady's insecurity of feeling that I was better than he was. He was always afraid that I would leave him if I became too successful. After Casey I never even thought about another man again.

The Creation of Enron

Some time in the spring of 1985, rumors started flying that InterNorth was being taken over by a gentleman named Erwin Jacobs. I wasn't a big enough player in the organization to know all of the details, but it was crystal clear that people in Omaha were nervous. Mergers usually meant that you couldn't count on keeping your current position, and of course there could be layoffs.

There was one weekend in the spring that we all worked the entire weekend without going home. I remember we didn't even get to take a shower or change clothes. We were copying documents for due diligence we were told. I don't think at that point in my work career, I had ever worked such long hours.

By July 1985, we knew what was going to happen to InterNorth. Since we were buying a company ourselves we were less attractive as a take over target. Sam Segnar, our CEO and the InterNorth Board had made an offer to buy Houston Natural Gas (HNG). That was the company led by Ken Lay that our strategic group had looked at a few months earlier.

The acquisition seemed to be a great move for all of us since it appeared that we were the ones in control and it would be the officers of InterNorth who would be making the decisions about people and where the company would ultimately be located. InterNorth had just completed a new corporate headquarters building across Dodge Street from our current building in Omaha and it didn't seem reasonable we would be going anywhere.

What was going on behind the scenes was something that I found out much later from Ken Lay himself. In the years to come, Ken would reveal in conversations I was involved in, that in fact he was asked by Bill Strauss himself to step in as CEO of the company. He did this to stop the political war that was raging between the Inter-North board and Houston Natural's board. Bill Strauss was the chairman of the InterNorth board and highly thought of by all of the InterNorth people.

Eventually, however, everyone from InterNorth discovered that we were not the ones in the driver's seat at all. I will never forget sitting in the old Orpheum theatre in Omaha hearing Sam Segnar tell the employees that a significant part of the company would move to Houston as it was the Energy Capital of the world and it made more sense to have an energy company in Texas.

I had done a lot of traveling to Texas in my internal audit days and actually liked the people there and thought they were friendly. I also had not grown up in Omaha so I wasn't as concerned as many of the people that had been raised in Omaha. I also liked Ken Lay who Sam Segnar introduced to us at that meeting. He reminded me of my grandfather. Little did I know that he would in fact become a major part of my life. I don't remember a lot more about the meeting or the events that took place before I was asked to move to Houston.

I was walking down the hall towards my office several months after the meeting at the Orpheum. My assistant called to me that I had a call from Jim Rogers. I knew he was "from Houston," but could not imagine why he would be calling me. Jim was in charge of all of the Interstate Pipelines including Transwestern and Florida Gas. "Cindy," he said, "I hear you are very good at Gas Accounting and I need someone to help me straighten out our Gas Accounting down here in Houston so I can discuss take or pay payments with our producers."

I understood the problem, as we had been dealing with a similar situation at Northern Natural Gas. Most pipelines had signed contracts with producers in the past to purchase their production or pay them for it if they could not take it. These contracts were signed when pipelines were desperate for gas production to run through their lines. Now that the entire pipeline grid was being deregulated, you could buy your gas cheaper from other producers not attached to your own pipeline system. There was also an abundance of gas production that had not existed in the past. Consequently, the take or pay liabilities held by pipelines were tremendous. All the pipelines were working with the producers to negotiate lower payments. If the pipeline had other issues in addition to take or pay, like Jim Rogers was dealing with, it was almost impossible to get the producers to even discuss a settlement.

He asked me if I would be willing to consider moving to Houston and taking over the Interstate Gas Accounting Group. I can't remember exactly what I said, but I know I was thinking how exciting that would be and that I wanted to do it. Not only was it in Houston, which I liked, but it was also a problem area. This was the first of many problems areas I would take on in my career at

Enron. I always enjoyed fixing something, but wasn't that good at maintaining an area that was doing okay.

Obviously given the situation with Casey, Grady and I had been having some issues in our marriage during that past year or so. I had been promoted quickly and had been successful enough that I was, just like Grady feared, starting to think that I didn't necessarily need him or anyone else for that matter.

We went through some counseling during our time in Omaha. The pizza venture was not as successful as we had hoped, and he had landed the job as a freight salesman for Churchill Truck Lines in 1982. Grady was great in sales. He has always had the ability to create personal bonds with people easily. In just a few short years he developed a strong client base in the trucking industry and Holmes Freight Lines had noticed. He was offered a similar position, but with more money and a company car at Homes Freight Lines in 1984.

There were a lot of issues we were dealing with. Grady was building his client base and progressing within the trucking industry. I had been sharply focused on my career with InterNorth and now this opportunity in Houston gave me even broader career horizons. In a way, I thought this might solve the problems. It was like a separation, but we didn't have to call it that.

I still have sad memories of our relationship when we go back to Omaha to visit. I certainly don't blame him for all of that. We were both pretty selfish and all wrapped up in our own worlds. I didn't even ask Grady if I could move to Houston. I just told him I wanted to move and gave him all of my reasons it made sense for me—not us.

Looking back, that was just a continuation of the self-centered person that I was becoming. I was already addicted to the success and the money I was earning. Of course, that was nothing compared to what was to come. God must have been hopeful that I would, at some point, realize the blessings he was sending my way.

Grady went with me to visit Houston to see if we wanted to move there. There wasn't anything about the trip that wasn't first class. We were greeted with a bottle of champagne in our hotel room and were treated to a wonderful dinner and tour of the city in a limo. Houston was incredible. It had so many classy restaurants and beautiful tall buildings. I was ready to go live there with no hesitation. As I look back and think about that decision I am embarrassed. I didn't even consider what Grady wanted. I knew I wanted that kind of life and I was going for it.

Grady stayed in Omaha and I stayed in a hotel in the Galleria area of Houston for more than a year. Later I moved to my own apartment on West Alabama. Grady wasn't ready to move. He still liked his job and we had moved into a new house on a small acreage in West Omaha not more than a year before. In addition, both of us were a little wary of up and moving without really knowing how well Enron would do.

I came back to Omaha every other weekend. Enron had worked out a deal with Continental Airlines for round trip tickets so it wasn't that expensive to come back. The only inconvenience was I had to pack up my things every two weeks when I came back to Omaha that first year.

The job I accepted was located at the Continental Resource Company (CRC) building, across the street from the Transco Tower in the Galleria area. The new Enron Building, which was downtown, had been leased and it was a gradual process for everyone to move out of the old Houston Natural Gas building. I was one of the first InterNorth people to move from Omaha to Houston, so I started making friends from HNG immediately. After all, they were in charge and their stock had gone up after the merger of the two companies, so they were all very happy.

The only issue I ran into early on was the guy who was currently running the Interstate Gas Accounting Group, and the financial people who worked with him at the CRC building. Understandably, they weren't that thrilled with my presence. Getting them to cooperate with the things I felt needed to be done was hard. After all, they had created the problems I was brought in to fix. I am not sure I would have acted a whole lot differently had I been in their shoes.

When I came to work in Houston I actually reported to Rod Hayslett. Rod worked for Jim Rogers and was responsible for the entire Finance Group for the Interstate Pipelines, which included Transwestern and Florida Gas. Rod had been a long-time employee with Florida, and was well respected within the organization. He had a very supportive management style and I enjoyed working for him. We would work together off and on until Enron filed for bankruptcy in late 2001. Actually, we were both on the administrative committee of the 401(k) when Enron filed for bankruptcy.

The problems that existed in the Interstate Pipeline organization were not that hard to fix. It required knowing what issues were causing the low accuracy of invoicing, getting people to take accountability for results and measuring those results. Something I learned in the audit department.

Unfortunately, the guy who ran the gas accounting group was not going to make the cut. He eventually left Enron and bought an 18-wheel truck and started his own business hauling freight. He was the kind of person who believed if you made an effort you were a good employee. I on the other hand, had learned to focus on results, and eventually we got the results that we needed. I was quickly learning what it took to get ahead.

There were others in the organization that didn't stay. I remember I tried to get the head of the accounting department to work with the rate department. They needed to work together to insure we had all of the best information for billing. In response to my request, he puffed up and told me that he was big and mean enough to do things on his own and he didn't have to work with the rate department on anything. I definitely had to deal with culture challenges. It was a good warm-up for the things I would face later in my career.

My personal life consisted of work and more work. Sometimes in the evening I would go for a run around the Transco Tower running track or occasionally go to dinner with someone that was in town from Omaha. But normally my life revolved around work and going back to Omaha every two weeks to see Grady. I am not sure what Grady did while I was gone. We never really discussed it, or if we did I don't remember.

One weekend in 1987, I flew back to Omaha and Grady picked me up at the airport. I noticed the flags were flying at half staff. I had no clue what had happened. Grady had to explain to me that one of the United States' naval ships was blown up by terrorists. I realized then that I was only involved and focused on the Enron world. The rest of the world just didn't exist for me.

About a year after I arrived in Houston, Jim Rogers asked me to meet him in the company cafeteria for lunch. The group I had taken over had made tremendous progress in that year, and we accomplished what I had been asked to do. I actually was fitting into the culture very well and I felt very comfortable with my decision to move to Houston. Working in Jim Rogers's organization was lots of fun. He had mobilized a fantastic team. Actually, that is when I first met Mark Frevert, who was in marketing for the Interstate Pipeline organization at the time, and who would ultimately become a very close friend.

That day, as I stood waiting for Jim at the top of the escalator that led to the cafeteria, I thought about the last year and how exciting it had been to be in Houston. I was nervous because I wasn't sure why he wanted to speak to me, but felt good about what I had accomplished. After we greeted each other I followed him into the cafeteria and we went through the food line to get our lunch before we sat down in the main room to eat. He handed me a bonus check. This was my very first bonus. It was for $600.

I had never gotten a bonus before and that seemed like a lot of money to me then. He was very happy with my performance he told me. It seemed like a dream that I was doing a good job for a company like Enron in the fourth largest city in the United States. God was certainly blessing me with incredible opportunities and I still wasn't thanking Him. I really thought I was doing it all on my own.

When I agreed to come to Houston, one of the things I asked of Jim Rogers was that I be considered for a job in marketing at some point in time. Thinking back on that I am not exactly sure why that seemed so important to me. I think in my mind anyone in gas marketing was more important to the organization and therefore, made more money. Not long after the lunch with Jim there were changes taking place in the organization again.

The Intestate Pipeline Group was going to be organized by company rather than by function. I had moved to Houston to take the lead on both Transwestern and Florida Gas accounting, and now it looked like they were going to split the two companies' functional groups apart and create another vice president of finance for Transwestern. Rod Hayslett of course would be the vice president of Florida Gas and Stan Horton was named the president. The president of Transwestern was to be Dan Ryser and he was to choose a new vice president of finance. That job would include the gas accounting area so I became a candidate.

The finance job included not only gas accounting, but the finance, planning groups, and the general accounting groups reporting to it as well. The finance and accounting areas were not my strengths so I felt lucky I was even considered for the job.

All of the candidates interviewed with Dan for that position. When I was offered the job I couldn't believe it. I was now a vice president. I remember Jim Rogers reasoning with me that this was a better move than the marketing track I had originally asked for. Little did I know that by taking this promotion, a move into marketing was all but gone because of the level that I was promoted to within the organization. It would prove to be impossible to move into a marketing job in the future and still keep the title of vice president.

The most exciting part of the Transwestern job was that I got to know Dan Ryser. I thought he was a great person and a strong leader. Dan had been with Inter-North, but I had not known him then. His expertise was in the "liquids" area, however, he was the kind of person who could catch on to anything because of his leadership style.

Dan eventually moved to Enron Capital & Trade and I lost track of him. By the late 90s he left Enron to go to work for Dynegy. Dynegy was a company that employed many ex-Enron people and had a similar business model as Enron. He did well at Dynegy. I have always been appreciative of him for promoting me to an officer position within Enron.

It was at this point in my career that Grady and I finally decided that Enron was going to make it and I wasn't coming back to Omaha. Enron's New York trading scandal, which I didn't really understand at the time, was behind the company. It also appeared to me, that I was fitting into the Houston environment and making a lot of friends. In addition, it would have been impossible for me to go back to Omaha and make the kind of money I was now making in Houston.

Grady had finally gotten tired of his job in Omaha and he realized that my future was much better in Houston. So, the decision was made that we would permanently move to Houston, and we immediately started looking for a house. Houston was so enormous that it was almost overwhelming. The housing market was cheap because of the oil bust that had taken place in the mid-eighties. We could buy a much larger house than we had in Omaha.

Grady quit his job, we sold our house in Omaha and we bought a new house in Conroe, about forty miles north of Houston. The house was a two-story brick with three fireplaces. I am not sure why anyone needs three fireplaces in Houston, but we thought it was kind of cool to have them. Grady didn't go back to work for a while because he took on the role of general contractor to build an additional garage and a swimming pool.

We were now both committed to Houston and there would be no looking back. The rough times seemed to be behind the company and I was an officer now. Grady even gave our snow blower to my brother-in-law and told people he was never going back to a place where he would need to use it again. Little did he know that years later we would need that darn snow blower!

My new job was exciting. Transwestern was the first in the industry to file a gas inventory charge. This charge was a subsidy to the actual price of the gas, which was added to allow the pipelines take or pay recovery. All gas pipelines across the country were undergoing radical change. They were going from what was called a "rate base" pricing structure to more of an open market where prices were set by supply and demand. Enron was leading the charge for energy deregulation.

The gas inventory charge, which Jim Rogers was sponsoring, was supposed to help the pipelines move into an open market but allow for a legitimate add-on charge that would help them recoup all of the old take or pay costs incurred in the past. About the same time that I was involved in this effort with Transwestern, a then, little known Jeff Skilling was working as a McKinsey consultant on the Gas Bank concept. This concept would eventually win Ken Lay's admiration and become the core strategy of a new business unit within Enron—Enron Gas Services, which soon became Enron Capital and Trade Resources, or ECT.

Not more than a couple of months after I was promoted to the vice president of finance for Transwestern, the organization changed again and the entire financial area was organized into a centralized corporate function. This was the first experience I had with corporate functions. I learned quickly that centralized corporate functions weren't respected by the businesses. They were viewed as too much overhead and a lack of control by the business units.

With this new organization structure I was promoted again. I was asked to take on all of gas accounting for the entire corporation including gas measurement. That included my old Northern Natural Gas position that I had when I left Omaha. Finally, the organization had made the step to include the Northern Natural Gas group in the company. This was the first step in integrating Northern into Enron. The entire organization, that I was now responsible for leading, numbered more than five hundred people.

I am not sure how that even happened and who was pulling for me at that point. I was now a vice president over all the gas accounting groups and gas measurement at Enron, reporting to the corporate controller, who was then Jack Tompkins. I was being asked to work with McKinsey to reorganize and trim costs. This would prove to be the first of many times I would work with McKinsey. It was easier to use a third party to help make hard decisions and McKinsey was Enron's consultant of choice in that area.

The consolidation of all of the gas accounting functional groups was done for just that purpose. Bringing all like functions together across the organization allowed us to take advantage of economies of scale. The problem with "centralization" was that the operating companies always felt like they had lost control. I learned during this effort that it was critical to have a functional organization that included someone who was respected and focused on the needs of the head of the operating company.

When I was told I had gotten the gas accounting and measurement job there were a couple of things that I remember vividly. Rod Hayslett, my good friend and mentor, was not named as head of the corporate financial planning and budgeting group. Instead, Melinda Tossoni, who I had worked with in Omaha, was named to that job. I was devastated and I experienced for the first time the loss of someone in the organization who I had grown to trust and depend on.

Rod came out okay because he had been with Florida Gas so long that he was too valuable to lose, but I now had to spread my wings without his support. I would find that not only did I lose a supporter, but I now was working with one of the hardest people I had ever had to get along with so far in my career.

Melinda Tossoni had also been one of "Chuck Radda's favorites," who I mentioned earlier was the finance officer for InterNorth. Melinda was tough, but what made her harder to get along with was the fact that she was competitive and had a very good relationship with the president of Florida Gas. That created a challenge for me as she didn't like the way I was running gas accounting. This was the first political situation I would have to deal with in my career, but would by no means be the last. Little did I know at the time that Melinda Tossoni was a "piece of cake" compared to the colleagues I would eventually be working with. God was obviously preparing me for things He had in store for me later on.

The other issue that I had to face as a result of this particular reorganization was that I now had King Oberg reporting to me. King had been my boss in Omaha when I got the opportunity to come to Houston. I didn't have a lot of respect for King because I had seen him place the blame for some issues we had in Northern Gas Accounting on a co-worker of mine, when in my opinion he should have taken more accountability himself. Now he was working for me, and I didn't necessarily trust him. Not surprisingly, King did not make the cut of people I eventually kept and relied on.

The other result of this promotion was being able to go back to Omaha periodically since part of the group reporting to me was located in Omaha. I got to work with some of my good friends again, which was nice. The Omaha environment was hard, however, because the people who had stayed in Omaha were never going to move. Most people who would even consider moving had already gone to Houston. So, the people left in Omaha were constantly afraid that their jobs would move also. It was a difficult issue to deal with because I was never certain that those fears would not be realized, and if they were, that it was not perhaps what was best for the organization.

The first thing I was charged with was to work with McKinsey to identify the people in the organization I would keep and those who would have to go. Oddly, I managed to perform that task without a lot of emotional stress. I kept telling myself that this was life, and for me to be successful I needed to keep the very best people who could do the jobs with better processes and better management skills. It was actually "fun" to benchmark the organization with other best practices organizations and to identify the cuts that would bring us in line with those companies.

This was where I learned that you had to use data to get people to buy into what you were recommending. You could not simply accept the argument from people that Enron was different. I also learned that you had to identify your management team first and make sure that they bought into the philosophy of benchmarking. They had to be willing to take some risk in the number of people needed to do the job. I realized too, that you had to not only focus on the efficiency of the organization, but also the organization's effectiveness. It would be a huge issue if we could not deliver the internal and external customer service necessary to keep the operation groups happy. This experience proved to be a valuable lesson I used many times throughout my career.

I eventually brought someone who was extremely good at reengineering into the organization to work jointly with me and one of the operating companies. He would eventually follow me to several different jobs at Enron. He was one of the best managers I had ever seen.

His name was Drew Lynch. Drew was a master at getting consensus with a group and building loyalty. He would not only teach me a lot about reengineering, but also help me understand the politics of the organization. Drew would ultimately follow me to ECT in the early 1990s and to the Human Resources organization in 2000.

I gradually learned to put the organization's needs above my own. In my heart it was hard to let people go and tell them they were not the right person for the job. I remember rationalizing, however, that if we kept everyone Enron may not be in business. To survive, these tough things had to be done. I managed to get better and better at putting my feelings about people in the background. With each promotion those feelings got pushed farther and farther back in my mind. The organization was rewarding me for remaining focused on its survival and success.

It was also during this time that Grady's and my friend, Joe Nieto, came back into our lives. He and his first wife, Cindy, had divorced, and the business venture he left Omaha to pursue had not materialized. Joe and I started talking about a position in my organization in Omaha and he ultimately went to work in the Northern Natural Gas Accounting area. We had created a gas accounting trainee program and Joe joined us in one of those positions.

Enron was becoming known as a desirable place to work, particularly if you wanted to be well rewarded for your creativity and a willingness to work hard. In fact many people that came into my life expressed an interest in working for Enron. Of course, I loved my job so much that I hardly talked about anything else. It was fun to work for a place that everyone else seemed to want to work for too.

My Career Takes Off

It was during these early years of my career, in late 1988, that I met Rick Causey. Rick was a junior member of the Arthur Andersen team at the time, and was trying to sell consulting services to Enron to augment their audit work. Ultimately Rick would come to Enron to work and rise to become Chief Accounting Officer of the company. At the time, I was becoming known as a driver of reengineering in the organization because of the fact that I had experience with InterNorth, and with many of the Houston Natural Gas entities. I developed a track record of taking on challenges in the organization, and I was able to make hard decisions. I also was mobilizing an incredible group of people who would help me in other areas later in my career.

Enron was starting to figure out how to merge the Houston Natural Gas and InterNorth operations and capabilities, and beginning to build integrated computer systems that would ultimately replace the functionality of the systems that each entity used originally. Enron was very open to bringing in consultants to help us figure this entire issue out. That kind of work meant huge dollars to consultants. Rick and I spent a lot of lunches together discussing how we were going to change the world and of course improve Enron. Eventually we became very good friends.

As Rick describes it, I *"finally"* agreed to use some

of his Arthur Andersen summer interns to reconcile accounts that my group was responsible for cleaning up. They were a great help to us in getting agreement of Enron's gas imbalance accounts with other companies.

Gas imbalances were created when two companies had an agreement to help each other move gas into areas that they did not have a physical pipeline in, but had a market to sell gas. These kinds of agreements were growing in popularity with all pipelines due to deregulation.

Enron could purchase gas in Texas and deliver it to another pipeline company in Texas outside our distribution area. For example, if we needed gas in New York, the other company would deliver the gas to us in New York off of their pipeline. An "imbalance" was created and accounted for the difference between the gas we delivered in Texas and the gas we got back in New York. These accounts were kept on the companies' respective balance sheets as either liabilities or assets.

The whole imbalance issue was huge for all the pipeline companies in the energy industry. They were very difficult to keep reconciled on both companies' books. That was one of the first projects where I utilized a cross functional team to clean up an issue. The reason that was important was because I couldn't impact the problem with just the people in my group. Several groups across the organization were responsible for creating the imbalances in the first place. To solve the issue you had to get operations, logistics and accounting at both companies to agree. This issue gave me incredible experience pulling groups together across the organization, and I would continue to use cross-functional teams many times throughout my Enron career.

The imbalance problem actually presented a couple of opportunities for me. At the completion of our imbalance clean up project, the internal Enron newsletter featured our accomplishment and I was given a lot of credit. It felt good to be recognized publicly and I liked the attention. It was again during this massive project that people noticed that I not only had an attention to detail, but I had a personality not typical of an accountant. I even got to meet with one of the Enron board members who congratulated me face to face on our accomplishments.

This experience also allowed me to work with other pipeline companies in the industry who had imbalances with us. Because of this project I became a member of a gas accounting roundtable in one of the national gas associations and I got to know a lot of people outside of Enron in our industry. I really enjoyed the networking opportunity this presented. It came natural to me to meet and connect with other people not only on a business basis, but on a personal level as well. Enron was starting to make a name for itself in the energy industry, and it was fun to be a part of a company people were starting to emulate and admire. This was my first taste of fame inside and outside of Enron and it felt good to be recognized.

Eventually, I helped bring the Gas Accounting Group *"out of the closet"* so to speak. At least that was what Ron Burns told me. Ron was in charge of Northern Natural Gas in Omaha and took over as the president of the entire Pipeline Group when Jim Rogers left Enron. Jim left to become the CEO of Cinergy, a Cincinnati-based electric company, sometime in the early 1990s. Because we were fixing many of the issues attributed to gas accounting, people both inside and outside of Enron were noticing.

Ron was becoming one of my biggest supporters. He was this big handsome guy who everyone liked (well almost everyone). He remembered people's names and always spoke to employees in an upbeat and enthusiastic way. He had a "larger than life" presence and lots and lots of charisma. There were many people who would do anything for Ron because he always treated people so well and his management style was so empowering.

Fortunately for me, Ron recognized early in my career that I had difficulty speaking in front of a group of people. I was one of those people that would rather die than get up in front of a crowd and give a speech. I became extremely nervous and it showed. He recommended I attend the Toastmasters program and it worked. Later in my career, I would have to give many speeches, and thanks to Ron I learned to deliver a message to a group of any size with ease.

When I think of Ron Burns, a somewhat embarrassing, yet funny, incident comes to mind. I was traveling from Houston to Omaha one evening to attend a management meeting in Omaha the next morning. When I arrived at the airport I ran into a good friend and colleague I knew from Omaha. I had not seen her in awhile and we were both attending the same management meeting.

Nancy Gardiner was responsible for gas scheduling and was the vice president in charge of that function for all of Enron's pipeline groups. I was the vice president over the gas accounting and measurement groups at this time, and our functions worked very closely together, but she reported to a centralized operations group and I reported to a centralized accounting function so we did not actually interact with each other very often.

As we both boarded the plane we thought was heading to Omaha we were talking non-stop about everything from Enron to our personal lives. Our husbands, in fact, were going out together that night as they knew each other and both worked in the trucking industry. Once on the plane, we continued our non stop conversation. We were so consumed in our own world that we completely missed several important things.

We hadn't heard the boarding announcement because we were so focused on our own conversation. The plane we had boarded was larger than normal, the meal they served was much nicer and the flight time was over an hour longer than the normal Houston to Omaha flight.

As we descended for our landing, again we didn't hear the announcement of our arrival city. When we touched down and I looked out of the window I immediately announced to Nancy and everyone else in the rows close to us, "This isn't Omaha. Where are we?" The people seated near us broke out in laughter because they knew we were in Los Angeles, California.

Neither Nancy nor I ever lived that incident down. We did make it back to Omaha the next morning by taking a red-eye from Los Angeles back to Houston and on to Omaha. Ron Burns was attending the management meeting we were trying to get to and everyone at the meeting took joy in the story and sharing it with as many people as they could. In fact Ron shared the story with Rich Kinder who was COO of Enron at the time, and he presented both of us with an award at the all Enron management conference that next fall. We got T-shirts announcing "This isn't Omaha. Where are we?" I don't think that either of us ever saw Rich Kinder again that he didn't tease us. He would ask us if we were sure we knew where we were going and chuckle.

Eventually, in early 1989, another organization change was announced. We were trying decentralization again. Northern Natural was being combined into its own organization separate from the other pipelines. I was asked to move to Northern Natural Gas to run the combined gas accounting and contract administration organizations. The reorganization resulted in decentralizing my two groups from a corporate function into an operating group.

As a result of this organization change I began reporting to Rick Richard. Ken Lay lured him from the FERC (Federal Energy Regulatory Commission), and like Ron, he was friendly to everyone and enthusiastic. He had an empowering management style and appreciated the skills that people brought to the organization. I remember he had Nancy Gardiner and I read a book that he had read and believed in. That book, *The Female Advantage,* focused on the strengths that women brought to a corporation.

Within months, however, Rick left the company and he was replaced by Stan Horton. I had dealt with Stan through the years. In fact when Jim Rogers brought me to Houston I interviewed with Stan. He was in charge of rates and certificates for Florida Gas at the time. He worked his way up to the president of Florida Gas, and eventually he replaced Ron Burns over all of the pipelines when Ron moved to Enron Capital and Trade to work with Jeff Skilling.

Stan was not very friendly to me. He was always so serious and I didn't really enjoy working with him. I thought Stan could have gotten so much more out of people if he would have "lightened up a bit" and taken a stronger personal interest in his people. In hindsight, I realize that Stan helped me develop the thick skin I would later need to hold my own with Enron's energy traders.

In my opinion Stan was not a good manager, but perhaps he just didn't like me very much. I think he may have been proud of the way he treated me. Maybe he intended to "toughen me up" to prepare me for my later challenges. Regardless of his motives, this was the first time in my career that I would deal with someone with such a prickly management style. Unfortunately, I think some of his management skills, or lack thereof, rubbed off on me.

When you get yelled at repeatedly, you tend to respond by yelling at someone else, or at least I did. Stan managed me by fear and intimidation. I still remember his internal phone extension and every time I saw it on my phone's caller display I knew he was mad about something. He certainly never called to check in or tell me I did something good. In later years, when I worked directly for Ken Lay it would be so refreshing to get a call from him just to see how I was doing or even tell me that I had done a good job.

When we reorganized and I went to work for Stan, he told me my salary wasn't in the budget, and if I wanted to stay in the organization I would have to find cost savings enough to pay for myself. I reengineered the group I took over and generated savings enough to pay for my own salary and then some.

There were a lot of people who got along great with Stan. He was a strong advocate for the pipeline group. For some reason, Stan and I just didn't seem to be on the same page. In some ways the fact that I could never seem to please him hurt my feelings as I tried so hard. I know that most people run into a manager like this in their career. Up to this point I had been lucky I guess.

In May of 1991, my grandmother died. My mom and dad were in Houston visiting us when it happened. We all left to go back to Kansas for her funeral. It was sad that she was gone from my life, but all of the family gathered at her house after the funeral. We all had spent so many incredible times in that house. We looked at pictures and told stories and laughed and of course cried a lot. "Mom," as we all called her, would have been proud to see all of the love we had for her and for each other. To this day we still gather as a large family for all major holidays and of course the great-grandchildren are having children of their own.

That next Thanksgiving, my mother and dad came to Houston to be with Grady and I. We rented a movie to watch that afternoon after we had all eaten way too much turkey. My dad and Grady had taken a nap and I decided to run the movie back to the rental store. Unfortunately, as I was stopped on Highway 105 in Conroe, making a left turn, a car hit me from behind.

I hadn't seen the car coming, but people who witnessed the accident told the police he was weaving in and out of traffic erratically before he hit me. It was later determined he was intoxicated. My car was totaled. The seat I was in actually broke away and I landed in the back seat of the car. One of the officers at the scene called the house, and Grady and my mom and dad came to make sure I was all right. They took me to the hospital, but I was only a little sore.

I have always believed there was a guardian angel in that car protecting me. I even remember thinking that I saw my grandmother in the seat next to me when the car hit me. Luckily I only had a stiff neck the next day. Everyone at the accident was surprised I wasn't hurt worse because the car that hit me was estimated to be traveling at least sixty mph. I could have easily been killed. I am sure God was there watching out for me.

It was during this time of my life that I started running. I turned forty and I felt fat, and I had all of the stress of working for Stan. I would take off on a run and be gone for a couple of hours. I was eventually running enough miles that I decided to train for a marathon. I am convinced that people who run a marathon have "stuff" going on in their lives. I had Stan Horton going on in mine.

Eventually, in January of 1993, I ran my first Houston marathon. I would go on to run two more in later years. Each time I know there was something driving me to prove to myself I was good. Because of all of the running I lost a lot of weight and I was wearing a size four. I also read a great book sometime during the Stan era that helped me through the Northern days. It was written by a female movie executive, Dawn Steel, and it was titled *They Can Kill You but They Can't Eat You.* It made me realize that people can do a lot of bad things to you but at the end of the day you survive.

After working for Stan for several years I did learn a few things. You have to pay your own way. In other words you have to generate enough value to the organization that you are worth having as an employee. I learned not to draw a box around my job because it usually involved others' responsibilities. Not everyone at Enron was a good leader. There were awesome leaders at Enron, but there were definitely a few that needed some work. Finally, make sure your superiors know what you have accomplished and toot your own horn—a lot.

Sadly, I also learned that if you really need to get something done and the people that work for you are not responding to kindness…yell at them! This warped management technique would cause me some problems as I moved into Enron Capital and Trade and worked for Rick Causey who was nothing like what I had learned from Stan. Also, after I worked with Terrie James, and after my long time assistant Bobbie Power left me, I would realize that I needed to change. Finally, during the last part of my career I would be fortunate enough to have one of the best managers I have ever seen as my teacher—Ken Lay.

I am sure that the experience with Stan was a blessing from God even though it was a rough time. It taught me a lot, but most of all it taught me no matter what, I would survive.

The Move to Enron Capital and Trade

In 1994, my friend, Rick Causey, was at Enron Capital and Trade (ECT). He had been hired by Jeff Skilling sometime in 1992. Jeff was starting to build his Enron Capital and Trade team and Rick was brought in from Arthur Andersen to run the accounting and back office. It appeared that ECT was going to become the place to be in Enron. Many of the more "progressive" people that had been in the pipelines were moving to ECT. When I say progressive, I mean those people who were perceived to be the higher performing, more innovative and less rigid people.

In addition, there appeared to be a lot of talent being brought in from the outside into Enron Capital and Trade. In fact, they hired an information technology guy from New York. Jenny Rub, a friend of mine from the pipelines, was currently working for Rick Causey in the contract administration/gas accounting role. She was being asked by the new IT guy to move to his organization. Jenny was a perfect fit for the new job and decided to take it, so Rick Causey was looking for someone to replace her. I am sure that Jenny recommended that Rick speak to me about the job she was leaving. It was a blessing to be able to move away from Stan into the environment that appeared to be where all of the growth was now occurring.

Not only were the people in ECT exciting, but the environment that was being created by Jeff Skilling was exciting as well. The first big controversy that other Enron employees outside the ECT organization focused on was the staircase that was opened up between the 30th and 31st floors to enhance communication. Those two floors were the ECT floors. People outside of ECT complained it was too expensive. In reality the open staircase was an awesome idea. The original stairway was just like any other building. It was not conducive to traffic between floors and the elevator actually took too long. After the initial stir, the open staircases were well accepted along with a lot of other ideas that emerged from the new ECT environment.

In addition, ECT was creating an open work space environment that also improved communication. That meant that everyone sat at a workspace out in the open and very few people had offices. When someone actually was in an office their wall was glass so they weren't hiding behind an office wall. There were snacks and drinks on the floors to encourage people to mingle and communicate in the break areas. All of these things were extremely controversial among employees in other groups, but what those things did was create one of the most innovative cultures ever.

The Enron Capital and Trade performance management process was also causing quite a bit of discussion and debate. Eventually, this process would be implemented throughout the entire Enron organization. Unlike a more traditional annual performance review done by only your supervisor, in ECT, an employee's performance was determined by a process that involved conducting a self-evaluation and soliciting feedback from supervisors, peers and people throughout the organization who the employee worked with over the previous performance period. Then, each supervisor would represent his or her employees in a series of performance review meetings.

During these meetings, groups of supervisors from various parts of the organization would discuss their employees' accomplishments, and rank each employee on a scale of 1–5. Ones were outstanding performers, or "water walkers." Fives were at risk of being let go. This is where the term "rank and yank" started.

Enron's performance review process led to a true meritocracy that focused on rewarding performance. However, at various times in Enron's history, the company forced supervisors to rank a percentage of employees in each category, thus requiring them to define some of their subordinates as poor performers, or "dead weight." At other times, when it was determined that the company had sufficiently trimmed the dead weight and the workforce was full of strong to superior performers, the forced ranking was lifted.

Forced ranking or not, however, bonuses and promotions were always tied to performance rankings, so it is easy to imagine how rigorous and raucous these meetings could become. Every employee had to hope their supervisor could withstand the pressure and would fight on their behalf for a favorable ranking.

I was a little concerned about the performance evaluation process, but I also knew I had a strong foundation of how to measure your worth to the organization in my previous roles. Also, I was sure it had to be better than working for someone who didn't support me. Ron Burns was now in ECT, but I didn't contact him about the role Rick Causey had open in ECT. I specifically wanted to get the job on my own, and I did.

When I look back on that job change I am sure that it was another step in the plan that God had for me. This was definitely a move that enhanced my ability to continue moving up the Enron corporate ladder and become familiar with the culture that would eventually become Enron's culture.

The ECT environment was fun and exciting. I loved the accountability, and the performance evaluation process was fair and actually the best I had ever experienced. The combination of Jeff Skilling and Ron Burns as co-chairs of the company was good. They both brought different skills to the organization. Ron was a people person, focused on the organization and its structure, while Jeff was extremely bright and creative and focused on breaking regulated markets and building new businesses. Putting the two of them together was brilliant, but it didn't last long.

Usually, the bottom line person in a combination like that doesn't see the value in the people person. I had experience with this because I was more of a people person and always felt my value wasn't as great or perceived as great by the bottom line managers. In fact, I believe I was occasionally referred to by some people as "fluff."

Ultimately, Ron Burns left Enron and went to work for Union Pacific as their CEO back in Omaha. Ironically, I didn't speak to Ron again until the day that Jeff's departure from Enron became public in the summer of

2001. I was visiting with Rosie, Ken Lay's assistant, outside of his office on the 50th floor when she answered Mr. Lay's phone. It was Ron. Ken was on another line at the time so Rosie handed the phone to me, and it was great to hear Ron's upbeat voice again.

Working for Rick Causey was fun. He was not only a friend; he was also an incredible manager. Rick was always fair and treated people with respect. He also had a real talent for getting consensus in the organization. I think that is the single most important skill I learned from Rick. Up until that point in my career I wasn't into consensus. It was much faster just to tell people what needed to be done. What I found however, is that consensus was much better and longer lasting. Rick was probably the best at it of anyone that I knew.

It was during my first couple of years in ECT that I first met Terrie James. I remember the Monday morning staff meeting where she was introduced to the management team—she was so darling and she sparkled. She had been hired to work on public relations and speech writing for Jeff Skilling in ECT. I didn't work with her directly when I was in my role in ECT, but I would get to know her very well and she would come to play a major role in my life later in my career.

Because I was involved in reengineering projects in the past, I took on a primary role in reengineering the back office support of Enron Capital and Trade. The back office was a term used to describe the support functions of the organization. These were functions such as financial accounting, gas accounting, contract administration and risk management.

In the performance evaluation process, the back office

people were known as non-commercial because we didn't have a direct impact in creating the deals. That was important because all the non-commercial people were ranked together. We of course had a lower salary schedule that our jobs were based on and our bonuses were lower than the commercial jobs. That was the case because we didn't directly impact the revenue of the company. It always made sense to me, but I know some people in the support organization had some issues with that.

The reengineering project I was involved in lasted several months and resulted in reorganizing people, changing processes and putting IT systems in place that created savings of nearly thirty percent over the entire back office. I took a major role in the project and I worked closely with McKinsey again. Unexpectedly I was even featured in a book written by John Katzenbach titled *Real Change Leaders.*

John was a retired McKinsey partner and actually was more of a people person than most of the McKinsey partners I had met in the past. In fact, the whole message behind the book and the reengineering project that we completed emphasized that it took a personal and very people focused approach. This approach was not typical of most McKinsey led projects. Most McKinsey projects were heavily bottom-line focused.

John recognized, like others had in the past, that even though I was focused on the bottom line and results, I also had a personality that was empathetic with the employees. It was interesting that my ability to focus on detail and results mixed with my people skills seemed to be a major reason for my success—even in ECT. I was very proud that a McKinsey partner would recognize me in this way.

Soon after we reorganized the ECT back office, Rick Causey was asked to leave his current role and run the finance area previously held by Andy Fastow. Andy made it clear to everyone that he was a very close friend of Jeff Skilling's. I am not so sure that was true, but Andy certainly had people believing it. He used that belief to get his way many times. It was common knowledge that you better do what Andy said or you might have to deal with Jeff. Andy was hired from outside of Enron and had gotten creative with the financial area. Years later he would receive an award from *CFO Magazine* for excellence.

Andy moved to Enron Energy Services to lead the new "retail" business unit that Jeff was creating. Andy actually tried to talk me into taking a role in that organization, but I was happy where I was and didn't seriously entertain the offer. Rick moved over to take Andy's place and they brought in another Arthur Andersen partner to take Rick's position in the back office accounting area.

I stayed in Enron Capital and Trade after Rick left and I asked for all the responsibility for the functions that had been reporting to Rick, except for the financial and general accounting. Rick's replacement, John Echols, came in and was in charge of General Accounting. John was not the manager that Rick was, and I soon learned he was also somewhat political. He would prove to be quite a challenge for me over the next year.

My new responsibilities involved a lot more contact with the trading organization. This is when I first met Kevin Hannon. For some reason, I sensed Kevin wasn't as bad as he was made out to be. Oh, don't get me wrong,

Kevin yelled and screamed at people, and most people were deathly afraid of him, but I could sense that somewhere in that scary person was a good man.

At one of the ECT Christmas parties he introduced me to his wife, Christine. They'd just had a new baby boy, and I asked her about their new son. She immediately volunteered that Kevin spent a lot of time with him. That's when I knew my suspicions about Kevin were right. I looked at him and announced that now I was sure that there was in fact a "soft side" to Kevin Hannon begging to come out. He gave me a smile and I knew I was right. Kevin Hannon was a nice guy deep down.

I was soon to have that premise tested, however. Several months after I took my new responsibilities, there was a several million dollar discrepancy in the risk books and financial books. I was in charge of the risk books. John Echols was in charge of the financial books. John, I was finding out, was not someone I could trust. Somehow, he convinced the guys that the problem wasn't in the accounting books, but in the risk books, and I was to blame.

Thanks to my previous cross-functional experience I was able to pull a team together that included people in John's organization. We worked long hours for several weeks to determine not only what caused the issue but which number was correct. We also identified what needed to change to insure that the out of balance never happened again

The most challenging part of this whole project was giving Kevin an update every day. He was a grouchy person on the exterior and I got huge doses of that side of Kevin Hannon daily.

Dealing with Kevin on this project was like having to work for Stan Horton again, only ten times worse. At least Stan refrained from profanity. I know I was called a "f—ing idiot" at least ten times in the course of the project. He made me so upset that I went home and cried many times after working a ten to twelve-hour day. Grady was so mad at whoever this Kevin Hannon was, I think he wanted to kill him. I just kept plugging through the issues and finally we identified what needed to happen to fix the problem.

Working the hours that we did and the added stress of speaking to Kevin everyday took a toll on me. I was exhausted. I remember early one morning when I was driving to work on the interstate I almost had a horrible accident. I went to change lanes and another car was in my blind spot and I didn't see them. When I did finally notice the other car, I had started to move over in their lane, overcorrected to get back in my lane, and almost rolled the car. I am sure, again, there was a guardian angel with me in the car that morning. After all, I had a project I had to finish!

At the conclusion of the project I insisted the team meet with Kevin. I wanted everyone who put in so many hours to sit in front of him and share our hard work. I was hoping that Kevin would express his thanks to the team personally. Kevin sat at the head of the long conference table in the conference room on the 30th floor. The entire group sat around the table facing him with somewhat fearful expressions.

Everyone had a part in presenting to him what we did to prevent the problem from occurring in the future. After the presentation was complete he did actually express his appreciation to the team and the meeting was over. Everyone of the team walked out of there with a little more respect for Kevin and a little less fear of him as well.

Kevin never told me that he appreciated the work that I did. I didn't expect that from him, but I knew I had now gained his confidence and respect just by the way he looked at me. I also knew that I could now consider Kevin a friend. When I eventually moved out of Enron Capital and Trade to work for Ken Lay, I made sure that Ken knew Kevin by encouraging Ken to invite him to lunch. Kevin and I did stay in touch until sometime after Enron filed for bankruptcy but, like many friends did, we stopped speaking when all of the lawsuits started to appear.

Not too long after that particular project for Kevin, I was asked to sign a three-year contract to lead the back office of ECT. My responsibilities were to complete the transformation of the wholesale business. That was important I was told, because as we went into the retail business in Enron Energy Services, the wholesale business would explode into more transactions than we could currently handle. That growth would require yet further improved processes and systems.

It was then that I knew for sure that I had won Kevin's respect. Jeff Skilling must also have supported me, to offer me a contract, and the wholesale group was definitely the place to be at Enron. God was truly blessing me again; however, I didn't give Him a thought or thank Him for what was going on in my life. After all, I was working very hard so I believed I deserved every good thing that was happening to me.

Working for Ken Lay

Sometime during my Enron Capital and Trade days, I was asked to be on the board of the Juvenile Diabetes Association by Nancy McNeil and Rebecca King. Rebecca ran community relations for Nancy. Using cross company teams we increased the Enron-wide participation in the annual Houston Walk for the Cure by nearly five hundred percent. It was the largest employee non-profit effort outside of United Way, and I took the lead for growing the effort within Enron. I worked on this in addition to my role in Enron Capital and Trade. Of course I could only have done that thanks to my awesome assistant, Bobbie Power, who also got extremely involved in the fundraising effort.

In mid-1996, because of my involvement in Juvenile Diabetes, I was asked by Nancy to attend a Juvenile Diabetes Luncheon and speak about our participation in their major fundraiser walk. Ken Lay was there and he sat down at the table next to me. As he pulled out his chair it reminded me of other times I had been seated next to him.

I sat at a table with Ken Lay in the past at several management conferences, and asked him to share the whole Enron story for everyone seated at the table. I always enjoyed hearing the events that led to the formation of Enron, and I knew other people who had spent less time with the company enjoyed the folklore.

The Enron management conferences were lots of fun. You were able to interact in person with vice presidents and managing directors that you worked with from all over the world. There were two nights of dinners and parties. Everyone had opportunities to really get to know each other and in some cases stay up until the early morning hours debating business strategy or simply talking. These events created important bonds that helped improve teamwork and communication among the top managers of the company.

I remember one conference in the mid 1990s where I had a blast dancing with Rich Kinder most of the evening. At that point in my career, Rich supported me in the organization and he was a lot of fun to be around. At another conference, after several drinks, Jim Prentice, who had run Human Resources in the early years, told me that I received Casey Olson's stock options many years ago by mistake and they had decided to let me keep them. Actually, this was a mistake made by the old InterNorth organization right before the merger occurred, and Jim had been in charge of Human Resources at the time.

When I think back, receiving those options had to be God working. I probably would have never gone to Houston had the company taken those back from me. Receiving those options was one of the primary reasons I decided to take a risk and move to Houston back in 1986.

My favorite memories of management conferences however, were when I was able to sit at a table with Ken Lay. I loved the way he made everyone at the table feel so special and valuable to the company. This came naturally to Ken because he genuinely cared about the employees of Enron. Unlike other CEOs I have dealt with, Ken would always direct the conversation to others at the table instead of dominating the conversation about himself.

At this particular Juvenile Diabetes luncheon in 1996, Ken Lay was again very warm and welcoming to me. He expressed his appreciation for all the work we had put forth to elevate Enron to one of the Juvenile Diabetes best walk teams in the city of Houston. He must have known I was working in Enron Capital and Trade at the time because he asked me what I thought was an interesting question.

Along with the usual questions about what was going on in general at ECT, he asked me how I thought the traders behaved and how they treated other people. After the experience that I had just gone through with Kevin Hannon, I probably could have given him an earful, but I told him that they, at times, were pretty rough with employees. I just assumed that he had heard a lot of "gossip" and just wanted to see what someone in the "ranks" might say.

It did impress me that he seemed sincerely concerned about how employees were being treated. There are times I have thought back to that lunch and wondered if I should have been a little more critical of the treatment employees received from the traders, but I am not sure that would have made any difference. I think Ken was starting to realize that the culture of Enron was changing. With the growth in the trading business came more and more traders that were very self-focused. That was just the demeanor of any trading organization. It almost had to be for them to perform the kind of job they were responsible for.

I learned later when I went to work for Ken Lay directly, that he was always genuinely concerned about the employees. In fact, he often told us that he wanted Enron to be a place where a person could use their "God given" talents to accomplish things they didn't dream they ever could. I would also imagine that Ken was growing a little concerned about the shift in culture of the company even though the new trading business was making a lot of money for Enron.

In late 1996, not too long after that Juvenile Diabetes luncheon, I got a phone call from Beth Tilney. She was calling to ask me if I would consider meeting with her to discuss a job opportunity in corporate, reporting to her. I had not met Beth yet, though noticed her from a distance at the last United Way event that was held in front of the Enron building that same fall. I was impressed Enron hired a woman at that level in the company. She had been brought in to manage Enron's marketing and advertising functions, and help build Enron's brand. I was excited to meet her.

The next day I went to her office on the 50th floor where we had lunch together and discussed the job opportunity that would report to her. I liked her immediately. She was warm and friendly, and I was impressed that she had worked at an advertising firm in New York prior to coming to Enron. She told me at this meeting that she had been asked by Ken Lay to speak to me about the job.

The position would be responsible for leading the community relations team. This was one of Nancy

McNeil's responsibilities, and Beth explained that Nancy was leaving the company. The other part of Nancy's job, which was running Mr. Lay's office, would be taken over by Rosalie Fleming.

My concern about the job offer was that I had just committed to Jeff Skilling that I would spend the next three years focusing on improving the Enron Capital and Trade back office. That was an incredible opportunity for me and in my opinion, this job Beth was offering me was much smaller and less important than the job I currently had in Enron Capital and Trade. Because Nancy had been known as "Ken's assistant" I feared that was basically what I was going to become. At the time, I really did not understand that the community position was a critical component in building Enron's brand.

I asked Beth if it would be okay if I spoke directly to Ken about the position since I would be working so closely with him, and she enthusiastically agreed that was a good idea. I left her office knowing the next step would be to meet with him.

The meeting with Ken occurred within a couple of days. As I walked into his office, he had me sit at his table and of course Rosie offered me something to drink. Ken's office was large and bright with numerous pictures of his family scattered on bookshelves and on end tables. I also noticed a picture of Ken with George and Barbara Bush displayed on the coffee table in front of the couch. The table we sat around was a beautiful wood- grained round table with a large heavy glass dish in the center full of chocolate. In the years to come, as a comfort for issues we were dealing with at the time, I would have my share of that chocolate!

The first thing I said to Ken after we sat down was "Do you know what I do? I am not sure why you are asking me to consider this position." Of course he gave me his all familiar huge smile and chuckled. He immediately started relaying to me why the job would be perfect for my talents. He told me he had seen me grow the Juvenile Diabetes effort, and he knew that I had the talent to do that in the entire community relations area. He wanted to have community relations basically reengineered.

After I left his office I was more interested than ever. He made the job sound so important, and I would be able to make improvements to what currently existed. I told him my only concern was that I had just signed a three year contract with Jeff Skilling to work on the back office of ECT. I also shared with him that I wasn't too excited about doing anything to make Jeff mad at me, and possibly leaving ECT for a job in corporate could do just that. I was definitely interested, but asked him if he and Beth should decide I was the person for the job, would he please work it out with Jeff. So, in essence, I left the decision with Ken and Jeff and I felt like if Jeff had a say in the decision then I was covered with him.

The other person I felt I should speak with was Nancy McNeil since she was the one leaving the job. I had heard she was getting a divorce from her husband, Ed, and I wanted to understand if the position demands had anything to do with that. When I met with Nancy I certainly did not get a "go for it" feeling from her. In fact, she discouraged me from taking the job. Despite what she said, I left her office sure that if Beth did formally offer me the job I was going to take it. My only nagging concern was why Nancy wouldn't be more supportive.

We had attended Christmas parties for several years where Nancy and her husband were also there. In fact at the last party involving that group something very strange had happened. Rich Kinder and his wife, Anne, were also attendees at this particular party. That previous October, Grady had given me a very nice three-carat diamond ring for our twentieth wedding anniversary. Rich came up to me at the party and asked to see the ring sometime during the evening. I, of course, showed it to him and commented that I think Grady might love me a little. Rich's response was surprising. He immediately added, "Or he is feeling awfully guilty about something." It wasn't until years later that I wondered if he himself could have been the one feeling a little guilty as he ultimately divorced his wife, Anne, and married Nancy McNeil.

After I accepted the corporate position of community relations I figured out that Nancy wasn't happy when we spoke. Rich did not want me in the job either, and Ken even told me later that Rich wasn't supportive of him hiring me. I always wondered why, but never really knew. Rich Kinder didn't speak to me again.

When Kevin Hannon found out I was leaving ECT, he told me he did not want me to go. That confirmed it—I really had won his respect. I remember I had some input on who would replace me. My recommendation was a friend who had worked with me in the ECT organization. She had a very different management style than I had; she was a very "hands on" manager and I felt she could probably do a much better job than I had done.

One of the most disappointing things happened between us. She did in fact get the job, but instead of being supportive of me, she complained about the job I had done in ECT. That experience hurt my feelings, but it taught me that you don't really know a person, and also how fierce the competition was among women. There have been many studies done on this subject and it happens everywhere, not just at Enron. It is just a reality that a large majority of women have to face in any work place.

Lucky for me, Rich Kinder left Enron shortly after my move from ECT to corporate. Jeff Skilling was moved to corporate as the COO to replace Rich. Jeff then started elevating many of the people I worked with in ECT to corporate. Things were definitely good, and it certainly appeared I had made a great move to my new position in corporate.

Ken Lay was right—the community relations position was a natural for me. I had some issues early on with some of the people who worked under Nancy McNeil. People in corporate did not respond well to the bad management skills I carried over from my years working for Stan and the traders. My management style included showing little patience and using profanity when people didn't perform. I had definitely picked up some bad habits and I really didn't blame the team that had been in place under Nancy for running for the hills.

At the time I had become pretty arrogant about my accomplishments, I believed I was doing everything right and the people who had already been in the community organization were doing nothing right. Now I look back on the way I treated people and I am the first to say I could have handled things much better.

Gradually I built my own team. It was an unbelievably talented group of people, many of whom had been in

ECT, including Terrie James. The team understood what I expected and could even tolerate my management style. We were awesome together and I never felt any competition among all of the women in that group—ever. We were friends and everyone supported and really liked each other. This was the most fun I had ever had at Enron, and Ken Lay had been right—I was a natural for this job because of the team and the passion we all had for it.

There were several specific projects our teams created that stand out in my mind. In 1998 Ken was the overall Chairman for the United Way campaign for Houston, and our team put together the most unique United Way kick-off event in the history of Houston United Way campaigns. We invited the entire city to join us in forming the first human rainbow. Five thousand people showed up. We gave each of them a colored T-shirt and they very orderly walked onto a large field near the Transco tower to form a rainbow. Everyone stood there for several minutes as pictures were taken. This event made not only the front page of the *Houston Chronicle,* it also headlined news channels across the country and was entered into the *Guinness Book of World Records.*

Another year we kicked off our Enron internal United Way campaign with a "Want to be a Millionaire?" game show. It was the year that our stock price hit an all-time high at the time of $80 per share, and the employees were very happy. The reception we got was pretty incredible. Employees were cheering and laughing. Jeff, Ken, Joe Sutton and Jackie Martin, who was head of the Greater Houston United Way, were the "lifelines." Employees were chosen to answer the questions, which of course were tailored specifically for an Enron audience.

For the 2000 United Way campaign kickoff, we held a basketball tournament in front of the Enron building between operating companies with the winner playing the team consisting of Ken Lay, Joe Sutton, Jeff Skilling, Rebecca Mark, and Clyde Drexler of the Houston Rockets. Unfortunately, Clyde couldn't manage to lead the team to the championship and the Enron Energy Service team took the tournament. In every one of these events, the excitement, participation and level of contribution was the envy of Houston's corporate community. The camaraderie we were building at Enron was also evident. Employees across different business units were getting to know each other, and these kinds of events continued to help encourage the innovative culture that other companies envied.

In total, our employees gave several million dollars to the United Way, and most of our top executives were members of the Alexis De Tocqueville Society donating $10,000 each, annually. It wasn't just about having a lot of fun it was also about helping a lot of people and our employees were becoming known for not only being extremely talented but also very philanthropic.

Enron sponsored one of the most successful Earth Day events in the country, and gave free office space to "Teach for America." We were involved in and sponsored the largest MS150 bike team in the state of Texas which raised thousands of dollars for Multiple Sclerosis. Our employees' participation and passion for the nonprofits in the city was certainly recognized and appreciated.

I remember, in 1998, we sponsored *The Civil War,* a musical production at Houston's Alley Theatre. As part of our sponsorship, we decided to host a large party before one of the performances. It was to be a first-class event, and all of Houston's officials and business leaders were going to be invited. I wanted every aspect of the event to be perfect. Unfortunately, on a Friday, when we were scheduled to send out the invitations, Houston experienced one of its trademark flash floods. No one on my team could get to work that morning, but I was so insistent that those invitations be mailed out that day that I demanded everyone get to the office despite the risks of navigating flood waters.

Thanks to Terrie James, who always pointed out to me when I was being less than reasonable, I backed down. Most of the team worked Saturday to have the invitations ready to mail out that next Monday. That incident showed me a couple of things. First, I was lucky that Terrie worked for me and was willing to confront me when necessary, and second, with a dedicated team, things can get done without the hysteria.

Quickly we set records in fundraising for every nonprofit we got involved with, and in volunteerism among employees, all the while reducing our overall community relations budget by nearly twenty-five percent. Enron had become a model that other Houston corporations sought to emulate.

For two years our team recruited Enron employees to volunteer for many of the city's nonprofits. We adopted a different nonprofit each year as part of our United Way campaign and used that as a vehicle and springboard to place our executives on boards of area nonprofits. It was a remarkable domino effect. At the time of the collapse of Enron, we had almost all of our top one hundred executives involved and on the board of at least one nonprofit in the city. We also utilized our "Bring your Child to Work Day" as a day we adopted children from the non-profits and brought them to work.

As a result of all of our efforts, our employee matching program nearly doubled in the course of a few years. In addition, we were giving nearly $6 million a year to the United Way. Enron was involved in every major non-profit in Houston, and the hours our employees spent volunteering for nonprofits more than tripled in a little more than five years.

It also became clear that what we did in the community was a great way to earn positive PR for Enron, and the corporate PR department became our strong ally. Our community programs were generating nearly $15 million in earned media or free media for Enron every year.

Ken ultimately became a member of the Committee to Encourage Corporate Philanthropy. Our community programs received recognition in one of their newsletters in the summer of 2001. We were unique because Ken had the vision of how important the community work was to a corporation's brand and business opportunities.

The things Enron did for people certainly went beyond our community activities. Most people were not aware of the Flying Angels program where we transported many sick people to Houston on our corporate aircraft so they could utilize the medical facilities at MD Andersen Hospital. Many times our executives would have these patients on board with them as they returned to Houston from meetings across the country.

Our aircraft was also used countless times to take employees to funerals of their families or pick up employees who were stranded in places either here or overseas.

Unfortunately, the use of the corporate aircraft has been portrayed as a perk for executives only, which was the farthest thing from the truth. Oh, don't get me wrong, there was abuse by some executives, but it would have been fairer had there been reporting of some of the good things we did with our aircraft.

In my community role I was also responsible for helping Ken with many of the efforts he got involved in around the world to promote Houston. Ken firmly believed that if Houston was viewed as a world-class city, then we could attract the world-class talent we needed to work at Enron. Ken co-chaired, with the Greater Houston Partnership, an economic development conference in Tokyo in 1998. I was responsible for coordinating the details.

I flew to Tokyo several times for meetings with our Japanese counterparts. I usually didn't have time to see anything in Tokyo so I turned around and flew back to Houston within twenty-four hours. The conference included the late Senator Lloyd Bentsen, the CEO of Toyota, and Malcolm Gillis of Rice University just to name a few. I realized after that conference that Ken Lay was not only highly thought of in Houston, but he was also considered a player in the international markets.

Ken spent much of his spare time at the conference in business meetings with several prominent Japanese leaders. The conference proved to hold another challenge I had to deal with. I found out that Ken Lay was allergic to shellfish and he could die if he ate anything that had even touched shellfish. That was more difficult to monitor than one might think since I didn't speak Japanese

and nearly all of the food in Japan included some kind
of shellfish.

Ken was also chairman of the Governor's Business
Council, an advisory group of CEOs from all over Texas
who met with Governor Bush quarterly. I was responsible
for working with the governor's staff to set up the meetings in Austin. Because of that assignment I got to know
Joe Albaugh and Karl Rove, who both have been on President Bush's White House staff. Bush was a charismatic
governor and it was fun seeing him in that setting.

After one of the Governor's Business Council meetings I was fortunate to attend a very small dinner party
at the governor's mansion. I sat at the table next to Laura
Bush. There were only ten of us and it gave me the opportunity to see a close up view of the Bush family. I have
always had a lot of respect for them as a family. After the
collapse of Enron, I was disappointed that George W.
Bush didn't give Ken Lay more support, but I am sure the
politics of "Enron" were very uncomfortable for him.

Through the Governor's Business Council meetings I
also got involved with the governor's education initiative
team, and became friends with the CEO who lead that
effort, Charles Miller. He owned the Georgia O'Keeffe
compound in Santa Fe, New Mexico, and I was invited
several times to join the education group there for meetings. Charles' wife, Beth, was involved with John Denver's environmental foundation, and the compound was
amazing. They grew their own food and they had their
own water purifying system. Charles and Beth enter-
tained lots of well-known people there, and were good
friends of Ken Lay.

Through the Governor's Business Council I had the

opportunity to meet many of the Texas CEOs. One of my favorites was Herb Kelleher who was the CEO of Southwest Airlines. He was a character, standing in the back of the meeting room smoking in a non-smoking room. I could certainly see, through him, how Southwest developed their unique culture.

In 1998, Ken Lay was heavily involved with helping Drayton McLane get the new baseball stadium approved for Houston. Drayton owned the Houston Astros and he was considering moving the team to another city if he could not get a new stadium built in Houston. Many professional team owners during this time were trying to get new stadiums in the cities they called home. Ken was concerned that if we did not keep the Astros in Houston it would be even harder to recruit the kind of talent we needed at Enron.

Getting the stadium built involved a community ballot and a vote by the Texas legislature. The African-American community was a key to winning the community ballot, and Ken called on three of his friends in the African-American community to help. That is how I got to know Howard Jefferson, President of Houston's NAACP, Reverend Bill Lawson, pastor of Wheeler Avenue Baptist Church, and Al Green, a well-known judge in Houston at the time, who has since become a member of the United States House of Representatives.

I quickly became involved in this effort and worked with Drayton McLane's staff to gain commitment from the community for the stadium. Drayton McLane ultimately became a friend. He is a wonderful Christian man and it was a great experience for me to get to know him and his staff.

The other bright spot in the project was the friends I made in Houston's African- American community. Some of my dearest friends today include the three people Ken originally called on to help him. Howard Jefferson became an advisor and a dear friend. He educated me on where the power base was in the African-American community in Houston. I found he had unbelievable insight into politics at Enron as well. He told me that he could tell I was raised by good parents by looking into my eyes and seeing no prejudice. Actually, I think if you go back in the genealogy of my mother's side of the family, we have African-American ancestors.

I also got to know Reverend Bill Lawson. Reverend Lawson was loved and respected by everyone in all communities in Houston. He had a calming effect on people, and I don't think I ever heard anyone, black or white, have a negative word to say about him. Both of these men stood by Ken Lay and remained his and my friends to this day.

The baseball stadium passed in large part thanks to the African-American vote, and Ken's and Drayton's commitment to diversity. Later the Enron management team worked with the Houston Astros to secure the naming rights to the new stadium. It was named "Enron Field" in April of 1999. This was a huge springboard for all kinds of community efforts for Enron.

We worked with the Astros to create the Enron Power Blast that earned thousands of dollars for the Boys and Girls Club of America. This program was one of the first in the country to donate money for every home run that was hit by the home team. Grady and I personally had the privilege of co-chairing an event at the field for the

Houston nonprofit, Search. The event brought in close to a million dollars for the charity thanks to many Enron people that attended and supported us.

Because of Enron's involvement in the new stadium, a lot of employees secured favorable seats at the field. I remember it was a thrill for the employees who got to throw out the first pitch for the home games. An employee of Enron Energy Services was able to sing the National Anthem at one of the games. Enron Field was huge goodwill for the company and with Enron's employees.

Because of the relationships I developed in the African-American community I became passionate about supplier diversity within Enron. During the stadium construction both Ken Lay and Drayton McLane had committed to the African-American community that they would insure that thirty percent of the dollars spent building the stadium would be with minority suppliers. We hired Reuben Brown, who was a prominent member of the African-American community, to do just that and it happened!

I became extremely confident in Ken Lay's commitment to this effort. At one point we were getting resistance from Haliburton, a major contractor for the construction, to secure minority vendors for the project. I threatened that if they did not honor the thirty percent commitment Ken Lay would pull his support of the project. Ken wasn't even in the meeting. I was becoming comfortable that I knew how Ken felt about a lot of things, and I was confident that I could represent his wishes without asking his permission. It wasn't until I met with Ken late in 2005, before I testified for him in his trial that he found out about what I had done in that meeting.

Ken had not changed one bit in those last four years. When I explained to him what I had done in that meeting years ago, as always, he gave me that huge grin, chuckled and told me that he was always comfortable with how I had handled everything.

In early 1999, Grady and I bought a townhouse in downtown Houston. We were spending a lot of time at community events in Houston in the evenings. The townhouse gave us a place to stay so we didn't have to drive to Conroe, which was more than forty miles from downtown. Not only was it convenient, but it was a good investment. Eventually, we spent more time in the Houston townhouse than the house we had in Conroe, which we only stayed in on the weekends. Actually we stayed there only on the weekends we didn't go to Colorado.

When Ken Lay was nominated and received the Horatio Alger Award in 1998, we were among the friends that were asked to fly on Enron's corporate planes to Washington, D.C., and attend the ceremony. What an incredible time for Ken. Everyone in attendance was so proud of him. This award was impressive when you realized who has received it in the past. Unfortunately, the Horatio Alger Association has taken Ken's name off of their Web site despite the fact he raised the most money of any nominee up to that point.

The Horatio Alger Award recognizes people who have gone from rags to riches and given back to the community. Oprah Winfrey and Henry Kissinger were two recipients from previous years. In fact, in 2001, when Ken was preparing to chair the Horatio Alger events the next year, we attended the festivities with him and his wife, Linda. We sat next to Henry Kissinger and his wife who had been flown to the event onboard an Enron plane; Henry was a very good friend of Ken's.

Both Grady and I were honored that we were able to attend an event like that. In fact, Grady wrote Ken a letter after the weekend. He expressed his appreciation and shared with Ken that he was especially impacted by the stories of the people being honored and the scholarship recipients.

Grady was raised by parents who had not encouraged him to do anything he wanted to do. Basically Grady felt like the American dream was there for anyone but him. I will never forget Ken's response to Grady's letter. In that letter he gave Grady encouragement for his accomplishments, and expressed his own appreciation for our friendship. I think this was the first time I realized that we were actually becoming friends with both Ken and Linda Lay.

I would learn later as I continued to work with Ken Lay that he always wrote personal notes to people. Everyone that truly knew Ken grew to love him because of his kindness and thoughtfulness given so freely to everyone. I have run into countless people who were associated with Ken in some way—his doctor, his ski instructor, his landlord. They all loved him. If you had any personal contact with him at all you thought the world of him.

During 1998 and 1999, I was focused "outside" of the Enron building. We were growing our community presence and hence, our community commitment as a part of Enron's brand. It was in mid 1999 that I wanted to get more involved inside of Enron helping build our commitment for Enron's supplier diversity and workforce diversity. With my experience in the African-American community in Houston, I heard a lot of complaints about how hard it was for minorities to get into Enron to even be considered as a supplier. We had also just gone through an audit by the Department of Labor. They had looked at our hiring and promotion practices of women and minorities and we were dealing with the issues identified in that audit.

The person that was in charge of diversity for Enron was a good friend of mine who was a very bright and talented African-American woman. She was finding it difficult to get management to pay attention to the issues. When she chose to leave the company, I asked to take the lead in these areas when she left because of my outside experience with the stadium.

Using a model that had proved effective in the past, I formed cross-organizational teams that gathered the statistics for each operating company and determined goals for improvement in both the supplier and work force areas. It was embarrassing when we determined that across Enron we were spending less than one percent of our supplier dollars with minority firms. Ken Lay had been the driver of the thirty percent commitment for the stadium and here in his own company we were only at one percent. Thirty percent became our goal and we reached that goal within a year and a half.

At the same time all of this was going on, Beth Tilney was asked by Ken Lay to form and lead a Vision and Values task force. The purpose of the group was to encourage everyone in the organization to know and live by our values. Beth asked me to be on the task force and we addressed many issues including workforce diversity. It was unfortunate that with the Enron Capital and Trade culture spreading across Enron, living the values was becoming a challenge.

Enron's values included *respect, integrity, communication and excellence.*

> **Respect:** We treat others as we would like to be treated ourselves. We do not tolerate abusive or disrespectful treatment. Ruthlessness, callousness and arrogance don't belong here.

> **Integrity:** We work with customers and prospects openly, honestly, and sincerely. When we say we will do something, we will do it; when we say we cannot or will not do something, then we won't do it.

> **Communication:** We have an obligation to communicate. Here, we take the time to talk with one another...and to listen. We believe that information is meant to move and that information moves people.

> **Excellence:** We are satisfied with nothing less than the very best in everything we do. We will continue to raise the bar for everyone. The great fun here will be for all of us to discover just how good we can really be.

Ken personally composed those values, and I believe it was Ken's hope that he could embed these deep into the Enron culture before he left. If that happened, I think Ken thought he'd leave Enron with a legacy that would sustain the company for a lifetime.

However, there was a kind of tension developing across Enron. The ECT culture, which was where the majority of Enron's growth in revenue was occurring, did not embrace the values like the rest of the organization. Many of the very successful traders had habits that did not sync up with the values. Employees were becoming cynical because unless all the employees in the organization adhered to the values they were meaningless.

Unfortunately, the very group that was spurring Enron's growth and defining its image did little to uphold the company's values. The Vision and Values task force efforts involved people from each business unit that had some level of influence in their organization. We hoped that with each business unit represented we could come up with programs that would embed the values in every single organization.

I was now responsible for community relations and workforce and supplier diversity. As a result of those responsibilities and Ken's focus on them, I was put on the executive committee for a short time. That is until that call from Ken in late 1999 when he informed me that I would not be on the executive committee going forward. This brings me to where I started this story. My promotion to Human Resources and that day in late 1999 at the Hyatt when I was asked if the employees should invest all of their 401(k) in Enron stock and I sat down thinking that I had done a good job.

It had been quite a ride up to this point in my career at Enron. I had been fortunate to have had some unbelievable opportunities, and I grew more and more loyal to Ken Lay. Working for him was a dream job. It was just like running your own business when he trusted you. In addition, I had gotten some incredible opportunities in the Houston community thanks to Ken. In retrospect, even though I had not given God any credit for all of the good things that were happening to me, He was there with me all along, and everything that was happening was part of His plan for my life. There are times now that I wish I could go back and live all of that over again knowing that He was working in my life. What joy I would have had realizing He was there right beside me.

I was also fortunate to have gotten the opportunity to meet and deal with a number of influential people across the country because of the relationships Ken had with them. I will never forget the night Ken asked me to touch base with Elizabeth Dole about something. He called her Libby. I also got to speak to Paul Newman when Ken joined his group of corporate philanthropists. I had the privilege to deal with Clyde Drexler, Carl Lewis and Troy Aikman all because of Ken Lay. I think a lot of us who worked directly for him understood his far-reaching influence and circle of friends; he was definitely admired by many people.

Eventually, I was nominated by Ken to be on the first female Greater Houston Partnership roster. I knew nearly every CEO of the major companies in Houston, Texas, and had worked with many people all over the country and the world. Now I was hopeful that I could make an impact in the Human Resources organization for Enron.

As I look back on these experiences today, I know that God truly blessed me. God had given me talents. He put me in a creative and dynamic work environment where I could develop those talents. He had also given me the opportunity to work with many incredibly gifted people and to work for a company that valued its employees and creating new businesses. I also was collaborating with people who were doing incredible philanthropic work in the Houston community. I was so privileged to meet them and to be in a position to help to facilitate their work. My work was rewarding at many levels.

Everything was part of God's plan, and when the time was right He would bring me to Him and I would be able to tell this amazing story. A story that would start to reveal not only the truth about Enron and Ken Lay, but also the truth that God really does have a plan for us much better than any of us can truly imagine for ourselves.

My Role in Human Resources

In late 1999, my first major role in Human Resources was to focus on developing a new compensation structure for the entire company. Jeff Skilling wanted to enhance the executive compensation to include more stock option potential for high performers. The rationale surrounding this structure was to reward employees for adding value to our stock price. Not only did the top executives receive stock options, but several layers of management also received stock options based on Enron's stock performance.

Everything we did was market researched and blessed by Towers Perrin. Towers Perrin was and continues to be the leading provider of human resource compensation and consulting. Even though it seemed the Enron compensation structure we were developing was extremely generous, it was competitive with other companies in the technology world and critical if we were going to continue to attract the talent from the colleges that had a choice to pursue other technology or investment banking opportunities.

That project was huge. We literally revamped the entire structure for Enron directors, managing directors, vice presidents and executive vice presidents. It took the HR team four months to finalize the entire matrix and get Enron Board approval. It was definitely a learning experience for me as I had not been involved in compensation prior to this project. Thank goodness for a very talented person on the team who was an expert in that area. She provided most of the direction and expertise as we finalized the project and got everyone's approval.

The annual Wallstreet analyst meeting was in January of 2000. I didn't have a role in the meeting, however, most of the executives did. Unfortunately, this particular meeting was a huge focus of the government's case against Ken Lay and Jeff Skilling. This was the first meeting of its kind that I ever attended. I remember I sat next to Rick Causey near the back of the meeting room. There was a sense of excitement from all of the analysts that were there. They all seemed to want to get the information they were hearing to someone first. It was almost like you were on the trading floor of the New York Stock Exchange.

Scott McNealy, who was the CEO of Sun Microsystems, attended the meeting. He was there to add credibility to the presentation our Broadband group was making about the deals they were creating with Sun. His presence was a surprise for the analysts, and only helped to escalate the excitement that you could sense in that room.

The Enron stock climbed over $15 a share that day. After that meeting the entire executive team had a gain of over $15 per stock option they had just received. Everyone in that room believed that Enron was truly a great company, and with our new Broadband business we were a part of the new technology world. Across the board, analysts were putting a strong buy on our stock.

The biggest issue we had in the company now was staffing Broadband. Because our stock had climbed over

$15, Jeff realized that Broadband was critical to the continued growth of the company. Jeff asked me after the analyst meeting to work with Mark Koenig to determine the break out of our stock value to the business units. He already knew the answer, but wanted us to show the number of officers in each business unit compared to the business unit allocation of the stock value.

Mark Koenig was in charge of investor relations for Enron. He was a good guy, but always seemed "nervous" to me. Mark worked closely with my group and got very involved in the Sunshine Kids, a nonprofit organization focused on terminally ill children. Unfortunately, Mark was one of the Enron executives that plead guilty and cooperated with the government in Ken's and Jeff's trial. His former assistant and friend testified at the trial that Mark had told her he did not believe that he was truly guilty, but felt pressure to do what the government wanted.

With the information that Mark and I put together for Jeff he could show to the entire management team that, with Broadband becoming a larger percentage of our stock value; it made sense to move some of our talented people into that business unit. At the Monday morning executive committee meeting that next week, Jeff presented the chart that Mark and I developed to the management team, showing them the break out of stock price and headcount. It was clear to everyone in that room that we needed to move talent to Broadband. During the next two weeks we moved almost eighty people from other business units to the unit that everyone believed was going to insure that Enron stay on the top of the list of most innovative companies.

That movement of people was a huge project that our HR team facilitated. The

Broadband business leaders were required to give presentations and interview the top people in other business units. The movement was strictly voluntary by the individuals, so it required them to be bought into the viability of the Broadband strategy. At the end of the two weeks not only had eighty people moved, but most people now understood the business strategy of the new Broadband business unit. As I think back on that process, I find it very hard to believe that all of those talented people moved without truly believing in the new business they were going to be a part of in the future.

Soon after that project, Joe Sutton insisted that I take a trip to India to visit our Dabhol plant. I was gone almost a week, and even took a day to fly to Agra to see the Taj Mahal. That was one of the most memorable experiences that I had working for Enron. Not because it was so beautiful, but because India is filled with so much poverty. I know Joe wanted me to become familiar with India because he had spent so much time there when he worked for the Enron Power group building the plant. I found it enlightening to see a third world country, and it truly made me appreciate what we have here in the United States.

That trip also showed me how talented our people were, not just in Houston, but all over the world. We were definitely hiring some of the best and brightest everywhere, and Enron was quickly becoming one of the most desirable places to work in the world.

I think a lot of people would agree with me when I say that a huge reason we all loved working at Enron is because we felt like we were working with some of the smartest people in the world—and we were. We also believed we were changing the world by creating innovative solutions for not only the energy industry, but the technology world as well. The internal meetings we were involved in and even the performance management sessions we held semi-annually were motivating because of the talent and ideas generated each and every day. Having the contact with all of those talented people is truly one of the things that I miss the most about working for Enron. Many of us believe that there will never by another company like it again.

The next big project that our Human Resource team tackled was to reengineer the entire HR organization. I brought into HR some of the people who helped me reengineer other areas of the company in the past. When we benchmarked the number of people in HR to other best practice companies, it was clear we were overstaffed. We had nearly five hundred people in HR, worldwide. We implemented new computer systems, brought people in from the business to run areas of HR, and we developed new programs for employees. We ended up reducing the HR costs by more than $29 million annually, and had improved our data capabilities and employee benefits. We improved our human resource capabilities so much that Goldman Sachs was starting to talk to us about helping them do the same thing.

Thanks to an unbelievably talented woman, Kathy Schultea, and her team of people, HR implemented an employee information system that rivaled anything that was currently on the market. It required that employees update their information about their job experience, languages they spoke, and any other kinds of data usually found on a resume. That allowed us to be able to go into the system and find employees internally when a particular skill was required for a certain job. Because the employees knew what it was used for they were more willing to keep their information current.

Another one of the responsibilities of my HR role was the Analyst and Associate program. That program had been extremely successful, and it fed top graduates from schools all over the country into our workforce. The best and brightest were coming to work for Enron from all of the top schools in the world. We were hiring approximately thirty new people every six months into this program from schools like Harvard, Kellogg, Wellesley, University of Texas, and University of Chicago, to name a few. Not only were we hiring talent from these schools, we were getting the best talent from these institutions.

Enron had been named *Fortune*'s Most Innovative Company, and we were on *Fortune*'s top 100 Companies to Work for list. We promoted our employees based on accomplishments versus tenure, and our compensation was competitive with any other major corporation out there. We could show many examples of current vice presidents at Enron who had started in the analyst and associate program and within five years were promoted and making close to $1 million per year.

The woman who led the program had done an incredible job building it, but she was not respected by all of the groups it was now serving. I made a huge mistake when I replaced her with an individual who did not have the support of everyone involved in the program. While I still believe the woman I selected was the right person for the job, I made the fatal mistake of not getting consensus from everyone before I made the move.

Needless to say, that move made a few key people very angry, including some who were close to Jeff Skilling. Jeff started the program, and it had grown out of the Enron Capital and Trade environment. Rightly so, he was very passionate and protective of it. I eventually learned from that experience that I probably would not be able to recover my credibility with Jeff. I, in effect, had just signed my death sentence, and no matter what I did, I never believed I could recover.

In late 2000, I thought Grady and I needed to buy a new house. As I look back now I am not sure what was wrong with the house that we had. I initially started looking for a house on the lake in Conroe, but found a house in the Woodlands that I didn't think I could live without. It was a show home with almost 7200 square feet, and it was five times more expensive than our current house.

Grady tried to talk me out of buying such a large house but I wasn't listening. I wanted this house. We paid over $1.7 million for it, and bought most of the furniture that was used while showing it as well. I remember having a bit of buyer's remorse about it, but that didn't stop me. I wanted a house as big and beautiful as other Enron executives had built or bought.

I was making a lot of money and I was certainly spending it. It was nothing for me to go shopping now and walk out with thousands of dollars in clothes. I remember flying into Colorado one weekend and I just decided I wanted a new Jeep, so on the way to our house we stopped at the Jeep dealer and I wrote a check and walked out with a brand new, yellow Jeep Wrangler.

Life was unbelievable for us by this point. I recall that the realtor who found the new house for us and sold our old house in Conroe commented, "You sure have lived a charmed life." We were certainly feeling bulletproof. Fortunately, God had a different plan for us, and we were going to start finding out all about it very soon.

In October of 2000, I went to meet with Jeff to tell him I wanted to fix the problem that I had created with the Analyst and Associate program. I had hired a woman from an investment bank in New York to oversee the program and I had suggested she report directly to Jeff. She was very talented and I thought that it would send a positive message about the program to the employees if she was reporting directly to the CEO. I was now hearing a lot of noise about the way she was handling the program, and it wasn't positive.

I told Jeff I would like to take the program back from her and fix the issues. He told me "No." It was then that I realized that my career with him in charge was all but over. He not only told me no, but that I was going to report to the Chief of Staff, Steve Kean, going forward and he was not sure what my role would be. He asked me to come back to him with what I wanted to do.

There it was. He had now accomplished what he tried to do in 1999. I was off the executive committee and reporting to Steve Kean. This time Ken Lay was getting ready to leave and Beth Tilney was not going to be able to help me. This would have been a perfect time for me to turn to God, but I still wasn't acknowledging that I needed anyone to help me.

After thinking about the situation and what I really wanted to do, I concluded I was the most passionate about the programs we developed for employees. I also had kept the responsibility for community relations, which I was thankful for, so I told Jeff that I wanted to continue to be responsible for employee programs—community relations, diversity and co-lead the Vision and Values task force with Beth. Executive compensation was already being handled by a very talented person in the organization and the business unit HR heads were fairly autonomous with their business units.

This move would give these people who were currently reporting to me an opportunity to take the reigns of their areas without me, and report directly to the chief of staff. I felt this made sense because I rationalized that with me not having Jeff's support, I would be hurting them if they continued to report to me. Besides, they were all excellent at what they did and quite frankly didn't need me.

It wasn't until July 2001, nearly six months after my meeting with Jeff in October 2000, that all of the changes in the HR responsibilities were actually announced. In that same announcement a lot of other changes in the organization were officially communicated. Ken Rice, one of Jeff's long time friends and the CEO of Broadband, had left Enron. Kevin Hannon, who was had also been in Broadband went to the international group, and Jim Fallon, a former trader in Wholesale, took over the CEO role in Enron Broadband. It was clear, by this point, that Jeff was settling into his new CEO role and putting his stamp on the organization with people that he trusted.

Immediately after that meeting with Jeff in October 2000, several things occurred. Bobbie Power, my long-time assistant, finally got tired of my arrogance. It had gradually gotten worse as all of my promotions occurred.

As I look back, the demands that I placed on her were unrealistic.

I expected her to be able to get us a first-class upgrade every time we flew to Aspen. Things had to be done immediately and they had to be perfect. If they weren't, I was sarcastic and down right hateful. I really didn't want her to leave. She had been with me for several years and I thought the world of her. Her departure shook me up and I realized that I wasn't a very nice person anymore. Secondly, I wasn't feeling very well. I was actually having a lot of female problems and had to have surgery to get some relief from the way I was feeling.

Ken and Linda were suggesting other options for me to pursue outside of Enron. Linda had set up a potential interview with the Houston Museum of Fine Arts. I didn't realize it at the time, but Ken was also looking at other opportunities outside of Enron, as Jeff took over as Enron's CEO.

From a national standpoint, Geroge W. Bush had been elected as president of the United States in a very controversial election, and in January 2001, Grady and I were invited to attend the Bush Inauguration in Washington, D.C., I am not sure how many planes Enron flew to Washington for the weekend of events, but I think it might have involved every plane we had. We transported a lot of dignitaries to the event, including the first President Bush and his wife.

Of course the festivities were unforgettable. The day of the inauguration it was cold and rainy, and fairly uncomfortable to be outside. We skipped the parade for that reason, but stayed for the entire inaugural ceremony on the steps of the capital. The "Black Tie and Boots" ball the night before had been unforgettable and we had stayed up later than normal for us. For that reason, we skipped the entire list of "balls" the next night, and went to dinner then back to our hotel room for an early evening to bed.

On the return trip back to Houston we were not cleared to take off for several hours because of an ice storm that had occurred the night before. Grady and I were on the plane with Kevin Hannon and Greg Whaley along with several other people. Greg was then the CEO of the trading organization. Grady was well acquainted with the Enron pilots. He always liked to visit with them, and even sat in the jump seat when we were on the planes.

He and the pilots decided to de-ice the plane themselves with brooms and scrapers. It worked and we ended up being cleared to take off much earlier than if we would have had to wait in line to get de-iced. The next Monday morning, Kevin Hannon told the entire management committee that Grady had de-iced the plane. I remember Jeff Skilling looked a little shocked, but it got a good laugh from everyone at the meeting.

Ken had recommended to Karl Rove, who was now on the president elect's staff, that I and several others from Enron be considered to become representatives on the Bush presidency transition team. In November of 2000, when Bush was elected as president, Ken and Enron were huge contributors to his campaign, and Ken wanted to have some Enron representation on that committee. Unfortunately, no one from Enron was chosen.

I waited until bonuses were announced in late January of 2001 to decide what I should do about leaving

Enron. Surprisingly, I got my full bonus for the prior year. Because of that, I decided to stay at Enron and stick it out for a while. It was during this time that I started to back off of the hours I was working and spent more time with Grady and our first dog, Chelsea.

I was starting to realize that I was happier when I was with Grady than at the office with all of the issues that I was currently dealing with. We even went out and bought another dog so that I would have one. Chelsea had gradually become Grady's dog because he took her to work with him during the day.

When Jake became a part of our family he was quite a challenge and demanded more of my attention than I thought he would. That was actually good because it took my mind off of the situation at Enron and gave me a project to work on. I guess the most important thing about Jake however, was that he loved me no matter what happened. When I got home from the office and he was there, it seemed to take my mind off of every bad thing that might have happened that day.

At work I focused more and more of my time on the Vision and Values task force, and adding employee benefits. Ken had a vision several years before to have a place working mothers could bring their children in close proximity to their work. In the summer of 2001, we worked on and opened our new child care center. It was first-class and the employees loved it. They could walk across the street and have lunch with their kids or just drop in for a visit any time of the day. We actually were one of the first major corporations at the time to offer this kind of on-site child care.

We also were working with the building administration people to design the common areas of the new building to make them inviting and creative. The new building would be connected with our current building by a large sky ring over Smith Street. Our plans for that ring included a large ticker tape lighting system that would display stock prices and other pertinent news of the day. A rock climbing wall was planned for the first floor area to encourage employees to take a break and get creative. As I now hear all of the things Google has developed for their employees to encourage innovation, I have to think that we at Enron were already doing those things in the late 1990s.

We implemented a program that, in partnership with Dell Computer, gave every Enron employee a computer for their home. The program was called "Click at Home." Now so many jobs can be handled remotely. Our plans with this program included increasing the amount of telecommuting that we could offer employees so, in some jobs, employees could actually work at home. Again, this was pre-2000. We were definitely on the right track with our benefits, and we continued to attract the best people from all of the best schools.

I was still working with Beth Tilncy on all of these things. Because of Beth and my incredible team it was still fun, and we were making a difference in our employees' lives and giving our employees the environment that encouraged creative thought and innovation.

Taking advantage of the relationships I had developed outside of Enron, I also worked to form a Human Resource Roundtable across the city of Houston. The roundtable provided a forum for all of the Human Resource executives of the large companies in Houston to meet quarterly. Our goal was to improve the image of Houston so we could continue to recruit outstanding talent from around the world. The Greater Houston Partnership and City of Houston were also a part of the group. One of the people on my HR team facilitated the group, and he continues to lead that group today.

Back in March 2001, I had started thinking about leaving Enron again—much more seriously than I had in the past. I was tired and still didn't feel great. I sold as many of my options as I could. I also converted my 401(k) to stable assets. I wanted to be ready to leave when I finally decided that was the thing to do. Even though I was having a lot of fun creating the culture we had, I didn't think that in the long run I would continue to fit into Enron after Ken left and Jeff became CEO.

I started traveling to companies that wanted to talk about how Enron had created our culture. Beth Tilney and I were meeting with CEOs and their representatives all over the country. On the outside I got a rush being told how great Enron was and showing them how we got there.

We had companies like American Express, Charles Schwab, Cisco Systems, Delphi, and Methodist Hospital in Houston all interested in how we became so innovative. On the other hand I felt like my resume and the relationships I was developing would allow me to find another job somewhere else when I decided to leave.

We also formed a small HR team that started to focus on how we could partner with a third party and offer our human resource capabilities to other companies as a profit center. The team we assembled in Human Resources did a tremendous job reengineering the HR functions at Enron and there appeared to be a market for our capabilities in those areas outside our company.

One of the people on that team was Bob Sparger. Bob and I had a history together as he had come to work for me years ago when I was in charge of the Enron Capital and Trade back office. We did not see eye to eye when he worked with me to reengineer Enron Capital and Trade, and actually left Enron for some time because of the way he was treated by me and others. I must admit that I treated him pretty badly during our first experience together. Despite that, he returned to work at Enron in the HR area as we started to re-engineer that group.

He was now an integral part of the team inking the deal with Accenture, which would give us a partnership to offer Enron's HR capabilities through a new entity owned jointly by Enron and Accenture. Without Bob, this would not have happened.

Bob would, in the coming years, be one of the few members of my old Enron HR team who would check on me periodically and stay connected. He would also help me in all of the investigations. Because of things I confided in him about how I felt about Jeff Skilling as he was starting to take over as CEO, Bob understood that I was considering leaving Enron early in 2001. Bob is a great example of someone that truly forgave, and I have looked up to him ever since and hope that I could do the same.

We actually inked the deal with Accenture right before Enron collapsed. This would have formalized our partnership to market HR products to other companies. I was excited about it not only because it transformed HR into a profit center, but it could have presented a way for me to leave Enron as there was a need for someone to run that business.

In general we had created one of the best employee benefit packages in the country, and we had transformed a typical HR function into a highly respected part of the company. Again, this happened because of the creative culture that we encouraged at Enron and the unbelievable talent that worked there.

In the mid-year 2001 performance review process, the business people made a mistake in how they handled the overstaffing issue in Enron Energy Services and Enron Broadband. Consequently, employees' perception of the performance process worsened because it appeared that it was being used as a rank and yank tool for management. Employees were also extremely upset with our values because what we were professing was far different from the reality of what they saw every day. Because our stock price was much lower than the year before, employees' morale was very low.

All through 2000 and 2001 Beth Tilney and I tried very hard through the Vision and Values task force efforts to influence Jeff Skilling to focus on our values. We even handpicked people for the task force who we perceived Jeff respected, but also emulated our values. Michael Kopper, who eventually pled guilty to theft from Enron, was actually one person who both of us were sure lived the values and had Jeff's respect. We were both shocked years later after the Enron collapse to learn that in fact Michael was taking money from Enron in partnership with Andy Fastow.

The California energy crisis had been heating up since early 2001, and it started to appear to Beth and me that Ken Lay was not totally comfortable with the way Jeff was handling the public relations surrounding it. We actually thought we were seeing a crack in the support of Jeff by Ken. It was because of the California issue that Ken asked Beth to get more involved in public relations at a corporate level. Even though Mark Palmer was promoted into the corporate PR role after Beth went to Enron Energy Services, Ken continued to consult with Beth on many issues.

Beth and I were confident that together we might be able to influence Ken to reconsider having Jeff as CEO; we were both concerned with the direction Enron was taking under Jeff's leadership. We had just become aware of an external survey sponsored by the corporate public relations group that indicated Enron was now being perceived as self-serving, not trustworthy and more arrogant compared to the year before. When you love a place as much as we both did, it was very disturbing to see what the outside perception of Enron was becoming.

Our stock had fallen dramatically by the early summer of 2001. Jeff cursed at an analyst under his breath on a conference call when the analyst wanted to know more about Enron's balance sheet and it appeared the analysts in general were losing patience with him. In addition, he told a very bad joke in California that compared the state with the Titanic and it wasn't well received. Finally, several of the new businesses that Jeff had touted so strongly were struggling. Enron Broadband Services, the business Jeff suggested a year earlier was going to be worth billions to the company, was especially suffering due to what Jeff referred to as a "total meltdown" of the telecommunications industry.

Beth and I were growing more and more concerned about Enron's reputation, and in a moment of desperation, and probably some insanity, we tried to garner support of doing something about Jeff from Mark Frevert. Mark was, and continues to be, one of my best friends, so I felt comfortable going to him. Mark was also highly respected in the organization. He had come back from running Enron Europe, was responsible for its success, and was working back in Houston in the Wholesale group with Greg Whalley (ECT was renamed Wholesale sometime in 2000).

Of course, Mark wasn't interested in helping us get rid of Jeff. I am not sure that he knew how serious we were. He told us that he hoped he didn't ever make us that mad at him for anything he did; he didn't want us to gang up on him too. He laughed at us and we left his office trying to figure out another angle.

Photo Gallery

An Early Family Photo of me with my dad and my
sister with my mom.

At our wedding in 1975

One of the many non-profit functions Grady and I attended
with Ken and Linda Lay.

My officer picture taken shortly after my promotion to
Enron's Executive Comittee in early 2000.

Running my second Houston Marathon.

Grady and I at the Presidential Inaguaration in January 2001.

Beth Tilney and I talking to Drayton McLane.

Grady and I with president George W. Bush at a "Celebration of Reading" fundraiser in 2001.

Two Months after Ken Lay died I lost my two year old
Great Pyreneese "Tika".

One of our fall Jeep trips with Rick and Bitsy Causey.

Grady and I with my parents, my brother and his family and
my sister and her family in 2003.

Our "family" Christmas picture taken in 2006. Grady and I
with Koda, Banjo, Chelsea and Jake.

With our friends Mark Frevert, Marion Ragland and Dan
and Judy McCarty in December 2000.

A little five year old boy, Jake Nieto, who saved me.

Grady and I celebrating New Years Eve with our dear friends Jim and Pam Alexander.

Jeff Skilling Leaves Enron

It was early August 2001, and Grady and I had planned another week in Colorado. We were getting away as much as we could. With my new downsized role and the incredible team that I had built, it was easier to leave without being missed. I still was not feeling very well, and I was starting to think more seriously about leaving Enron again. I don't know what it was about being in Colorado that made me start to reevaluate where I was and what I was doing with my life, but it happened a lot when I was there in that serene setting.

During that particular week in Colorado, I went on several of my long runs and did a lot of thinking about my priorities and my career. I didn't have God in my life then, or so I thought, so I didn't ask Him for help making the decision. I just "felt" it was time to leave and do something different. I called Ken Lay's assistant, Rosie, toward the end of the week and set up a meeting with Ken upon my return. I didn't tell her what the meeting was about. I knew though, that I was going to tell him I was leaving Enron.

As usual I walked into Ken's office and immediately sat at that big round table that I had been at so many times over the last few years. I wasn't nervous because I knew what I wanted to do. I began our discussion by explaining to him that I had not been feeling very well lately and I wanted to back away from a full-time schedule. I told him that with everything I was involved in with diversity, the Greater Houston Partnership, and the meetings I was having with other CEOs around the country I felt like there were some opportunities for me outside of Enron that I might be more passionate about.

I didn't even mention that I also was not happy with the direction Jeff Skilling was taking Enron. In fact, I didn't even mention Jeff as a reason I was leaving. Ken let me go through my speech that I had rehearsed. Then he smiled and simply said to me after I finished, "He is leaving. And I need you to stay and help me rebuild Enron."

At first I couldn't believe what I was hearing. Here I was ready to leave and now Ken needed me to stay and help him. I immediately knew who "he" was even though Ken did not call him by name. Emotionally, I was a wreck. I didn't realize how much stress had built up within me because of how Jeff had treated me and others.

It was then that I spilled my guts about everything I felt Jeff did to me. How he had been rude to one of our community relations people who simply wanted to give him a brochure she was distributing to all employees—that brochure announced our new matching gift hotline to make it easier for employees to get a personal gift matched by Enron. I told Ken that Jeff was in a relationship with a friend of mine outside of Enron; how even Drayton McLane and Howard Jefferson confided in me they really didn't care for him. Of course, in retrospect, nothing that I shared with Ken would be cause for Jeff to not operate effectively as CEO of Enron but I believed Jeff did not represent the values Ken had built the company on.

I had been very careful not to share any of these things

with Ken before now because after all, he had selected Jeff for the role, and I felt my responsibility was not to trash Jeff but to try and help him develop the qualities I was sure Ken wanted to see in Jeff as CEO. Ken was well aware of the strategies that Beth and I had used to try and get Jeff on board with our Vision and Values. He was also well aware of the challenges that we encountered in that mission.

I shared with Ken the encounter I had with Jeff one evening on the 50th floor. Jeff came into my office to ask me to look into an HR issue for him. When he asked me if I could do something for him I said, "Sure, anything you need." His response was surprising as he looked at me and said, "Anything?" in a very inappropriate way. Of course I immediately added, "Anything within reason." Looking back on that conversation today I am sure Jeff was just trying to be funny, but I was so mad at him at the time that I assumed he had other motives.

Ken was surprised that Jeff would say that to me so I went on and shared things I really didn't know for sure about Jeff and other women. It's ironic now that I have looked back on that conversation with Ken and felt bad about those things I shared about Jeff. That was exactly what the government did to all of us. I was painting Jeff guilty even though I did not know for sure. I would get a taste of that kind of treatment when, after Enron filed for bankruptcy, the Justice Department was convinced Ken Lay and I had been involved in an affair.

Of course I wanted to know why Jeff was leaving, and as I remember it, Ken didn't go into a lot of detail. I think I read into our conversation more than actually occurred.

I was convinced that Ken and the board wanted Jeff to go because I did, but I really don't think that was the case.

I wasn't sure why Ken told me Jeff was leaving. I suppose he knew that it would be hard to get me to agree to stay unless he told me the person that had made my life so miserable the past months was going away. He cautioned me that I could not tell anyone, not even Beth, because it was not widely known. He even voiced his own surprise at sharing the news with me. Of course, I told him I would stay.

It was very difficult leaving Ken's office with basically a gag order. I had news that I knew would make many people in my circle of friends extremely happy. I was ecstatic and immediately I started thinking of all of the things we needed to do. Jeff was leaving, Ken was back, and I would be back also. Even though this was all good news, I managed to keep the information Ken shared with me to myself for several days.

When the news about Jeff was finally announced publicly the internal reaction was very positive by a large majority of the Enron employees. It didn't even cross my mind for a minute that the external perception would be different. That, of course, proved devastating for Enron.

Internally, everyone I was close to was excited. We were in the Ken Lay camp, but forgot there was a very strong Jeff Skilling camp within Enron as well. Jeff's resignation split the company down the middle. The pipeline people and others in the organization who had been at Enron for a long time were very happy. They had seen Ken Lay overcome countless obstacles for Enron to become one of the world's leading companies. They all felt their hero was back in charge, and the issues people had about the performance review process, the stock price and the lack of adherence to the values they saw in the new businesses were going to be fixed by Ken.

A large majority of the employees that were in the wholesale organizations and the new businesses of the company came to Enron because of the innovation that Jeff Skilling introduced to the company. Many of them had joined Enron in the last few years, and they admired the business models that Jeff had introduced. Those people felt betrayed and angry that Jeff would "just leave." It was actually telling of their character and "deal mentality" that they were so quick to "cut him loose." Perhaps because they didn't have a strong emotional tie to anyone, they were quickly thinking about who would replace Jeff. Of course we all were speculating on our next COO, but the traders were very vocal in calling for one of their own.

Beth and I went to dinner to celebrate with a couple of other friends the day it was announced. We all had become concerned about where Enron was heading under Jeff's leadership. We all stood ready to do whatever Ken needed us to do to get Enron back on track. Again, none of us, as I remember, thought about the negative perception that the outside world would have to Jeff leaving his position as CEO.

Ken Lay held an employee meeting that next week to discuss Jeff's departure and Enron's future. When Ken entered the Hyatt's large ballroom and stepped on stage, he received a rousing standing ovation from more than three thousand employees. He didn't even have to say a word. They stood up and just started clapping. The employees wouldn't quit and I remember thinking how great it was that Ken was back. Jeff was gone and everything was going to be wonderful again.

During this employee meeting, Ken announced that he knew we needed to work on our values. He wanted people with questions or concerns to call Cindy Olson or Steve Kean. I was already starting to work with a small group of people to quickly pull together an employee survey to send out internally so we could evaluate all of the employee concerns.

Shortly after Ken stepped back in as CEO, Steve Kean came to me and told me it didn't make sense for me to report to him any longer. Ken trusted me and he didn't need to be in the middle of that. Steve began his career at Enron as a regulatory lawyer who was instrumental in Enron's fight for open markets in natural gas and electricity. He was amazing to watch when he talked about deregulation because he was so incredibly passionate. Steve Kean was also truly one of the best leaders at Enron, and Jeff was justified in trusting him as much as he did. I have always thought a lot of Steve for stepping out of my way when Ken returned as CEO. It takes a big person to do that. I found out years later that Steve wrote a very thoughtful letter to Ken about the state of the company when Ken returned as CEO.

We knew there were a lot of employee morale issues stemming from the performance evaluation system that was held mid year. Morale in general was an issue because the stock price was lower than anyone wanted to see. Ken had been out of the loop for awhile, so we thought it was important that he understand how the employees felt. I didn't even think about how far away from the day to day business Ken might have gotten. I am sure while we were worried about the employee's concerns he was starting to uncover issues in the business.

When I got back to my office after the employee meeting, Sherron Watkins, who would become well-known as the "Enron Whistleblower," was sitting outside of my office. Hilda, my assistant at the time, had her take a seat in a chair outside my office while she waited for me to return from the employee meeting. It took me nearly two hours to make it back to my office after the employee meeting. When I saw Sherron sitting there, I remember feeling irritated that she was waiting on me since I had been delayed in returning from the meeting that morning. I was trying to get out of the office early to catch a plane to go with Grady to Wisconsin for the weekend and I knew I had to leave soon to make that plane.

Sherron had a single page letter in her hand. When we walked in to my office she laid out the folded paper as I sat down next to her at my conference table. She started the conversation by explaining that she had a letter she had sent to the people in charge of collecting employee questions prior to the employee meeting. She wasn't surprised that it had not been read because it was long and she had signed it "anonymous."

I knew Sherron had worked for Andy Fastow when she first started working at Enron. I also knew that she had previously worked at Arthur Andersen. I had known her since those early days of her career, but quite frankly, I had lost track of where she was currently working.

I quickly scanned through the one page letter she handed me. I had only heard people mention the Raptors and LJM. I wasn't familiar with all of the points she was making to know any of the details. I asked her if Rick

Causey and Andy Fastow had gotten a copy of the letter because of her reference to accounting and she responded that she didn't know for sure. She told me what she really wanted was for someone to look into her concerns other than Rick or Andy to determine if she was correct in her allegations. The contents of the letter seemed serious enough that I encouraged her to meet with Ken Lay.

I was concerned that she would communicate her issues to Ken in a way that would cause him to not take her seriously. Ken always gravitated to good news and this letter was not positive. I had also heard Sherron had a reputation of being somewhat dramatic. I encouraged her to think through her presentation to Ken and keep a logical, calm tone when she explained her concerns. She agreed that she wanted to meet with Mr. Lay, so I called Rosie and had her schedule a meeting between Sherron and Ken on Wednesday of the next week.

I told Sherron that I would check with her on Monday when I returned from my trip out of town to ensure that she had not changed her mind about the meeting. Her most immediate concern was that Ken was considering Andy Fastow for the COO position. Since Jeff left, Ken announced that as CEO he would name a new COO to work with him very soon. I felt like the allegations Sherron was making, if correct, should be known by Ken before he made that decision.

When I returned to the office on Monday I sent Sherron an email from Rick Causey that Rick had sent to Ken regarding her allegations. I asked Sherron if the explanation given by Rick was sufficient and did she still want the meeting with Ken Lay. Sherron called me almost immediately and told me that she did, in fact, still want to meet with Ken. I was so focused on getting the employee survey out to employees and I felt she was in good hands with Ken. I set up the meeting and went on with all of the other things that were on my plate. I felt comfortable that if there were any serious issues Ken would let me know.

After her meeting with Ken, Sherron was not comfortable working with Andy Fastow any longer. Ken called me to see if she could work in my group. He asked if I would also work with Sherron to get her computer back to Andy as he was requesting it be returned to his group. Sherron moved to an office on my floor the next week.

I was so naïve about what was going on. I really thought that Andy wanted Sherron's computer because he did not want to have to buy another one. So I had Sherron work with IT to copy all of her files on a new computer. In essence she gave Andy back an empty computer. I've since found out that Andy most likely was destroying files to cover his tracks and he wanted to destroy her files as well.

In late August, we finally sent out the "Lay it on the Line" survey that we had been working so hard on. The employees had grown so distrustful of management that they voiced their concerns about answering the survey honestly without repercussions. We had to send out an email emphasizing to everyone that their answers were in fact confidential.

The results of the survey were compiled within a few days. The major issues the survey identified included the stock price, the PRC (Performance Review Committee) process, and employee morale. Those results were no surprise to Beth or me. We could sense it before we even asked the employees what they thought.

Grady and I flew to Aspen with Ken and Linda for the Labor Day weekend in 2001. I reviewed the results of the survey with Ken on the way to Aspen. All four of us were upbeat for the future of Enron. In fact, Linda Lay commented that we were going to address the issues in the survey, get the stock price back to $90 a share, and then Ken was going to run for mayor of the city of Houston. Little did any of us know what would happen during the next ninety days.

I was getting letters from headhunters to the tune of at least one letter or call per week after September 1. I remember sending Ken one of the letters with a note expressing my concern about how many other executives were receiving these kinds of offers. He returned the letter I sent to him with a note back to me asking again that I not entertain any of these offers and "please stay." I really wasn't looking for a compliment from him, I was in fact very worried that we would lose a lot of great talent if we didn't pay attention. Clearly, at that point, we were all worried about keeping all of our good people.

Early the morning of September 11, 2001, as I drove the short distance from our townhouse to the Enron building, I heard a small plane had hit the Twin Towers in New York. Like most people I wondered how a plane could be so off course that it would hit a building in downtown New York City.

I arrived at my office on the 16th floor of the Enron building just in time to see the second plane hit the other tower. Instantly, everyone watching the monitor outside of my office knew it was not an accident. We had huge TV monitors hanging from the ceiling all over the floor and everyone quickly turned their full attention to what was unfolding on those screens. This was the worst thing that I had ever seen. It was like we were watching a Hollywood movie. As we were focused on the horrible national drama that was unfolding, we were unaware that huge Enron issues were starting to be discovered as well.

After September 11, my focus was on issuing a report to the employees summarizing the results of the "Lay It on the Line" survey. Secondly, my group started working on what we were going to do to address what Enron would contribute as a corporation to help the families of the 9/11 victims. This is when I personally got the first hint of a potential problem at Enron.

As we always did in disaster situations, we researched what other major companies were doing financially to help the 9/11 victims. After completing the research, we sent a recommendation to Ken Lay that put us in line with other major Fortune 10 companies. Ken called me to tell me he had to cut our recommendation dramatically. Even though he had agreed to $1 million, our recommendation had been for $5 million. We were all surprised. That didn't happen very often, and we thought something did not seem right, but we were not sure what was going on.

In the meantime, the *Wall Street Journal* had continued writing articles about Enron. They started when Jeff Skilling left, and they were speculating on who would replace him. The events of September 11 slowed their articles, but after the dust settled on their reporting of that national tragedy, the *Journal* resumed their reporting of Enron even more aggressively. Every day a new article would appear that made us feel like the *Journal* knew more about the company than any of us did.

Ken named Greg Whalley as COO and Mark Frevert as vice chairman to replace Jeff Skilling. He called both Beth and I to get our input on his decision to name the two before it was announced. He wanted us to think about the decision in terms of how the employees would react. I was comfortable that with Mark Frevert as a part of the team, Ken's choice was fine. Mark was an incredible manager and Greg had the respect of the traders. Together, I thought they would be great. But at the end of the day, however, Mark and Greg really never had a chance to make a real difference.

In late September, Beth and I were invited by Ken to join the executive team for a meeting at the Woodlands conference center. Neither of us was on the executive team but Ken spoke to us on a daily basis for our advice regarding employee and image issues. He trusted our judgment on the employee related issues, and wouldn't make decisions about any employee communication or meeting without our input. Ken asked us to come to the meeting in the Woodlands to present the summarized results of the "Lay It on the Line" survey to the group of Enron officers.

This meeting at the Woodlands was scheduled to bring the entire management team up to speed on the issues that were being identified by many of the new players. It was clear at that meeting that Beth and I were being viewed as a distraction by Greg Whaley. He felt the presentation of the employee concerns to the group was taking up valuable time they needed to spend on other, more important, business issues. Actually, when we realized months later what was going on in the rest of the company, he was right.

We presented our portion of the agenda and were then excused so that the rest of the day could be spent on other things. Both Beth and I were disappointed. Again, we felt that the employees and our Vision and Values were taking a back seat. We were well aware of many of the issues because the survey brought those to the forefront, and clearly the media reports we were dealing with were very serious. As always, we felt we had an obligation to the employees to communicate to them what was going on.

Finally, in mid-October, we issued a report to the employees informing them of the results of the "Lay It on the Line" survey, and what we were doing to address their concerns. By then however, it was clear that many things were going wrong.

At an employee meeting in October an employee submitted a question suggesting Ken Lay was "smoking crack." At that same meeting, one of the traders stood up and literally screamed at Ken about his support of Andy Fastow. Unfortunately, Ken defended Andy at that meeting, but within a few days additional information about Andy's activities was discovered and Ken and the Board placed Andy on leave. Amazingly however, Andy wasn't fired until well into 2002 and in true character, Andy was more concerned about his severance than what had happened to the company.

The *Journal* continued to be relentless on its reporting of Enron. By this time we were all sure someone was feeding them information. I was involved in a group that met to discuss the current PR crisis we were facing. Everyday we discussed what we believed would be the next shoe to fall, and what we should do in response. Jeff McMahon, who took over Andy's position as CFO when he was placed on leave, was involved in this group, but he was also uncovering the mess that Andy had left behind, so he was pretty busy. As it turned out, there wasn't agreement among our group on a clear strategy to address the *Journal*'s concerns and Ken ultimately grew very frustrated with what the *Journal* reported and our lack of response.

During this same time frame we were asked to start working on things we could do to conserve cash. Ultimately, in late October we sent a memo to Ken outlining several suggestions. We were planning the annual November Enron management conference, and the cost of this conference normally ran around a half million dollars. We recommended that we forego that conference this year. It was hard for Ken to let that go as it was a very important annual event in the company.

We had also been planning the first all-Enron Christmas party. In years past, each operating group had held their own party. This year we were planning an "over the top" party at Enron Field for everyone together.

The price tag was shocking to a lot of people. We estimated the cost of the party we were planning was a little more than $1 million. Actually, though, when you considered the cost of all of the Enron related parties in the past, we spent close to that in total. No one had really ever tallied the entire Enron cost until we started planning this one big party. Anyway, we recommended that we cut out the Christmas party that year as well, saving us more than $1 million in cash. Beth and I had to almost beg Ken to do this because he was so concerned how the employees would react.

Grady and I had gone to Hawaii in mid-October to celebrate our twenty-sixth wedding anniversary, but I spent a lot of time during that trip on conference calls back to Houston. When I got back from Hawaii I was faced with a key decision about the transition of our 401(k) plan to Hewitt from Northern Trust.

In my revised role as the head of Human Resources I was responsible for the employee benefits and the 401(k). We had determined over six months before that we were going to transition our plan from Northern Trust to Hewitt. The benefits group, led by Cynthia Barrow, had done an outstanding job keeping up with employee suggestions for the benefit plans. Many employees wanted to trade their 401(k) portfolios on a daily basis. Northern Trust was not responsive enough to our requests for the upgraded service levels that our employees were asking for, and we determined several months earlier to transition the plan to Hewitt because they could provide day trading on the plan and other services our employees wanted. By April 2001, Northern Trust service levels were at an all time low of 36% with abandoned calls of 15.8%. This service level, which represented how quickly and accurately Northern Trust answered our employee inquiries, was far from acceptable to us.

We spent the previous six months getting the communication materials together for the transition and laying out a very detailed plan for that communication. Now it was time to go forward with the change.

Two of the people that worked for me, Cynthia Barrow and Mikie Rath, had already sent various forms of employee communications out during the previous several weeks informing employees that they would not be able to conduct any buy or sell transactions in their 401(k) during the transition period. The transition was expected to last at least three weeks starting on October 29, 2001.

A couple days prior to the transition date of the 401(k), Cynthia and Mikie asked me to help them make a decision. The decision was whether we should move forward with the transition of the plan to Hewitt given the volatility in our stock price. Our outside counsel, along with Cynthia and Mikie, was recommending that we move forward with the transition even though our stock price had declined significantly.

Because of the situation with the stock price they all wanted me to make the final decision. In my opinion they had a valid argument for moving forward with the transition. All of the employees and ex-employees who were still in the 401(k) plan received a total of four e-mails and/or letters to their homes announcing the transition. If we did not move forward with the transition as planned, we had potential legal exposure if an employee or former employee did not get the letter canceling the transition. Because of the anthrax issue the postal service was dealing with after September 11, it didn't appear we would be able to insure communication would make it to everyone in the plan in time.

Before I made the decision to move forward or not, I called the two Human Resource vice presidents who reported to operating groups. These two were the most influential HR heads in the organization. I laid out the options and issues to them and they both agreed we should move forward with the transition as planned. I made one final call to a trader who worked in Enron Wholesale and potentially traded his 401(k) frequently. After giving him the same information I had given to the two HR vice presidents, he recommended we should send out one final memo to employees and move forward with the transition.

So, after all of the discussions, I made the decision to move forward with the transition. I made a point to tell Cynthia not to worry. I would take full responsibility for the decision and any consequences would be mine. I didn't realize then what the consequences would be.

We had done our homework, communicated at least twice to all participants to that point and had already spent a lot of time and money to effectuate the change in administrator. I didn't even consider asking what Ken Lay thought we should do. Looking back, that might have saved me a lot of grief, but given what he was dealing with, I felt confident this was not a decision that he needed to be involved in making. It would be in 2005 that I finally had a chance to share with Ken exactly what had happened, and how I had made the decision. Throughout all of the questioning I always told the truth. Even though many congressmen, senators and the media suspected a management conspiracy, I had made that decision and no one else.

Of course, after the Enron bankruptcy, this decision came back to haunt me. Because the stock price declined so significantly from a high in October of 2000 of $90 per share to below $1 before we filed bankruptcy, many employees unknowingly blamed the transition and ultimate lock down of the plan on losing their entire 401(k) value. They claimed that they were not able to trade out of their Enron stock during the two week-long transition period and lost their entire 401(k) value during that period of time. In reality, the stock price only declined approximately $4 per share during the transition period. Because many Enron employees were so loyal to the company that had been so good to them throughout the years, they simply could not sell their Enron stock.

The other surprising issue for many people was that it actually prevented many employees from buying more Enron stock. When we analyzed what really happened, with the stock declining approximately $4 per share during the transition period, employees actually bought more stock at about $10 per share immediately after the transition. Many of them probably thought it was a great buy at that price. Not more than a month later the stock would be worth less than $1.

I had been a member of the administrative committee of the 401(k) plan since January of 2001 or about ten months. The administrative committee was responsible for insuring that the investments offered by the 401(k) plan were strong performing investments. We had done a great job with the outside portfolio choices. Because of the performance of the Enron stock, we started meeting weekly after we transitioned the 401(k) to Hewitt in late October. Actually the transition of the plan was completed a week early because we, as a committee, strongly encouraged Northern Trust to expedite the process.

The committee was struggling with the question of what we should do with the investment in Enron stock as it continued its downward spiral. Of course, none of us knew exactly what was going to happen to the stock price. We felt if we recommended taking the Enron stock out of the investment portfolio and it rebounded, we would be in as much hot water as doing nothing. We hired an outside attorney to help us with this decision, but we never really got any sound advice from him. As a result, we continued to retain Enron stock as an investment option until well after Enron filed for bankruptcy and most of us had resigned from the committee.

The rest of October and November 2001 are a blur for me and probably for a lot of Enron employees. *The Wall Street Journal* continued to attack us daily about various issues they suspected were taking place at Enron. They started with the off-balance sheet partnerships run by Andy Fastow. They revealed details about Chewco, the Raptors and the Nigerian Barge Deal. At the end of the day, none of these things individually would have made a big impact on Enron's financial statements; however, together they all undermined Enron's credibility.

So many people have asked me what happened at Enron. I think it was this simple:

Andy Fastow was the bad guy. He embezzled money from the company through the partnerships he was managing. When Jeff Skilling left the company, a lot of people wondered why a CEO of the seventh largest company on *Fortune*'s list would suddenly leave for reasons that didn't make sense. *The Wall Street Journal* started digging into Enron and uncovered issues that financially were not big enough to really hurt the company. Our trading business however, required total confidence in our financial stability. Once there was any question—no matter how minor it was—in that financial stability, the lack of confidence impacted our stock price.

Once the stock price started falling, standard contractual clauses were triggered allowing all of the big banks that were so quick to come to the table with lines of credit, to call for their money. We didn't have the cash to repay every one of them and we had to file for bankruptcy. It would be just like if all of the creditors, mortgage lenders, credit card companies, etc., any of us have, asked for all of their money back on the same day. You just can't pay it all back that quickly.

In November 2001, prior to Enron filing bankruptcy, it appeared that Dynegy was going to make an attempt to acquire Enron. Chuck Watson, the CEO of Dynegy had always wanted Dynegy to be just like Enron. I wasn't excited about the potential take over. I had a prior experience with Chuck at a customer meeting when I was with Northern Natural Gas years before, which caused me question his character. I had no respect for him after that, and I knew I would have no desire to work in that organization if the acquisition went forward.

There weren't many people at Enron excited about the acquisition. I left Ken a voice message some time during the negotiations telling him that employees didn't want the acquisition to happen. I went on to say that we would rather file for bankruptcy. As I look back on that now I am not so sure that we would have felt the same way knowing what was about to happen. It is also clear now that Ken was trying to save the company, no matter the personal cost.

I didn't get involved in any of the due diligence related to the acquisition. Most of the work fell on the person responsible for executive compensation and the business unit HR heads.

During the due diligence, Ken Lay was entitled to a

$60 million severance payment if Dynegy completed the take over. His contract gave him the right to that payment because he would not be the CEO of the combined company going forward. The Enron traders were irate when they found out about that payment. In the end, Ken agreed not to take that money. I'm not sure all of the employees realized what Ken had done. That sent a huge signal to me and others that he was trying to save Enron regardless of how it impacted him personally.

In discussions I had with the Astros they told me Chuck Watson, during this time frame, had inquired about changing the name of the stadium in Houston to Dynegy if the acquisition occurred. Several of us thought that possibly Chuck's ego was so large that his main reason for the Enron take over might have been so he could have his company's name on the stadium.

Because it was clear that Ken Lay would not be the CEO going forward, Dynegy's head of Human Resources would have the lead job for the combined company and I would not be there going forward either. I continued to emotionally withdraw more and more. The other Enron Human Resource leaders were much more valuable to the organization. Since I was in charge of the employee programs, diversity, community relations and the vision and values task force there was not a lot of need for me to be that engaged in what was currently taking place.

Ken spent his Thanksgiving holiday working on the deal trying to make all of it fall in place. Unfortunately, Dynegy's board ultimately did not approve the acquisition and our bond rating immediately fell to junk.

Of course as our bond rating fell, the banks started

calling for their money. Enron filed for bankruptcy on Sunday December 2, 2001.

That same Sunday afternoon it was confirmed with the bankruptcy lawyers that we would not be able to ensure severance for the employees that we were going to have to layoff. The layoff was necessary to cut costs, and was the only hope that some form of Enron could survive.

We immediately went into emergency mode; by that time everyone was exhausted, but we still had a lot of work to do. We had to finalize the list of employees we would keep, and get all of the paperwork prepared for those who would have to leave. Our ultimate goal was to effectuate an orderly layoff throughout several days allowing employees to gather their things and say their goodbyes.

After many hours of agonizing discussion it was concluded by the management team and Human Resources that we would have to coordinate a mass layoff on Monday morning December 3. We knew that there would be anger and hurt, and we were concerned for the employees' safety, so we planned that we would coordinate meetings on all the Enron building floors at 10:00 a.m. The process we agreed on was unfortunately cold and simple. The people who would stay would be told prior to those meetings that they had been chosen to continue their employment. Anyone that had not been asked to stay prior to the floor meetings was required to pack their desks immediately and leave the building.

That Sunday evening when I got home from the office was a blur, and maybe one of those truly awful things that your mind attempts to forget. I don't remember anything about it. I don't remember going to bed or if I even slept. I don't remember driving to the office the next morning, but I do remember the sick feeling in my stomach when I did walk into my own office that morning. I also remember talking to Beth and both of us agreed we were glad Ken was out of town starting to work on the details of the bankruptcy that day and didn't have to witness the layoffs. It would have broken his heart.

I have got to say that Monday, December 3, 2001, was one of the most horrible days of my life. I agreed to be the executive to hold the floor meeting on my floor that morning. I had tried to hold one daily throughout the last several weeks in an attempt to keep the employees apprised of any new developments. Even though the meetings during the last few weeks were difficult, I knew the one that Monday would be the worst. It killed me to stand in front of all of our employees that morning and tell them they had to leave.

I asked that everyone on my floor meet outside my office. If they had not been spoken to by their immediate supervisor prior to the meeting I told them they would not be working for Enron going forward from that day. I was in tears as I shared the news with them. I looked into the faces of employees and friends who had trusted me over the years and I could see that trust was gone. There were so many questions I could not answer. None of us knew how much money they would get or when they would get it. We didn't know what was going to happen to Enron. Everyone was in a state of total shock.

At the same time, many executives and "key" employees received retention bonuses to stay. That is common practice in a bankruptcy to insure you have a work force in place to work through the potential recovery of the company. I didn't get one of those bonuses because I wasn't in a critical role. I was just lucky that I could stay and keep a small team in place.

The fallout from the employees that had been laid off was awful. We received a fax from Portland that an employee was threatening suicide. There was so much anger that the HR team received death threats and we had to have security on our floor for several weeks following the layoff.

I was not involved in determining the bonuses for those who stayed, or for that matter who would be asked to stay. Ken was protecting me again and I in turn protected as many people on my team as I could. We formed a small group, with everyone in offices around me on the north end of the 16th floor. Immediately, we began helping the employees that were laid off to try and find other jobs and file for unemployment so they had some source of income.

Later, I would see the blessing of not getting one of those bonuses as I would be asked at the congressional hearings if I had gotten a bonus to stay at Enron. It would have made it even worse for me to answer "yes" to that question. Since that day, most everyone who received one of those bonuses has been sued by Enron to return it as a preferential payment.

To this day I am just not sure why everything happened the way it did. Not knowing what employees were going to get and then handing out the huge bonuses to people who stayed was something we would never do under normal circumstances. I have been asked where Ken Lay was while all of this was happening. I don't know for sure, but

I strongly believe that Ken would only agree to the lay-offs and retention bonuses if he felt there simply were no other options to save Enron. I also believe, by this time, the bankruptcy specialists and lawyers were now firmly in charge of the company and they of course would have no feelings about the people that were let go.

Our small team was now intently focused on help-ing ex-Enron employees find jobs at other companies. In less than five days we developed a Web site so employees could post their resumes, and potential employers could post job opportunities. We set up job fairs for the Enron employees, as well as seminars so it was easier for them to file for unemployment. I remember we had so many out-side companies calling us during the following weeks to hire our ex-employees that we linked our voicemail with our e-mail so we would have a written record of who had called. We didn't want to miss any opportunity to place an employee with a new company.

We also spent a lot of time counseling with ex-employ-ees about their personal situations. Because this hap-pened so suddenly there were many people who did not have the money to carry them for the weeks or months it took to find another job. Sarah Davis, who was part of my small team and had helped build the analyst and associate program, was unbelievable in this area. She was so empathetic with ex-employees and did everything in her power to help them. She had been a strong employee advocate before, and the work she was doing with the ex-employees was crucial.

Kevin Hannon eventually worked with his church to set up a fund to give ex-employees relief financially if they were in jeopardy of losing their house, or just needed money for food. Sarah worked with Kevin for several months to make sure as many employees as possible were helped with this fund. I started trying to work with people in the community to pull together a high visibility Day of Healing for the employees, but no one in Houston was interested.

We were doing all of this as everyone else started working on figuring out the bankruptcy, and what was going to survive going forward. By this time the attorneys had all of us so scared that no one was talking to anyone.

Our little team's mission was actually a labor of love. We all felt fortunate, but at times guilty that we still had jobs. During this time I had no problem reconnecting with my work and putting in as many hours as it took. We all felt like we were doing something that was very important. At the end of our project we helped almost one thousand ex-Enron employees find jobs, and JP Morgan Chase moved one of their functions from New York to Houston just to take advantage of the Enron talent in the city.

Ken Lay left the company on January 23, 2002. He called a meeting of all of his direct reports in the executive conference room and told us he was leaving, wished us luck and walked out the door. I didn't get a chance to say goodbye, but I know I couldn't have gotten through it without crying. I also knew that would not be the last time I would see him, and "Goodbye," just wasn't an appropriate thing to say to someone you would see again, hopefully very soon.

Seeing Ken so tired and broken was hard. I knew there was no other choice. He had to leave. For Enron to have any fighting chance of going forward there had to be a change in leadership. I thought back to the last five years of my career at Enron, which involved almost a daily contact with this man. Never once did he treat me badly. I had made mistakes, but I had been harder on myself than he had been. Even when we had introduced the Enron logo and found out the yellow wouldn't copy after we had just rolled it out to the world, he didn't get angry. We simply had to fix it and he told Beth he liked green a lot. (Green was the color that replaced the yellow with in the logo.) Yes, Ken Lay had been the best CEO anyone could have ever asked to work for, and I knew I had been lucky to have been there beside him.

Beth Tilney decided to leave about that same time. Things were going to heat up for her because her husband Schuyler was working at Merrill Lynch, and along with many of its employees, had been an investor in LJM. They had also been friends with the Fastows. It was hard to see Beth leave. In some ways, Beth leaving was harder on me than Ken. We worked a few offices from each other and she had been a strong daily support system for me. I knew I would miss Beth a lot.

Ken made sure that I had the lead for the entire Human Resource organization before he left, but it wasn't the same at all. I was reporting to Jeff McMahon who had now been named COO. Jeff was an outstanding leader, but he was reporting to Stephen Cooper who was an outsider appointed by the creditors as interim CEO. The Enron we all loved was gone. Now, the attorneys, the creditor committees and the bankruptcy specialists were running the company. It wasn't clear until several years later that the winners in all of this would be all of these people. They would milk the Enron bankruptcy for hundreds of millions of dollars that could have otherwise gone to help employees. Ken had been out of the building much of his last month before he retired but knowing he was never coming back caused most of us to finally lose hope and face the reality Enron would never be the same.

The Lawsuits

There were not many things I remember about working at Enron after Ken left except for the lawsuits, and the fact that you could walk around one of the old Enron floors and see empty desks on the entire floor with computers and papers still on the desk. It was as if something had come along and just made the employees vanish. I guess, in a way, that's what happened.

One afternoon, I, along with my friend, Terrie James, who was one of the people I managed to save, took off to explore all the floors in the Enron building. Most floors at that point had no people, but everything was still the way it was left. We brought back to our little space on the 16th floor several pieces of art that we thought we should keep track of. We believed there might be opportunities for this art to someday hold a place in the Smithsonian.

One piece we salvaged from an old Enron Capital and Trade floor was a huge painting of Albert Einstein painted by the late Denny Dent. He painted it on stage during the kick-off the ECT Innovation campaign in April 1998. It was significant because Enron would go on to be *Fortune*'s Most Innovative Company for six years in a row. I'm not sure what eventually happened to the painting after I left Enron, but now that the artist has passed away it is truly a collector's item.

What was so sad about all of this was that we had created an environment in and around the building that was so alive and exciting. The lobby had always been filled in the mornings and at lunch with the energy of employees. The Starbucks in the lobby was a popular place for employees to hold small meetings because they were surrounded by the electrifying atmosphere.

Even the elevators were fun. We had installed Enron TV in each of the elevators and "The Building Guy," one of our employees dressed as a contractor, communicated with the occupants of the elevators between clips of CNN. We were in the process of building our new tower during the few years prior to Enron's demise, and he had shared progress on the building and other Enron trivia and current events. We were one of the very first buildings to have something like that in the elevators. Now it seems like every building I am in has something very similar.

Outsiders would come into our lobby and comment on the energy they felt. Now it was like a ghost town, and instead of hundreds of employees streaming into the lobby and out the front doors for lunch, everyday it was eerily quiet.

Yes, things were quiet, except for the hundreds of reporters who seemed to be in front of the Enron building every single day. It was miserable to come to work because you had to make your way through the cameras and reporters who were all trying to get as much dirt as they possibly could. I remember hearing that many employees tried to talk about all of the good things that Enron had been about, but rarely did the news media pick up on their stories. Believe it or not, there were, and are today, many employees who loved Enron and miss what we had.

Reverend Jesse Jackson got extremely involved in what was going on with the Enron employees and their retirement funds. Since Ken was gone, no one else really wanted to deal with Jesse, so I met with him a couple of times with Stephen Cooper. Cooper didn't like those meetings and just the very short time that I had to work for him made me miss Ken Lay even more. Ken always treated Jesse, or whoever he was meeting with, with the utmost respect. Now I was working for someone who made it clear with his actions that he was not interested in becoming involved in the media hype or community outreach surrounding Enron and its employees or former employees.

Cooper was also critical of everything that had gone on at Enron in the past. One day when we were sitting in the Enron board room, he went on and on about what had gone on in there before he arrived. There was so much I wanted to say to him. I wanted him to know the truth. Enron was a wonderful company. People loved working there. We had some of the best and brightest.

He didn't really know or care what happened at Enron, but he probably wouldn't have listened anyway. After all he made his living picking the carcasses of bankrupt companies. The less I had to deal with him the better. Besides, at that point, my life was pretty caught up in all of the aftermath of the bankruptcy—all of the lawyers and the U.S. Labor Department.

In mid-January 2002 the lawsuits started to appear. I was named in at least two of the major lawsuits. The Tittle lawsuit was a class action suit that charged the board and the 401(k) administrative committee with fraud. Of course, because of my role in Human Resources and the administrative committee, I was a major target. The promotion and position I had fought so hard for was now coming back to bite me.

Also, because Sherron Watkins came to me originally, their claim against me included that I knew everything in her letter she took to Ken Lay was accurate. I learned later that she actually took a seven page letter to Ken which I had not seen. They thought I had seen that detail and in turn, they claimed I should have taken my knowledge of the information to the administrative committee. The Tittle lawsuit was later joined by the United States Labor Department suing everyone involved in the 401(k) plan.

Sherron was still working in my group. No one was willing to hire her. I think people were scared of her. But, I continued to try to help her find a job within Enron. Ultimately one of Stephen Cooper's people hired her to work on the bankruptcy, but she didn't stay long after that. She would go on to write the book *Power Failure* and was named one of *Time*'s 2002 Persons of the Year.

The Newby case focused on 16B officers, or the top officers of the company, for insider trading. There was talk early on that all those named in the lawsuits would have all of their assets frozen. Luckily that didn't happen to everyone.

Since I had been a 16B officer, or an insider, when I was promoted to the position in Human Resources, I was in the middle of that lawsuit as well. Fortunately, however, I was only a 16B officer from November 1999 until January of 2001 before the real trouble started.

The other thing that saved me in that lawsuit was that I was getting ready to leave Enron.

In fact, luckily, after my meeting with Jeff Skilling in late 2000, I was so mad at him that I told my good friend, Bob Sparger, that I was going to leave Enron. I also confided in Bob that I had gotten investment advice from the asset manager at our bank. Both he and my cousin, who also was knowledgeable about investments, encouraged me to sell my Enron options because I was so heavily invested in one single company.

Years later Bob would tell me that in an interview he had with the Enron Federal Task Force he told them why I sold my options. To this day he and I both believe that because of Bob and the knowledge I shared with him about what I was doing in 2001, I escaped an insider trading charge.

After I had that discussion with Jeff late in 2000, I got serious about leaving Enron. I started getting our finances together so I could leave, which included moving my entire 401(k) to the stable asset fund, and exercising all of the options that were above the option strike price. I then took those proceeds and invested in fairly conservative bonds. Actually, Jeff had done a huge favor for me, even though I was devastated at the time because of the way I was treated. Perhaps in reality God did me a huge favor. It's amazing the way He uses other people to save us.

In January of 2002, Cliff Baxter killed himself. Cliff was a brilliant person. He was in charge of corporate development for Enron and a close friend of Jeff's. I remember he was not one of Andy Fastow's fans. He and

Andy had many disagreements about business deals, and I think Cliff saw what Andy was truly like.

Cliff left his home in the early morning hours of that day in January 2002. He drove a few blocks from his house and put a gun to his head. Everyone was in shock that he would take his life. Cliff would have had to endure the torture of seeing what eventually happened to Enron and to Jeff. He would have had to testify and be interviewed repeatedly by the Justice Department. There were certainly times that I could understand to some degree why he might take his own life. After Grady and I started going back to church my perspective changed. I wish that Cliff had felt God's love, and understood that nothing that happens to us in this life could ever take that away. Bad things do happen to good people.

I have realized that each of us ended up dealing with the loss of our company and our lives in our own way. Many people got back on their feet and started new businesses. Some turned to alcohol. Sadly, some people divorced, some went to counselors, and some people just kept on going, taking one day at a time. Some of us renewed our faith. I am so glad God got my attention. Through Him the loss of Enron became a blessing for me in many ways.

It is interesting to see what happens in bankruptcy. The lawyers come out of the woodwork like roaches at night. I soon had "my attorneys." Actually it took me awhile to even figure out who my attorneys were because there were so many that wanted to help. I had attorneys in Houston, Washington, D.C., and I think even in New York.

In the end, the Houston attorneys stuck with me

through all of it. Of course, it wasn't because they liked me necessarily. The firm certainly profited from the Enron "matter." They represented about a dozen of us who were involved in the civil lawsuits. Thanks to the insurance money, which covered our expenses until late 2005, they ultimately built a new office space on the top floor of the Chase Tower in Houston.

I didn't realize at the time what a blessing having the insurance money was until I found out that those people who were not being accused of anything themselves or were not executives could not get access to it. Several Enron assistants, who had worked for the executive being accused of criminal activity, were asked for depositions or to appear in front of the grand jury and had to pay their own legal bills.

The Labor Department started taking depositions early in 2002. I was actually requested to appear in front of them twice, and I was always accompanied by two sets of attorneys.

The first Labor Department deposition wasn't all that scary for me. At that time, I didn't fully understand the implications of what I was getting ready to go through. During that deposition, they questioned me about the letter Sherron Watkins brought me, and what I had done to share that information with the administrative committee. I consistently told them that Sherron herself told me she was not sure if she was right about the allegations in her one page letter she brought me, and wanted Ken to kick-off an investigation to confirm she was correct in her assumptions.

They asked about the transition of the 401(k) from Northern Trust to Hewitt in October 2001. The tremendous amount of Enron stock employees held in their 401(k) plans was an issue for them. They really didn't focus on the fact that employees had twenty different investment options that they were encouraged to review, understand and utilize. They also didn't understand the loyalty many employees felt to Enron and its stock, and the fact that employees were hesitant to sell their stock because the company had been so good to them in the past.

Bottom line, I believe the Labor Department thought I should have taken the information I got from Sherron Watkins (confidentially) in my Human Resource role and shared it with the 401(k) administrative committee. Then, based on that information, the Labor Department thought the committee should have sold all of the Enron stock held by employees in their 401(k)s. Given Sherron's lack of conviction and first-hand knowledge I still believe it would have been negligent to act on rumors. What if she had been wrong?

There were several issues with what they thought we "should have" done. First, the information I had was hearsay from a mid-level officer who wasn't necessarily knowledgeable of all of the deals. The second issue was that our committee didn't have the power to even execute a sale of all the Enron stock. Finally, any sale of stock by the committee based on knowledge that was not public could be considered insider trading. The only thing we could have done was stop employees from buying more stock by taking it away as an investment option. Even that option had downsides if the stock would happen to go back up.

At the time, any of these actions would have been met by significant employee resistance. Employees were continuing to purchase stock as it declined thinking it was an incredible buy. I know that our actions or inaction as it was, were reviewed, critiqued and ultimately criticized. Because of what we were faced with, I am sure new policies and laws have been put in place to help other committees in the future have a clearer idea of what they should or should not do. Believe it or not, the entire committee was trying to do the right thing for our employees. We found ourselves in one of those situations that does not allow for a solution with any positive consequence.

Later in the summer of 2004, I went to talk to the Labor Department again. They, of course, asked a lot of the same questions they had asked in their previous deposition. Because they had now talked and questioned many more people during the last two years, they did have some new questions on their list. They now had questions about the letter I had gotten from Margaret Ceconi in August 2001.

Actually, that letter was sent to Ken Lay and I was copied on it. However, I told Rosie to tell Ken not to respond to her. I felt comfortable I could handle her ultimate issue. Margaret was recruited by Enron Energy Services; she had been a director with GE Capital prior to coming to Enron. During the summer of 2001, Enron Energy Services started downsizing their staffing levels. Unfortunately, Margaret was caught up in that.

Margaret was furious and the letter she wrote was very bitter. The Enron Energy Services Human Resources people were working with her, but she did not get what she wanted. She wanted more severance money. She had been recruited away from GE to come to Enron, and in less than a year she was being laid off without a job. For that reason she sent the letter to Ken Lay.

The letter addressed the Enron Energy Services deals that she believed were not making money, the poor management she thought ran the group she was a part of, the use of corporate aircraft by Enron officers and even the loss of the coffee machines on the EES floors. The letter was a laundry list of everything she didn't like about Enron.

Because I had people in my group involved, I told Rosie that we were handling it. I doubt that Ken even looked at the letter. I was questioned why I hadn't taken her concerns to the administrative committee, but she obviously didn't have firsthand knowledge of the issues she brought up. On top of that, she was a disgruntled employee who wanted something for herself personally. Unlike Sherron, had Margaret not been laid off, I highly doubt that she would have said a word to anyone. The thought never crossed my mind that any of her accusations might have merit.

That is not what the Labor Department believed. They of course thought I should have brought her letter to the administrative committee. In turn, they believed that the committee would have used the information in Margaret's letter to liquidate the Enron stock in the 401(k). Of course, everything looks very different as you look back on the situation and know what the final outcome was.

At this point, the Labor Department was conducting their own investigation of Grady and I personally. They interviewed our friends and Grady's company employees. Several of our friends did not communicate with us for several years because they were so frightened at the tactics used by the Government. Friends that we spent Wednesday nights with at a local ice house were drug in front of the Justice Department. They were questioned about the conversations we had as we ate steak and drank beer throughout the last few years.

This was nothing compared to what others had to endure. It was rumored that Ben Glisan, Enron's former treasurer, who had pled guilty for his role in LJM, was held in solitary confinement while in prison until he agreed to testify for the prosecution in Ken and Jeff's trial. It was also rumored that David Duncan, from Arthur Andersen, pled guilty because the Justice Department discovered a piece of property his wife had inherited many years before had been undervalued on their taxes.

The tactics used by the government were dishonest and manipulative. They believed we at Enron were all guilty and they went about proving it any way they could. Many people had every detail of their lives scrutinized by the Justice Department in their hunt to find something to use as leverage to support their case. I have often reflected that God's decision to bring me to a deeper knowledge of Himself paralleled my experience of the U.S. Justice Department. I have come to love the Spanish word for the Holy Spirit, *abogado,* which is the same word used for defense attorney. I know that the God who became incarnate and died for me is still my biggest advocate. While there were powerful forces ready to go to any length to prove me guilty, the Judge whose opinion ultimately mattered was there interceding on my behalf.

Of course Scripture says it all in Romans 8:34–39:

Who is he that condemns? Christ Jesus, who died—more than that, who was raised to life—is at the right hand of God and is also interceding for us. Who shall separate us from the love of Christ? Shall trouble or hardship or persecution or famine or nakedness or danger or sword? No, in all these things we are more than conquerors through him who loved us. For I am convinced that neither death nor life, neither angels nor demons, neither the present nor the future, nor any powers, neither height nor depth, nor anything else in all creating, will be able to separate us from the love of God that is in Christ Jesus our Lord.

In January 2002, the congressional hearings started and I was on their list to testify. I had to fly to Washington, D.C., and be prepared by yet another set of attorneys in early February. Actually, Grady and I had planned a Super Bowl party at our house that we had to cancel. Instead of enjoying the football game with friends that weekend, I went to Washington and spent Sunday and Monday going over and over all of the questions I had already been asked by the Labor Department.

This new set of attorneys told me they had prepared many CEOs who had to appear before Congress. They had me sit in a mock court room and we went over and over the same questions and my answers. When I started the drilling on Sunday morning I was what they described as "Chatty Kathy." I was trying to be as helpful as I could by telling everything that happened, and at the same time make my case for what we had done. My lawyer coaches told me that no matter what I said they were not going to believe me, or for that matter even listen to what I had to say. This was the senators' opportunity to be on television and perform for their constituencies back home. Obviously, what they were telling me was so much for the whole truth.

When I was finally ready to testify on Monday my answers were now to the point, very brief and concise. No rambling and no additional information. I now understood that whatever I had to say would not change their minds about our guilt. I was an executive of Enron and would be crucified no matter what I did. I took comfort in one of the last things my attorneys said to me, "Every one of those congressmen and senators had more dirt in their past's than you could ever have." Perhaps this is the reason for one of Jesus's teachings: "He who is without sin be the first to cast a stone."

I really had not followed previous corporate collapses, so I was not totally aware of what was happening. I was supposed to appear in front of Senator Joe Lieberman's Committee on Governmental Affairs on Tuesday, February 5, at the same time Ken Lay was scheduled to appear in front of another Senate committee. The preparation was brutal. It was a good thing I worked for Stan Horton and Kevin Hannon in the past, as those experiences as least somewhat prepared me for what I was going to face in these two congressional hearings.

On Monday afternoon, shortly before the attorneys finished preparing me, I learned that Ken Lay was going to plead the fifth and not testify after all. Instantly I became the first Enron executive to testify that next day. That meant the media coverage would be on me instead of Ken. My friend, Terrie James, called me on Monday afternoon and literally begged me not to testify for fear of what would happen to me publicly. By that point, Enron and its executives had become the brunt of many late night talk show hosts. Terrie was so afraid that I would be the next target if I testified.

When I realized I had a choice of testifying or not, I went to my attorneys and told them if Ken was not going to testify, I would rather not either. They explained to me that Ken was facing criminal charges. His attorneys would have him take the fifth so he would not perjure himself in an eventual criminal trial. I, on the other hand, only faced civil charges and they felt my testimony would not be harmful to me in the future.

I don't remember how they convinced me to go forward as planned, but I agreed to go ahead and testify. The next day I was walking into that congressional chamber feeling a little frightened, but mostly numb.

What happened that morning, I can see now, was God putting His hand on my shoulder and letting me know He was with me. There in front of me was Jesse Jackson with a large contingent of ex-Enron employees. I had worked with Jesse in Houston when we were focused on supplier diversity for Enron and met with him several times after the bankruptcy. He liked Ken Lay a lot and because of Ken, liked me as well.

He actually gave me a hug when I walked into the room with my attorneys and asked me how Ken was doing. Even several of the ex-Enron employees came up to me and greeted me warmly. My attorneys were shocked at the reception I received from these people, but the best thing about this greeting was it put me at ease. I felt like

I had several advocates in that room—one of the most intimidating rooms I had ever been in.

I raised my hand for the first time pledging that I would "tell the whole truth....so help me God." The next four hours were anything but fun. I'm not sure where the term "testifying" comes from. It primarily involved me listening to all of the senators telling me and their constituents what an awful person I was. I got to say a few things, but no one really listened to what I had to say. I was evil because I was an Enron executive and had exercised $6.5 million in stock options throughout the last several years. The fact that I had been with Enron twenty-three years didn't even matter. The fact that I had worked my way up in the organization during those twenty-three years and might have actually deserved the compensation I got was not even mentioned.

That experience was truly the beginning of my understanding that no one was looking for the truth—they were out to get all of us. They had selfish career goals themselves, which is what they said was wrong with Enron. When it was finally over, my attorneys quickly escorted me out of the room and into a waiting car. They thought I did a great job. I was just glad that round was over.

I only wished that session would have been the end. Mikie Rath and I had Wednesday off. Mikie, who was involved in the 401(k) plan and the administration of the administrative committee, was testifying with me both days. The day was filled with more preparation with our attorneys. We went to dinner that evening, but neither of us had much of an appetite. We knew what we were going to be in for the next morning.

Thursday morning we went down to eat breakfast in

the lobby of the hotel. Both Rick Causey and Rick Buy were there getting ready to make their appearance in front of the Senate that morning. Rick Causey was there because of his role as chief accounting officer. Rick Buy had been responsible for Enron's risk management function. They would both be advised by their attorneys to plead the fifth even though they also wanted to tell their side of the story.

It was clear that morning that all of us were in a daze. I was thinking it had to be a very bad dream. Unfortunately it was all too real. I had gotten a taste of just how real it was on Tuesday. Mikie and I again traveled to Capitol Hill in a black limousine-like car with our attorneys. It reminded me of cars that the family rides in when going to a funeral. In a way, the mood was similar. We were escorted up the steps and into another chamber in the House of Representatives.

We took our places at that table at the front of the room facing the chairman and the other congressmen. Congressman Boehner started the session off, and the House got their turn with me. It wasn't any easier; in fact a lot of these people were even nastier. Many of the same things were said. Again, they talked at me and really didn't care about the answers I gave. I found that the women congressmen were the toughest on me. One of them even implied that the entire Enron bankruptcy was my fault.

Like the earlier session on Tuesday, my attorneys quickly escorted me out of the chamber and into a waiting car after we had been beaten on for several hours. This time I got to go to the airport and get on a plane back to Houston. At least that was over. *Now,* I thought, *maybe life will get back to normal.*

But, when I returned I realized my picture was plastered on the front page of the *Washington Post, New York Times* and *Houston Chronicle* and I'm not even sure where else. My attorneys told me they were keeping a scrapbook for me, but I have never asked them for it or listened to the tapes of the hearings. I was just hopeful that this was the end.

Being finished was only wishful thinking. When Sherron Watkins testified, the senators questioning her asked her a whole series of questions about me. I held my breath as I listened to Sherron answer those questions on live TV, but it turned out good for me. She told them, in essence, I did everything I could do with her letter and her computer, and I had done the right thing encouraging her to meet with Mr. Lay.

After her testimony however, Lynn Brewer, an ex-Enron employee from Portland, contacted me and sent me a tape of the hearing that she had recorded from her computer. The session took a break and a conversation during that break was on that tape. The tape revealed a couple of senators and/or lawyers discussing the questions they wanted to ask Sherron about my role in the administrative committee. It was clear they were not finished with me and referred to me as a friend of Lay's and discussed the things they thought I had done wrong. My heart sank after I received and listened to that recording, but it was prophetic and things were just heating up for me.

I was also getting some pretty strange e-mails from people outside of Enron. One email was from a person that claimed to be the whistleblower for the shuttle disaster. He praised me for the way I had handled and protected Sherron Watkins. Another email told me I was the one playing the piano in the whore house. I guess because of my nationally televised testimony I was attracting that kind of weird attention.

Around this same time Grady received an e-mail from a very good friend who was an attorney in Denver. The following is that e-mail. At the time both Grady and I thought Norm was crazy and was overreacting to the situation. It wouldn't be until later that we would realize that he was in fact very accurate in his view of what was going to happen.

From: 'NORMAN WRIGHT"
      <WRIGHTN@hro.com>
To: <golson@qts-services.com>
Sent: Friday, February 22,2002 1 1 :18 AM
Subject: ENR fall out

Grady:
I just happened to see an internet news clip from CBS because I have a web page that picks up news on my stock holdings of which ENR was one . The clip deals with Rep Waxman going after Cindy using a 1999 video clip from some meeting where she recommends only ENR in your 401 (k). She should nol have appeared before Sen. Liberman's committee. Everything she said will be cross checked and any inconsistencies used to beat her up, or even prosecute her. I hope she is getting good legal

advice, if not, she should look for an experienced and connected SECICriminal lawyer ASAP.

Obviously this case has high public profile with very ugly facts. ENR execs (and probably some AA people) will be going to jail before this is done. She needs to isolate herself from Skilling and Lay and laying everything out to her lawyer so that a good game plan can be devised is critical. This will not blow over. Too many people lost money, and unlike the telco's or dot corns, there is no easy market reason to lay off the blame (no pun intended). Plus, the Dems are all too eager to put some of this on Bush and Cheney. All of the money Lay, Enron and Andersen sprinkled with the politicians will now bounce back. The politicos will have to look like they are above reproach, which means others will be sacrificed.

Sorry to be so gloomy, but you (she) need to appreciate how very dangerous this case is. Other than that Mrs. Lincoln, I hope all else is going well.

                                                            Norm

The next shoe to fall was that letter to my attorneys from California's Senator Henry Waxman that Norm mentioned. That letter arrived less than a week after the congressional sessions and stated I had perjured myself in my testimony before Congress. They sent along a copy of the now infamous video clip from the 1999 employee meeting where I instructed employees to invest all of their 401(k) in Enron stock. Because I denied I had ever given the employees investment advice in my recent testimony, they reasoned I had lied and the video tape proved it.

Remember the question that Jeff Skilling had me answer at the employee meeting in 1999. Well, I couldn't imagine what video would show me doing that, but sure enough there it was, that 1999 employee meeting question. "Should I invest all of my 401(k) in Enron stock?"

"Absolutely...right, guys?"

This would be the first time those few minutes on stage answering that question would come back to haunt me. My attorneys downplayed it, but it seemed like they were the only ones who did. It was played on every national network several times that next day. I was now known as the blonde in the Enron video.

Leaving Enron for Good

In April 2002 several things happened that made me start to think it was time to leave Enron for good. I decided I should pay off the mortgage on the house we bought in 2000. My attorneys had finally convinced me that all of this "Enron stuff" was not going away, and the prudent thing to do was get as much of our money in our homestead as we could. In Texas your homestead is protected from creditors. Buying that expensive house was now looking like a brilliant move.

I met with the financial manager at the bank that managed our assets, and we laid out a plan to transfer money from our managed asset account to pay off the loan on the house. Later that afternoon his assistant phoned me to let me know that I could not access the funds in the managed account. Unfortunately, the money in that account was collateral for loans that Grady's company had taken to make an acquisition of another one of the bank's customer's in late 2001.

Grady, the bank asset manager and I were completely surprised by this. I now became very focused on what was going on with the acquisition Compass Bank had encouraged Grady's company to make. I felt strongly that I needed to go help him make sure we were protected personally.

In addition to that surprise in our personal financial

position, it was becoming clear that I had been perceived as too close to Ken Lay to have any credibility in the new company going forward. At the first employee meeting that Stephen Cooper held in April 2002, he received several questions about me and why I was still at Enron. It hurt my feelings to see those questions, but they made it easier for me to do the thing I had to do—leave Enron and go help Grady.

Jeff McMahon decided to leave Enron also. He had a similar issue. We both had been too close to the old Enron management. I actually asked Stephen Cooper if I could work part-time while I focused on Grady's company, but they didn't need me any longer. Robert Jones, who had worked for me in the past, was more than capable of handling the entire HR function going forward. I left Enron for good in April 2002 after nearly twenty-three years at the company.

Packing up my desk was a walk down memory lane. I had kept so many things that reminded me of the unbelievable career that I had enjoyed at Enron. The notes of congratulation on my promotions, the cards from employees thanking me for my support of them, and several florist cards from Grady telling me he was proud of me. I had also kept several notes from Ken that reminded me again of how much I had admired him.

Thankfully, I didn't have to carry the boxes out of the building myself. Bobbie Power, who was now working for Robert Jones, told me she would have them delivered to my house. That helped my actual departure just seem like a normal exit of the building. I didn't walk the floors to say goodbye to my friends because most of them were already gone. I told my HR team goodbye and left.

I knew they would be fine—they were all incredible. I got in my car for the last time, drove out of the Enron garage and drove directly to Grady's trucking facility. I was now ready to help him figure out the issues we had facing us, and live the next chapter of my life.

In 1998, Grady's company, Quality Transportation Services, was named one of Houston's 100 Fastest Growing Small Companies. He had grown his company to over $9 million in annual revenue. I was, and I am to this day, so proud of him. He started the company with one truck and by 2002 had nearly 150 trucks. He owned his own facility and had provided his employees very good benefits for a small company. In 1998, the bank, who had loaned Grady money in the past to purchase his trucks and trailers, started courting us personally to manage our personal wealth.

Our net worth at that time had grown and this particular division of the bank focused on individuals with net worth of $5 million or more. They were interested in acquiring us as customers for their managed asset division. They thought with us as clients I could potentially help bring them more Enron clients. At that time everyone in town was trying to attract the Enron money.

The bank president and their investment banker invited us to have lunch with them in the penthouse suite at their River Oaks branch. After that meeting, we agreed to move all of our personal assets, accumulated primarily from Enron stock sales, to Compass Bank for them to manage. That move proved to be a huge mistake for us, but at the time we were naïve and proud that a bank would be courting us.

From 1999 through 2001, Grady's company continued

to grow and move up the list of the 100 fastest growing companies. Grady had nearly one hundred employees and was running several million dollars in trucks and trailers. They had found a good niche in the beverage hauling business. Their major customers were Coca-Cola, Budweiser, Ozarka, and Dr. Pepper.

In 2001, our personal net worth peaked mid-year. We showed net worth of almost $15 million when you calculated future vested stock options. We purchased the house in the Woodlands and forty-six acres of land across the road from our house in Colorado.

We now owned a townhouse in downtown Houston, a home in the Woodlands and a home in Colorado with additional acreage. We bought a turbo Porsche and a motor home for travel. Grady was getting ready to race in the Vintage Series Races so he bought a race car in addition to the other eighteen cars he owned. We were addicted to "stuff" and I am embarrassed to say now that we were proud of how much "stuff" we had.

I remember going to Omaha that year for a fundraiser for the Cosmopolitan Club. This was a civic club that Grady belonged to when we lived in Omaha. They were having a live auction that evening to raise money for juvenile diabetes. One of the auction items was a dinner prepared by several of our good friends. The year before the dinner had sold for $1500 at the auction.

This year I decided I wanted it. So, I immediately bid $5000 for the dinner and of course I got it. This was a perfect opportunity for me to show everyone in that room just how much money I had. The organization ended up with $5000 plus a matching gift from Enron for another $5000. It was for a great cause and my friends still thank us for that generous gift, but since my motive was more about letting everyone know how successful I was, it makes me ashamed now.

As I have studied biblical scripture it is clear that the motive is more important than the generous act.

After Ken died and I saw all of the wonderful things he contributed to personally, many times without recognition. The list is a long one, but included the Horatio Alger Association, United Way, The Aspen Institute, and all of the arts organizations in Houston, to name a few. I have run into several people who talk about the personal money he gave individuals for their children's college education. It is almost sickening to know that many of these organizations have threatened to take or have taken his name off of their list of donors.

In mid-2001, Compass Bank introduced Grady to another one of their customers that owned both a distribution company and a truck line. They told Grady that their other customer needed to focus more of his time and resources on his distribution business and get out of the trucking business. They thought Grady should look at the trucking division because it could be a complement to his current business.

Grady had looked at an acquisition earlier in the year, but decided to pass. Because the bank brought this particular company to Grady and since they were also managing our personal wealth, he took a serious look at it. Looking back we were both naïve and again proud that a bank would suggest Grady look at this company thinking that they really thought Grady was a good business manager.

So, in October 2001, as the bank continued to push

Grady to do the deal, Grady signed the documents to purchase this new company that almost doubled his current size. What he didn't realize at the time was that the company he just acquired was actually not making money and was being subsidized by the distribution side of this customer's business.

We believe that the bank saw an opportunity to hedge their risk with this company by using our personal wealth as collateral. This gave the bank much less risk using our personal guarantee, not to mention the additional business they now had with the additional loans that Grady had to make to acquire the new company.

Because we had done business with this bank for so long and since we were now "partners" with them in our minds, we did not have all of the bank documents reviewed by an attorney. We really had not dealt with attorneys much at that point. We used a friend to help us with the closing papers for the company we acquired. Bottom line, we trusted the bank because they were also managing our personal wealth. We believed that they would not jeopardize the money they were managing for us personally by leveraging our personal wealth to grow Grady's business.

In essence that's exactly what they did. They increased the risk on our personal money by leveraging it to support additional business for them. In a way that's what happened at Enron. Again, we were naïve and very trusting. We made a huge mistake. Everything had gone our way in the past and we couldn't imagine that not continuing.

After the acquisition, Grady's company went from making as much as $20,000 per month to losing $200,000 a month. By the time I came into his company to help him in April 2002 after I left Enron, his company had lost close to $1 million. The revenues they counted on with the acquisition were just not there. They had acquired additional equipment that was in very poor shape without revenues to support it. There was a major cash flow problem and it was clear that to keep Grady's company afloat we were going to have to infuse a lot of our own money. So, here we were, I had left Enron, and we were now using what we had hoped was our retirement to keep Grady's company alive.

Grady had hired a new operations manager to help with the acquisition in March 2002. Unfortunately, he wasn't the right person for the job. He told us he needed us to inject at least another $600,000 to turn it around. He reasoned that we needed to clear old payables and buy new trucks and trailers to replace the "junk" acquired in the acquisition. After we put the additional money in the company he still had not fixed the problem.

Finally, in late 2002, we found a true turn around guy to come help us. Wayne Thompkins had a lot of experience in the trucking business. He helped us in a couple of ways. He not only helped us with the company, but he also shared his faith with us openly. I am sure now that Wayne came into our lives for this short period of time not just to help us with the company, but also because he showed me that God has a plan for us. He truly helped us realize that you take one day at a time and you turn it over to God.

What Wayne determined we needed to do with the company was drastically downsize the amount of equipment and the number of employees. We had to get costs in line with revenue. The other guy was trying to grow revenue to match the costs we had, but it just was not working. Wayne even downsized himself out of the company after only being there for two months. So, in May 2003, Grady and I, and a very small team of people tried to get the company back on its feet. Thanks to Wayne, we were taking one day at a time even though the company had now lost more than $3 million.

Unfortunately, when the bank loaned us the money to complete the acquisition in late 2001, they almost tripled the company's line of credit and cross-collateralized all of our loans and personal accounts. What that meant was we couldn't sell anything without having the money to satisfy all the loans we had with them. At that time all of our loans totaled nearly $6 million.

Also, when we signed the original loan documents, we agreed to have our personal managed asset account as collateral for all of the loans. We were so trusting of the bank that we failed to read the fine print and understand just how tied up they had us until we needed to unwind everything. That became clearer to me as I came into the company and started understanding the situation. The bank now owned everything we had that was liquid, and the money we had for retirement was now Compass Bank's. I suddenly realized how Enron had gotten its hands tied financially before the bankruptcy.

In March of 2002 the bank told us we were going to need to infuse more cash in to the business. Grady was starting to get frustrated with them and the situation he was in. The bank now needed us to sign for another personal loan to the company and insisted on taking us to dinner to get it done. I was so furious with them that I walked out without finishing my meal. In the end we were forced to do things their way. We owed them too much money. When we signed that document and others after that one, the bank had inserted a clause that held them harmless for anything in the past. Even though Grady had asked them if there were any significant changes in the documents they failed to disclose that particular clause to us.

Sometime during my transition to Grady's company, Ken Lay called to talk to me. I just couldn't do it. With everything I was going through with our personal situation and the emotion of Enron all I could do when Rosie called me was cry. That made me sad to think that this person who had been so much a part of my life was not in it any longer. Eventually both our attorneys encouraged us not to speak to each other. That was happening to many people at Enron. All of a sudden your friends were off limits because of all of the legal issues that existed.

I was also very angry with Grady at this time. *How could he let this happen?* I had worked so hard at Enron, made a lot of money and his company lost a significant amount of our net worth. Even though I was full of anger, something kept telling me to keep pushing forward. After all, Grady had been so supportive of me when Enron crashed and my world came tumbling down. It was only fair that I work this through with him.

It was like I was on a roller coaster. One day I would feel everything was going to work out and the next day something would happen to trigger the anger and I would explode at Grady. I am almost embarrassed to say that even though I know it was wrong not to forgive, I still occasionally blow up at him when things are not going the way I think they should. I truly understand when people say they are God's work in progress. I certainly am.

Jake Touches Our Lives

We had been friends with a couple, Joe and Julie Nieto from Omaha, Nebraska, for many years. We had known Joe since 1980 when he was married to his first wife, Cindy (he refers to it as his "mulligan" or "practice marriage"). Joe married Julie in 1989. They would go on to have four children in addition to Jeff who was from his "practice marriage" to Cindy. Joe, Julie, Jeff, Jenna, Jill, Jessica and Jake would visit us in Colorado each summer.

Jake was the youngest with three sisters, and he had the energy of all of them together. He always had an interest in cars, trucks and wanted to be an astronaut. Grady would take Jake to the race track in Aspen and let Jake put on his race helmet and sit in his race car at the track. I think he even took Jake for a practice lap or two.

Grady loves to tell the story of how we named our second dog Jake. He called Joe to inquire if they would be offended if we named our new puppy after Jake. Joe handed the phone to Jake and tells Grady "Why don't you ask him yourself?" Grady asked Jake if we could name our new puppy after him. Of course Jake was ecstatic and yells back to his mom and dad, "Grady and Cindy want to name their new dog Jake!"

In September 2002, we took both our dogs (Chelsea and Jake) to Omaha and stayed with Joe and Julie and the kids. One afternoon when the kids came back from

swimming, Grady and I and our dogs were in their basement. Jake comes running down the stairs to say hello
and let us know they were home. Our dog, Jake, started
growling at him as he appeared on the stairs. Someone
asked "Jacob Joseph Nieto, what did you do to that dog?"
His reply was telling as he blurted out "I didn't kick him
or nothing." Leave it to a child to tell the whole truth.
Jake was busted. He was always full of energy and smiles,
and even though he just might have harassed little Jake,
he was a kind, gentle, wonderful little boy.

Joe and Grady spoke weekly and were always engaged
in business discussions. Grady helped Joe expand his distribution and logistics business into the Houston market with a sizable contract. As Joe prepared to open the
Houston facility in the fall of 2002, he commuted from
Omaha to Houston and stayed with us while in Houston
for weeks at a time. I can remember some of the phone
calls back home to his wife Julie at the time as she voiced
concern with their Jake's abnormal abdomen growth.
Her concern was certainly valid based on the news they
received a few years prior.

In August 2000, Jake had a series of tests subsequent
to abnormal tests results as an infant in 1997. Shortly
before Christmas that same year Joe and Julie were
informed that Jake had Neiman Pick-C, a disease caused
by the body's inability to break down cholesterol, leading
to the accumulation of cholesterol and other fats in the
liver, spleen, and brain. Sadly, life expectancy is thirteen
years, with three to five of those final years experiencing manifestations similar to Alzheimer's and Parkinson's
disease. The news was devastating, yet Joe and Julie were
grounded in faith, and realized in our Creator's plan there

are no mistakes. What Jake was experiencing with a distended abdomen was in fact an early and rapid accumulation of cholesterol in his spleen, which made his little belly big.

The reality of how devastating this disease is revealed itself to me in the spring of 2001 when Grady and I met Joe and Julie in Tucson for a fundraiser that Ara Parseghian, a past Notre Dame football coach, hosted each year to raise money for the research of a cure for Neiman Pick-C. At the table was a couple from Phoenix who lost their precious daughter to this disease just one year earlier. I know it had to be hard for Joe and Julie because Grady and I found it very difficult to hear those parents describe their experiences. It was at that dinner we realized what Joe and Julie would eventually have to go through.

In December 2002, Jake was admitted to the hospital to have his spleen removed. He and his sisters questioned why he was getting fat. Since Joe and Julie made the decision early on not to share Jake's disease with his sisters, they had to refrain from making any mention of the actual problem Jake had. We went back to Omaha to use the dinner I had bought at the Cosmopolitan Club live auction months before. We invited several couples to join us including Joe and Julie. Even though it was an arrogant thing to do when I bid on it, that dinner was so special because we realized the seriousness of Jake's illness at the time, and wanted to show our support for the family.

When we arrived in Omaha that December we immediately went to the hospital to see Jake. His eyes lit up when he saw Grady and immediately asked where Jake and Chelsea were. We have to assume he was happy to see us, but the dogs took precedence at that moment. Jake's hospital room was full of pictures from his classmates and sisters wishing him to get well. He had lots of balloons in the room and since it was close to Christmas there were pictures of angels and Santas around. We brought a stuffed animal with us for him in hopes of cheering him up. While he was awake and alert his body was being ravaged and the Nieman Pick-C was attacking his liver. A transplant was scheduled using Joe as the donor. On the eve of the scheduled transplant surgery the doctors gathered with Joe and Julie to let them know that the disease was also now ravaging his lungs and other organs.

It was evident to Joe and Julie that God wanted Jake home, and no amount of modern medicine was going to prevent that from happening. At the age of five, Jake died on the morning of January 4, 2003, in the arms of Joe and Julie. In the moments before Jake died he was wiping tears from his mother's eyes, unable to speak because he was on a ventilator. He wiped them as if to say "Don't worry, Mom, I will be fine." Joe tells me now it was the closure needed for Julie to release him unto our heavenly Father.

Grady and I traveled to Omaha a few months later to spend time with them knowing the "quiet" was setting in and everyone was getting back to their normal routine. Of course, our main reason for going to Omaha was to be with them and comfort them, but we were the ones who left with a sense of comfort. We would come to learn more about Jake and some of the amazing things Jake said with reference to his spiritual beliefs as an adolescent.

Riding in the back seat of the family's minivan Jake

one bellowed to Julie, "When we're raptured, do you promise you will be with me?" or another time, again from the back seat of the minivan, "Mom, is Dylan's name in the Book of Life?" Dylan was his childhood friend and Jake wanted to make sure their friendship extended into eternity. Another time he was in the lobby of the dance studio, playing, waiting for his sisters to finish and was overheard sharing with another little boy, "Do you know you have to know Jesus to get to heaven?" Jake would finish his bedtime prayers with, "…and I pray that those who don't know you will come to know you, amen." It is evident Jake's life was shortened, but not incomplete.

On Sunday we attended church with Joe, Julie and the girls. Neither Grady nor I had been to a church in years except for our occasional appearance at Grady's parents' church at Christmas.

Their church is a non-denominational, Bible doctrine church and we spent the better part of ninety minutes engulfed in the Bible. I left inspired and full of questions (my accounting and auditing background I guess). That evening Julie gave me a Bible and we sat at the kitchen table until midnight and went through what was taught in church that morning. Like an answer to Jake's bedtime prayer, we came to place our faith in our Savior, Jesus Christ.

I am guessing that the angels above were rubbernecking and watching what transpired that day. If God keeps score for saved souls I would venture a guess that Jake got the assist for our two! Saved not because of who and what we are, but who and what Jesus Christ did for us on the cross and our faith in Him.

All the turmoil, trials, tears, lost fortunes we experienced up to that point, and to think God sent a very special little five-year-old boy to touch our lives. That weekend changed our lives forever, and I know that someday we will be able to thank Jake for that.

Before we left, Julie located the name of a pastor in the Woodlands that they had gotten to know through the Dallas seminary. His name was Dave Anderson. When we returned to Houston, I immediately found the church where Dave Anderson was the pastor. It was a church on the north side of the Woodlands called Faith Community Church. I will never forget the first day we attended this church or the first sermon. The topic of the sermon was on the book of James.

This book talks about the issues with the love of money, arrogance and pride. I cried. He was speaking right to me. I had become addicted to fame and fortune and here this pastor was quoting Scripture during his sermon that made me embarrassed for what I had become during the last few years of my career. I started reading the Bible that Julie gave me, and realized that even though I was raised going to church, I had so much to learn about what the Bible taught.

That first Sunday in church an interesting thing happened. As we were leaving the church we didn't really know anyone so we were making our way to the exit fairly quickly. Dave Anderson, the pastor greeted us before we walked out of the front door. He shook Grady's hand and asked him if they had ever met. Of course, Grady told him no, but also relayed to him that we had found our way to the church because of the death of a little five-year-old boy. Dave, we would find out later, had just lost his thirty-two-year-old son only a few weeks before.

We never missed church from that day forward unless we were out of town. We even started going to Sunday school and made new friends. What I noticed was how nice everyone was. These people we met were focused on helping other people, and that was such a contrast to the Enron world that I was a part of for so long.

The rest of 2003 we were busy trying to refinance loans, market Grady's company, trying to sell whatever real estate that would sell, and going to church every Sunday. Reading the Bible and attending Dave Andersen's sermons every Sunday gave me the strength to keep plugging away. I think I even started being nicer to people and not blowing up at Grady.

Grady's dad was sick with cancer and got sicker by the end of 2003. Hospice had come into their home to care for him by the middle of 2003. Finally, in late 2003, we reached a deal on our house in the Woodlands and we found a buyer for Grady's company.

God obviously wanted us in Colorado because the Colorado house did not sell. So, based on the doors that God closed and the doors He opened, we made the decision to sell our house in Texas and move to Colorado.

We lost more money by selling it then as real estate in that price range had not yet recovered after September 2001. This sale, however, allowed us to move on with our lives. The deal we cut on Grady's company wasn't that lucrative for us, but it allowed our employees to keep their jobs and there was the potential of a future payment to us if the new owner did well with the company. We inked the deal on Grady's company on December 31, 2003, at 7:00 p.m. We celebrated New Year's Eve that year by picking up a Wendy's hamburger on our way home from the office.

We had gone back to Wichita for a couple of days at Christmas 2003 because Grady's dad wasn't doing well at all. He was diagnosed with prostate cancer and congestive heart failure several months before. My entire family had gone to Colorado to stay at our house for the week after Christmas, but we couldn't join them until after we finalized the sale of Grady's company.

So that next day, after we inked the deal to sell Grady's company, we got on a plane and went to Colorado for a week. We were exhausted, but felt good that the company was sold and we had sold the house in Texas.

One of our priorities, as we were getting ready to move to Colorado, was to find a church that we felt as good about as Faith Community Church in the Woodlands. We asked Dave Andersen and Mark Rae, the associate pastor, to help us locate a graduate of the Dallas seminary that might be at a church near us in Colorado.

We had tried to find a church named Basalt Bible Church on a previous trip, but hadn't found it. On that trip we had actually gone to another church in the area, Christ Community Church, because it appeared to be very busy on that Sunday morning we were looking for Basalt Bible.

That church did not seem like the right fit for us. We were looking for a church where we could study and understand Bible doctrine. So, this trip we were going to try again to find Basalt Bible.

We had seen an *Aspen Daily News* article about the land the old Basalt Bible Church purchased, and the name of that church was now Grace Church of the Roaring Fork. That was why we were having such a hard time finding it! That's just how subtle God works sometimes. After seeing that article, I called information that Sunday we were in town and found out when and where the church services were held. They were meeting temporarily in the El Jebel Community Center so we went there hoping this would be the place for us to continue our walk in faith as we moved to Colorado.

What a friendly group of people we met. The worship team was small and unlike our church in the Woodlands, there was not a huge screen in front to show everyone the words to the music. It was a very small fellowship comparatively, but Terry Maner, the pastor, was warm and welcoming. We left the service with a good feeling about the church. But, it was that next Monday that God truly blessed us.

Since we didn't have much to do, we decided to go to a movie on Monday. No one goes to a movie at noon on Mondays. We do occasionally when we want to just escape the day, however, you just don't expect to see many other people there.

We got our large popcorn with lots of butter and a Coke to share, and sat down near the back of the theatre to enjoy the popcorn and the movie. Actually, Grady and I probably enjoy the popcorn as much as we enjoy the movie. Shortly before the feature started, Grady heard his name being called behind him. A couple from the church we had attended on Sunday was just sitting down behind us. I recognized the woman as one of the worship team, but did not recognize the man.

When the movie was over, we walked out with them and stood in the lobby visiting for almost an hour. Their names were Jim and Pam Alexander. Jim had taken a few hours away from work to meet Pam. We left the theatre even more excited about the church we had just attended on Sunday because of Jim and Pam. Little did we know at the time the blessing God had just given us by meeting Jim and Pam Alexander.

God Does Answer Prayers

When we returned to Houston from our weekend in Colorado we were in store for even more issues. We had not finalized the bank's paperwork and their involvement in the sale of Grady's company before we left for Colorado. We had kept them apprised of the developments, but we still had to sign all of the bank documents shortly after we returned after the holidays. These documents were primarily supposed to assign the receivables and payables over to the new owner of Grady's company. The bank was also taking a second lien on our Colorado land and Colorado house so they would have adequate collateral for the remaining loans.

Within a few days of signing the bank documents a couple of things happened. The bank decided not to honor the deal we had agreed to before we left for Colorado. Secondly, Grady's dad took a turn for the worst.

On Friday, January 16, 2004, around 10:00 in the morning, we got a call from Grady's sister. She told us their dad was dying and we should get home as fast as we could to see him before he passed away. Within fifteen minutes of that call the bank also phoned Grady and informed us that we needed to come by the bank to re-sign the new arrangement they had agreed to offer us. Grady wanted to see his dad before he died so we didn't stop. We headed straight for Kansas and told the bank to do what they had to do.

Grady's dad had been in the hospital until about a week before he died. During the time he was in the hospital, my mother and dad had gone to visit him. During one of those visits Grady's dad told my parents that he had noticed that Grady and I had really changed for the better. He went on to say we were nicer to others and more thoughtful. God was truly working in our lives, and it was comforting that Grady's dad saw that before he died.

When he came home from the hospital everyone tried to get him to sleep in a hospital bed in the front room of their house. He refused until the morning he died. He finally gave in, but within twelve hours he passed away. Grady has always believed that he knew he was going to die, and that was the only reason he gave in and agreed to sleep on that hospital bed in the front room.

Grady's family is not a close family. His brothers and sisters can go for years without really speaking to each other. Grady's dad's funeral, however, brought everyone together and it was a great family reunion. The four siblings seemed to put away their differences, at least for a couple of days.

This funeral was easier for me than funerals had been in the past. I think primarily because we knew Grady's dad was a believer, and we were believers and we knew we would see him again. Don't get me wrong, death is always sad, primarily because you know you will miss that person. Belief in Jesus Christ gives you hope though, that the person is going to be in a better place and that you will be with them someday.

After the funeral we spent a few days with Grady's mother then headed back for Houston to wrap up the sale of the company and the sale of our house in the Woodlands.

On the road back to Houston we got another call from Compass Bank. They wanted to meet with us immediately upon our return to Houston. We hadn't focused on the issue during the days leading up to and after the funeral, and now we had to face whatever the bank was going to do to us.

We both went to that meeting the next morning after we returned. As we drove to the bank we discussed that we were prepared for almost anything. We thought that they were pulling the plug on the sale and we were going to have to shut the company down and liquidate.

What a shock we had when we got there for our meeting. They actually said they wanted to work with us. Even though they had closed our bank accounts and all of the drivers' checks had bounced, they reopened the account and allowed the payroll checks to clear. The thing that changed in the deal was that the new owner of Grady's company did not purchase the accounts receivable or payables. We were to keep the responsibility for the payables and the bank would collect the receivables.

Another surprising thing happened during that meeting. The Compass bank president told me about a lawsuit the bank had just settled with one of their customers. This settlement involved a bank customer who had been introduced by him to another bank customer. The first bank customer had invested in the other bank customer's business. Eventually, the first bank customer had lost all of his investment as the other customer had filed for bankruptcy. To this day I can only think that he told me this because he was trying to justify to me that he was in fact an ethical lender. He prefaced this bit of information with the fact that he only had one deal cause him a problem in all of his years of banking.

Compass Bank had just settled for one hundred cents on the dollar with that particular bank customer that lost their investment. I couldn't believe the president was telling me all of this. Grady was certainly in a similar position. The bank had brought him another one of their customers businesses, and the acquisition of that business had almost bankrupted Grady's company.

I waited until we walked out of the bank to tell Grady what I had just been told. We immediately went to see an attorney that we knew in town. This attorney, in turn, did some research and determined the details of the lawsuit the bank president mentioned to me during our meeting at the bank, and what the exact circumstances were surrounding the settlement.

What that bank president told me had to be a gift from God. It just did not make sense for him to share that kind of information with me.

In March 2004, right before we left Houston, our attorneys filed the lawsuit against Compass Bank to recover the money we lost in the acquisition. The attorneys took the case on contingency and we left Houston with the hope that maybe someday we might recover some of that money.

I look back on that and I know that was God working in our lives again giving us the information to file the lawsuit, and allowing us the hope that someday we might recover even a portion of the money we had planned for with our retirement.

We spent the next five months wrapping up the sale of Grady's company, selling our house, downsizing our furnishings to fit in one house and getting everything moved to Colorado. We even decided that we needed to add another dog to our little family. Our vet in Houston suggested that since we were in a fairly remote area it might be good to have a larger dog to protect our two Cavalier King Charles Spaniels. So, as we moved to Colorado we adopted a Great Pyrenees puppy and named her Tika. Tika would prove to be just the thing I needed to keep me busy until I found something that I could do. We had never had a large dog, so training her was a challenge and an adventure.

We also stopped in Wichita several times to make sure Grady's mother was doing okay after his dad's death. It was a blessing that we had the time to do that. We helped her clean out her house and have a garage sale. One long weekend, when she was away for several days, we did a makeover of her house with new carpeting, new paint and even some new furniture. It felt good doing something like that for her. In the past we never had the time, or quite frankly the inclination to spend hours helping someone else. God was definitely working on us.

In May 2004, after we started to get settled in Colorado, we hadn't yet paid off all the Quality Transportation loans to the bank. We were still trying to collect a significant portion of the old receivables so we could pay off the final loans, when suddenly the bank started foreclosing on everything we had. Our attorneys had filed our lawsuit before all of that was taken care of, and the bank wanted us to drop the suit. Filing that lawsuit before we were completely clear of the bank gave them leverage to try and get us to drop it. It was a huge mistake to take that action before we had paid them off completely.

We were now faced with losing our Colorado property and the Houston facility we still owned. In all, they could take these properties from us which were worth a significant amount of money. We had only two weeks to come up with the money to pay off all of the loans with the bank totaling nearly $1.5 million. Our attorney filed a stay on the foreclosures that bought us another month.

In the meantime, our personal bank in Houston started working on refinancing the Houston facility. We had been trying for several months to refinance the Colorado land we owned adjacent to the property our house was on. No bank would touch it because they had been burned on vacant land deals in Colorado since 2001.

As we were moving all of our furniture to Colorado and trying to consolidate two households of furniture into one house, we needed to get rid of a few things in Colorado. We advertised a pair of bunk beds on an online classified service in our area. A nice couple with two young girls answered the ad.

They had just bought a home in Glenwood Springs and needed beds for the girls' room. When they came to the house to look at the beds we also discovered that he was a vice president at WestStar bank in Glenwood. They bought the bunk beds, but I believe God brought them into our lives for another reason. He was able to refinance the Colorado property within a couple of weeks, allowing us to come up with the money to pay off the Compass loans.

Even with the refinancing of the property in Houston and the property in Colorado, we were still going to need almost $400,000 cash to pay off the remaining loans. One more miracle occurred. We had filed our taxes in April. Because of the "Net Operating Loss" carry back provision, we were expecting a large tax refund from the IRS, but we had been asked for additional information by the IRS after the original filing and were not expecting the money to make it to us in time to pay off the final loans. Because the bank had cross-collateralized everything, we could not just pay off some of the loans, we had to satisfy every loan we had with the bank to get free on any of them. They continued to tell us to drop the lawsuit and they would work with us.

Miraculously, that refund arrived in the mail days before our deadline with the bank, and we were able to completely pay off all of the remaining loans we had outstanding. I truly believe that through the grace of God, all of the pieces came together so we did not have to forego the lawsuit. The experience solidified my faith, and the importance of patience. For those who believe that God has a plan, things seem to work out in time.

A couple of other things happened that summer. The Labor Department had been pushing for a settlement from me on the Enron 401(k) issue. I had been a member of Enron's administrative committee of the 401(k) with five other people from Enron. By the summer of 2003, I had been deposed by the Labor Department twice and testified in front of the Senate and the U.S. House of Representatives. All of this was primarily due to my role in the 401(k) administrative committee, and the fact that

Sherron Watkins had first brought to me her now infamous letter written to Ken Lay.

Again, the contention of the Labor Department and most of America, if they were following what the press had to say on this issue, was that I should have just known Sherron's letter was completely accurate. I should have then gone to the rest of the administrative committee of the 401(k)s and pushed the committee to sell off all of the Enron stock in the employees' 401(k) accounts.

Of course, as I mentioned before, the fallacy in that belief was first, Sherron's letter could have turned out to be inaccurate, and acting on inaccurate information could have caused us to sell the stock that could have rebounded to a higher price. Secondly, the use of information that was not public knowledge would have also created insider trading issues for us.

The Labor Department was pushing me for a settlement of $1 million. Unfortunately, or maybe fortunately, we no longer had that money. It had gone into keeping Grady's company afloat and to pay off all of the bank loans. Because we didn't have the money any longer, they investigated, along with the FBI, both Grady and I for money laundering. Grady jokes now that one might call what happened to our money laundering, but we forgot the part about getting it back.

Because the Labor Department continued to push for a large settlement from me, my attorneys decided that it might help if I flew to Washington, D.C., with them and sit down with Leslie Perlman and explain where our money actually went. Leslie worked directly under Elaine Chao, who was in charge of the Department of Labor.

So, we flew to Washington and spent an afternoon

with Leslie going through in excruciating detail "where the money went." On the plane ride back to Colorado I became more and more furious. I left those meetings with the perception that they felt I had done nothing wrong. In fact, I had the impression she actually believed that I had done everything I possibly could have, but politically they had to have a person to pin the blame on. I was the natural candidate because I was so visible with Sherrron Watkins and the infamous video.

I actually wrote a letter to President Bush asking for his help because it just wasn't fair that I should take the fall. I was naïve enough to still believe that everyone involved was looking for the truth in the whole Enron disaster. How foolish I was. I am glad I never sent the letter. It would have gotten a big laugh I am sure.

Miraculously, after this meeting in Washington, the Labor Department changed their position and now wanted a total of $250,000 from the entire committee of six people. I thought that was great news and fair for all of us to put in an equal amount. We had six committee members so we could each put in $42,500. Unfortunately everyone didn't want to agree to that.

Now my fellow committee members were not willing to share the exposure equally, and if I wanted the deal done I would have to agree to $75,000 of the total amount. It wasn't the money that was the big issue to me. It was the fact that my colleagues and friends must have felt like I was in fact guiltier than they were. It was clear that everyone was going to look out for themselves in all of this. Sadly, this just reinforced the reality of what happened to all of us. We had all been friends, working side by side to make a great company. With the fall of Enron, you lost your job, in some cases your house, but most importantly you lost your friends.

The Indictment of Ken Lay

In June of 2004, we were unpacking the boxes from Houston that finally arrived in Colorado. I was in the middle of moving boxes and packing paper up to my eyeballs when Grady called for me upstairs. I stopped whatever box I was unpacking at the time and ran up to see what he needed.

There stood an FBI agent with his badge out standing in the doorway. I can't remember exactly what he said, but the bottom line was I had to be in Houston to testify in front of the grand jury in two days. My first reaction was—I was not going to go. I had boxes to unpack and we couldn't afford an airline ticket booked at the last minute.

My attorneys in Houston thought differently. They got me a ticket and hotel room and I was on a plane the next day headed for Houston. I left Grady with all of those boxes to unpack alone. I felt bad that this Enron thing kept disrupting our lives.

I had not talked to Ken Lay since the day he left Enron. I missed him a lot, and I knew the kind of man that he was. Here I was now, in front of a grand jury that was about to indict the man I had loved working for, for so many years. My attorneys could not be in the room with me. I was on my own.

There were approximately twenty people, like you

or I, who were selected to hear a number of witnesses discuss various issues that the government zeroed in on. Their job was to determine who, at Enron, they would indict. The major issues they wanted me to address were of course the Sherron Watkins letter and the letter from Margaret Ceconi.

I knew Margaret because one of the guys she had dated was a friend of Grady's and mine. The grand jury again wanted to know if Ken Lay had actually seen a copy of her letter. I told them I didn't think he had seen it. I told them I told Rosie, Ken's assistant, to let Ken know I got the letter and that we were handling it in Human Resources; Margaret was a disgruntled employee wanting a larger severance and I could handle that.

I went on to tell the grand jury that she had been working with the HR people in EES. They had determined that there was nothing more they wanted to do for her or it would put them at risk with other people that were similarly situated. I hated to see anyone leave Enron that mad, so I started working with her personally on a potential contract position. She could use her General Electric experience to help us develop some advanced management training.

Unfortunately, she had run into a group of EES employees in a bar on a Friday night during our discussions. They had all been drinking. No one acted professionally from what I was told. There was a lot of shoving and words flying between all parties. After that incident Margaret called me and told me she wasn't interested in working at Enron ever again. That was the last time I spoke to her.

One of the questions the grand jury wanted me to

answer was if I was loyal to Mr. Lay. That was an interesting question. Somehow I felt like them asking that question meant if I said yes, I would say anything to protect him. Even though I had not talked to Ken for several years I told them that I had a huge amount of respect for Ken Lay and started talking about all of the positive things he had done for Enron and the city of Houston. I was immediately shut down by the federal prosecutor asking me the questions. They really didn't want to hear anything positive about Ken.

After about five hours of questioning I was finished. I left the grand jury hoping I had helped Ken, but I could just feel that he had a slim chance of escaping indictment. It was clear the government wanted him, no matter what, from the questions they had asked me. If I hadn't given them an answer that would help them they quickly moved on.

Shortly after I returned to Colorado, Ken Lay was in fact indicted. It broke my heart to see him in handcuffs. One thing I did notice about him walking with his hands behind his back was he still had a smile on his face, and the positive attitude I always admired had not gone away.

As Grady and I started to determine what we wanted to do with the rest of our lives, I felt it was prudent to test the waters to see if I was employable anywhere at all. In early 2004 I put together a resume and started working on a list of references. Even though I could not talk to Ken directly I called Rosie and ask her to get a message that I would like to include him in my references. Many people encouraged me not to include him, but working for him had been such a big part of my professional life.

I felt I needed and wanted him on that list because I believed in him.

Drayton McLane, who I had worked closely with as we built the new baseball stadium, also had been more than willing to be one of my references along with Gordon Bethune who was the CEO of Continental Airlines. Because of all of my Enron experience I had an impressive resume and an even more impressive list of references.

I sent out no less than two hundred resumes and letters to companies all over the country. All I got back were letters letting me know that there was nothing available. Of course, they would keep my resume on file. It wasn't a shock. I had a feeling that I was going to have a tough time finding anyone that would hire me.

Early in 2001, I, along with most of the employees at Enron, probably could have gone to work for any of the major companies in Houston and many others around the country. Enron was known to have some of the best employees anywhere. Having Enron experience on your resume was like gold. Unfortunately, by the beginning of 2002 that was no longer the case, for me at least.

When we had determined that in fact we were going to relocate to Colorado several months before, I started watching the *Aspen Times* online for anything that might be interesting. In April 2004, I actually did get a call from Colorado Rocky Mountain School (CRMS) in Carbondale, Colorado. They were looking for a director of finance for the school and I thought that would be a perfect fit for me.

The school headmaster liked my resume, but I think he had some concerns about the Enron connection. I had several interviews with him and the current director of finance. Finally in late June, they offered me the job and I accepted.

It appeared to be just the right job. It was a short distance down the hill from the house. Not a bad salary for the Roaring Fork Valley. The job was perfect and the timing was great. I think back on it now and I wonder if it wasn't God working in our lives again. I am not sure we would have been able to refinance all of the loans that we had, in such a short time, had it not been for that job offer. It came right as we were working with our Houston bank and WestStar Bank in Colorado to refinance the loans with Compass Bank.

Shortly after the loans were approved Ken Lay was indicted. I got a call from CRMS that they needed me in a meeting the next morning. I had agreed I would be starting my new job the first part of August, but they told me they needed me then for a short meeting. As I drove down the hill to Carbondale that morning I couldn't imagine what the meeting might be about. I thought possibly they wanted me to start earlier than agreed to work on the next year's budget.

When I heard the words come out of their mouth I don't think it registered at first. They were going to have to rescind the job offer because the CRMS board would not approve hiring me. I was also told that the indictment of Ken Lay was a determining factor in their decision. After Ken died, I found it interesting that he had donated a lot of money to the school. It was okay for them to accept his money, but not hire someone who had worked for him.

There it was again, that sick feeling in my stomach,

present so many times since the collapse of the company I loved. This time it was different. I somehow knew this was God saying to me that this was not what He wanted me to do. I felt like He wanted me to be patient, and He would ultimately show me what He wanted for me. I was beginning to trust God more and more. He was in control and His plan for me would reveal itself when the time was right.

I got involved in a Bible study at the church, started to work with someone from our church on some nonprofit ideas and focused on getting the house situated. Grady also worked at the Aspen Racing and Sports Car Club that summer while I finished unpacking and getting the house in order. He was paying off his past dues that we hadn't been able to afford the prior two years because we were just fighting to survive, but he was having fun back at the track.

Grady was one of the earliest members of the club, and always enjoyed his time there when we lived in Houston and came to Colorado for long weekends. He asked the club membership if he could pursue starting a corporate racing program at the track the next summer because he saw, while working there, how under-utilized the track actually was. During the process of developing a corporate racing program for the summer he got the idea of a winter driving school for high school kids for the winter season when the track was actually not used at all.

I helped him develop the business plan, the Web sites and brochures for both programs. By December 2004, he was kicking off a Winter Driving Program. The *Aspen Times* covered it and we hired a PR firm that got a lot of publicity for the program. We only had about seventy-five paying customers that first year, but the idea was catching on and Grady secured a car sponsor and a tire sponsor for the program. It was actually a blast working with Grady to build something from the ground up.

By March 2005, he worked out a deal with the club to manage the track and also hold his corporate racing program events during the summer. I was spending my time helping him. We only snow skied a couple of days that winter, but took some time off and traveled to Ireland with our good friends from church, Jim and Pam Alexander.

Jim and Pam gradually have grown to become our very best friends. We spend every Friday night with them eating Mexican food and drinking margaritas. We have continued to grow closer and closer to them, spending holidays with them and celebrating birthdays. We got to know Pam's mother, Betty, as she came to live with Jim and Pam in the summers. She was a hoot and we loved her. We spent as much time with her as we could until she passed away around Thanksgiving of 2004.

Pam grew up in the church as the daughter of a pastor. She, along with her oldest daughter, Amber, has one of the kindest hearts of any person I have ever known. Several years ago she fell down the stairs going to their basement and developed very chronic pain in her in body as a result. She has tried everything available to help with the pain she now has in her feet. I feel like Pam and I were meant to be together to help each other through the tragedy of losing our old lives. God gave me a special blessing with her in my life.

Jim Alexander and Grady have become very close as well. Jim is on the board of an orphanage in Juarez,

Mexico, and frequently takes clothes and furniture to the children. He also has adopted a family in Jamaica and has sent the two daughters to college and built them a house. He is probably the most generous person I know.

Being with Jim and Pam is so different. We now spend time with them in conversation about biblical scripture or what is going on in our church. It is a sharp contrast to the time we spent with friends in our Enron days where our conversations focused on the company and the latest deal or promotion.

During 2005 we got a couple more lawsuits behind us. Back in 2004, when we had paid off the outstanding loans with Compass Bank, we actually overpaid them and the only way to get any of the money back was to sue them again. It was amazing to us that before the Enron collapse we had never even retained an attorney, and now we had multiple attorneys working with us. We settled that lawsuit with them for a modest amount compared to what we believed they owed us, but by now we just wanted our normal lives back. Little by little we were working through all of the issues. We were continuing to get better at taking one day at a time and trusting God with whatever he sent our way.

The Corporate Fraud Trial
of the Century

In the beginning of 2006, the two big issues we had left to deal with were the original lawsuit filed against Compass Bank and the lawsuit by Enron creditors for the deferred compensation I got right before Enron filed bankruptcy. I deferred a $60,000 bonus I received in 1994, and in late November 2001, right before Enron filed for bankruptcy, I turned in the paperwork to get that money paid to me.

I wasn't going to even think about turning in that paperwork. I didn't believe there was anyway Enron would file for bankruptcy and besides it felt disloyal. One of the people who worked with me in HR left a form on my desk on a Friday afternoon in late November. I told her that I was absolutely not going to fill it out because I didn't want anyone to think that I was disloyal to Enron in any way. I knew that Ken would be aware of anyone turning in the request for their deferred compensation. When I returned to work on Monday she had left another form under the door of my office and told me that everyone she knew was filling out the form including my friend Mark Frevert.

Knowing that new information, I reluctantly proceeded with filling out the form that requested my deferred compensation. I remember thinking however, that it was surely a long shot that Enron would actually file for bankruptcy. Unfortunately, any payment by that time would be considered a preferential payment and would be subject to legal action by the creditors if in fact Enron was bankrupt. Now, Enron wanted that money back.

In the fall of 2005, a friend of Grady's called me about working with him to build a concierge business in Aspen. I immediately jumped on board. I put together a business plan, hired some good people and put together and started executing a marketing plan. It was just what I needed as I had spent most of the summer painting our fence and deck while Grady worked at the track. The business plan was motivating. It appeared there was an opportunity to make money, and I could use some of the skills I had developed at Enron.

Now with fall here and winter coming, Grady's winter driving program was gearing up, and he had secured several sponsors for a new high school scholarship program. The 2005 season of winter driving was a huge success. Grady taught more than three times the number of kids he taught the winter before. He hired someone to handle the reservations and I focused on my new business venture. Life seemed to be getting back on track, but I have now learned when you start feeling that way you get hit over the head again as a reminder that you are not in charge.

Thankfully our attorneys said it would be okay to reconnect with Ken and Linda Lay. So during the summer of 2005, I sent them an email and asked if we could have dinner together the next time they were in Colorado. Seeing them again was great. We all had gone through so much. We talked openly about our faith and got caught up on each others lives. We stayed in touch after that dinner and Ken asked me to help him with a nonprofit effort in Houston. I even flew to Houston several times to start that project with him and we continued to have dinner occasionally and exchange emails or talk on the phone regularly.

My friend, Rick Causey, and his wife, Bitsy, came to visit us in Colorado periodically, and we always stayed with them when we had to be in Houston. The long anticipated Enron trial involving Ken Lay, Rick Causey and Jeff Skilling was about to begin in January 2006. My attorneys told me there was little chance that I would have to testify because of all of the baggage I had, so I wasn't worried about that at all.

We sold our forty-six acres in January 2006, and at the same time we started the addition to our house that we had been planning for a couple of years. Grady's job at the track had gone well, and he accomplished a tremendous amount during the season. The concierge business had been fun, and we had made some real progress in Aspen in the first ski season.

Shortly after we returned from Wichita after spending Christmas 2005 with our families it happened again. Things started falling apart.

First, Grady discovered that two of the other members at the Aspen Racing and Sports Car Club were cutting each other side deals and he called them on it. Since the track is member-owned Grady was adamant about looking out for all the members, not just the ones who showed up regularly. The two members he caught cutting the deals were on the board and lobbied the other board members to replace him as the track manager.

I had to fly to Houston in early January 2006 for a week to pull together the last of the documentation for the experts who would testify on our loss in the Compass Bank lawsuit. While in Houston I met with Ken Lay's and Rick Causey's attorneys. Because of everything I was dealing with I couldn't stay involved in the concierge business.

Both Rick and Ken were getting ready to go on trial later that month and they both wanted me to testify for them. My attorneys were wrong when they told me that there was only a slim chance of me having to testify at all. Many potential witnesses refused to testify for the defense. The government prosecutors did a great job pressuring people that it would be in their best interest not to testify.

Some people got on the stand for the prosecution and told the jury things that were not true to protect themselves and their families. Some of them were in fact threatened with prosecution themselves for things like IRS issues or possible insider trading. As I mentioned previously, one of the prosecution's star witnesses was actually held in solitary confinement for a long period of time until he agreed to testify to what the prosecution wanted him to say; there was another person who pled guilty because the prosecution found that a piece of property his wife had inherited many years before had been undervalued on her tax returns—they were threatening to prosecute his wife if he did not cooperate.

I knew the government had tried their best to find something on me. We were told by both Grady's employees and our friends about the interviews and questions they were asked. If they had found anything they could potentially use on me they would have already brought it forward.

I felt it was the right thing to do to help both Ken and Rick. I believed that they were two of the most moral, ethical people I have ever known. I didn't believe that either of them would ever do anything to hurt other people intentionally. It was after I became a believer that I also knew these two people had a tremendous amount of faith. I wanted to tell the truth for both of them.

Years later, Rick's wife, Bitsy, wrote me to tell me what Rick had said about me after I had spoken to his attorney and offered to testify for him. He had said to her, "Isn't it interesting that the only person that was willing to testify for me was a woman. She was the only Enron person strong enough."

Rick decided to plead guilty before the trial started. His attorneys convinced him that if he went to trial it was a Hail Mary whether he would win or not. In other words, his chances were probably less than 50/50 that he would not end up with a life sentence in prison no matter what. The public opinion was so incredibly strong that there would be no possible jury that could hear the truth.

The evidence that the government held against Rick included a document referred to by the government prosecutors as the "Global Galactic Agreement." I actually remember my attorney's asking me what I knew about "Global Galactic" sometime early in 2002. I told them I thought it was the huge computer system we were developing. Was I ever wrong!

The Global Galactic Agreement was supposedly a document initialed by Rick Causey that guaranteed from

Enron that the partnerships or special purpose entities that Enron had setup (run by Andy Fastow) would not lose money. Suspiciously, this document was produced by Andy Fastow himself. He had supposedly kept it in his safe deposit box. The strange part was the document was only a copy, and a copy cannot be analyzed for handwriting authenticity. Even though I believe Rick when he says he did not initial it, experts could not validate Rick's claims.

Janie, Rick's oldest daughter had just graduated from high school and was in her first semester at the University of Texas. She had a huge role in his decision. He was being offered five to seven years in prison if he cooperated with the government, and pleaded guilty. Janie asked him to plead to ensure he could walk down the aisle with her when she got married. Rick told us that he saw us in our 50s and still leading a good life, so there would be many years for him and Bitsy to enjoy the rest of their life together after he got out of prison. He decided to plead on one count of reporting irregularities, but on nothing else, and the government accepted that.

It appeared that the government seemed to just want Rick out of the way. With him pleading guilty, they basically had control of whether or not he testified. Curiously, they never called him to testify in the trial against Ken or Jeff, probably because they did not want to have him testify that he believed the Global Galactic Agreement was a fraud by Andy. That would have cast some doubt in juror's minds about a key issue. Jeff Skilling had supposedly signed that agreement as well, and if Rick told the jury he did not sign it in his testimony that could shine doubt on Jeff's guilt.

During the week prior to Rick making his decision, Ken Lay called me several times. Ken knew I was close to Rick. Because he could not talk to Rick directly, Ken wanted me to communicate with Rick that he was sincerely concerned for Rick and his family, and wanted them to know that he understood that Rick needed to do what was best for them.

Having Rick plead was obviously going to make the trial for Ken and Jeff more difficult, but I believe that Ken honestly thought that he and Jeff would be found innocent. Ken didn't want Rick to plead because Ken thought that there was a good chance they would all three be acquitted.

During one of our trips to Houston, Ken asked me if I thought Rick would testify for him. Rick had always told me he would testify, but he would always tell the truth. Ken told me that he knew it would be a difficult decision because if he testified for the defense, the prosecution could retaliate by asking for a sentence term of seven years instead of five for Rick. Ken told me that if the tables were turned he would testify for Rick. He also shared with me that he didn't think that Jeff would do the same. I know that Ken cared deeply about Jeff, but I think that statement from Ken validated my misgivings about Jeff and confirmed for me that Ken recognized Jeff's shortcomings. At the end of the day, Rick was never called to testify by either the government or by Ken.

Seeing Rick plead guilty was hard on us as we were such good friends with him and his whole family. We also knew he pled guilty for something he did not do because of the threat of life imprisonment. I don't think I have ever seen anyone, except for Ken Lay, go through what he did with his head up and with a positive attitude. Ken shared with us that at the end of the day there is only one judge for all of us and he knew in his heart that he had not done anything wrong.

The situation with Grady and the Sports Car Club became more heated. Grady threatened to go to the county about an issue at the track in an attempt to get the board to pay him the money they owed him. All that he accomplished was making the two guys he caught cutting each other deals furious with him. In late February, Grady was locked out of the track and couldn't finish his winter driving program.

None of the threats worked and the club continued to owe him money for his work as manager, but they were not going to pay him. So we had to retain another lawyer. At least we were getting better at knowing when and how God is talking to us. Not too long after all of this happened Grady went to Bible study and the topic was Psalm 39 which states:

"I said, I will watch my ways and keep my tongue from sin, and I will put a muzzle on my mouth as long as the wicked are in my presence."

Grady came home from Bible study that morning talking about how appropriate it was that they would study that particular psalm. He had certainly not put a muzzle on his mouth with the guys at the track and he was paying a high price for that.

In March we went back to Houston for depositions in our lawsuit against Compass bank. That moved us one step closer in that issue. While we were there I met with Ken Lay and his attorneys. It was clear, during that Houston visit, that Ken Lay was now going to call me as a witness for the defense and they needed me back in Houston in early April.

My attorneys advised me all along not to testify. At some point however, they stopped encouraging me one way or the other. They realized I was going to help Ken regardless of their advice to me.

We did take a week away from Colorado and Houston and went to Mexico with Jim and Pam and their girls. Puerto Vallarta is a wonderful town and Jim and Pam had purchased a timeshare there almost twenty years ago. It was a great week and a welcome break from what was going on in the other parts of our lives.

When Grady and I were in the airport leaving Puerto Vallarta we were waiting for our plane. A couple with two teenage daughters sat down in the gate waiting area across from us. The mother and daughters got up to do some last minute shopping in the duty free shops leaving the man alone. Grady had brought one of our bags with the Enron logo on the side. The gentlemen seated across the aisle from us commented that we had a collector's item in that bag, and of course, that opened up a conversation about my role at Enron.

He was the executive director of the United States Chamber of Commerce and told the story of having to give back a contribution that Ken Lay had made to their organization. He thought Ken Lay was a good man. I told him he was right, Ken Lay was a good man and I was going to testify for him when I returned. He was glad to hear that he was not wrong about him.

When his wife returned she joined in the conversation and I told her about the book that I was writing. I told her about the trials we had gone through and that I

wanted to let people know that through my experiences I
have learned that you have to turn your life over to God
because you are not the one in control.

They both seemed to understand because they nod-
ded in approval. She told me that she had a saying that
just about boils life down to one question. Do you want
one pork chop or do you want two? What she meant by
that is, in the scheme of our lives you really can't do much
about anything else.

After they walked away I thought, *She's right. We aren't
in control so let God work in your life according to His plan.*

After we returned to Colorado from our week in
Mexico we immediately headed for Houston. I was told
by Ken in a conversation before we left, that they were
going to have me testify that next Tuesday. When we got
to Houston on Monday evening I met with Ken's attorneys to review the areas they needed me to address in my
testimony.

Ken's attorneys decided that they didn't really need me
to address the Sherron Watkins's letter again. They felt
comfortable that her testimony had not hurt Ken because
of the angle they had used in their cross-examination of
her. Sherron actually sold stock after she had brought her
letter to me and I had sent her to Ken. The defense's case
stressed that, if in fact, Sherron's allegations were factual
versus hearsay, she herself should have been charged with
insider trading.

She had sold more stock than Martha Stewart, yet the
government hadn't charged her with a thing. The defense
used that to show the jury that her letter therefore, should
be treated as hearsay. If her knowledge was not treated as
fact in her case, then it should not be something Ken Lay

would rely on for a factual state of the company. This made total sense to me as I knew that Sherron's intent was for Ken to perform an investigation to confirm what she believed to be true.

The issue that Ken's attorneys did want me to address in my testimony was whether or not I knew if Ken Lay had seen the letter from Margaret Ceconi. I did not know for sure whether Ken had seen her letter, however, my previous experience with Ken led me to believe that if I told Ken I was handling something he let me handle it—period.

Ken's attorney's wanted my testimony to put at least reasonable doubt in the jury's mind whether or not Ken saw Margaret's letter. That issue seemed easy enough, and I felt comfortable with what they wanted me to do. They also asked me to share with the jury the major community programs Ken Lay had encouraged and sponsored.

It wasn't until Thursday of that week that the court wrapped up with Jeff Skilling's testimony. Therefore, I wasn't called until Thursday morning. Grady and I were a little concerned that I wouldn't be called for sure until the next week but luckily, I was put on the stand at 2:00 the afternoon of April 20, 2006.

The court took a break right before I went on the stand. Jeff Skilling and Ken Lay shared a room near the courtroom where they, along with family, friends and attorneys gathered during the breaks. I was actually getting a little nervous so I didn't socialize much during the break. Jeff spoke to me briefly.

That was the first time I had seen or talked to him since before he left Enron in August of 2001. He told me he wasn't supposed to speak to me until after I had testified. So, we only exchanged hellos. I was so focused on getting on and off that stand that I don't remember for sure what transpired in that room.

As the break ended one of Ken's attorneys walked me into the court room and into the witness box. I was seated between the judge and the jury. Grady sat down in the second row of the courtroom with my attorney. Between the rows of spectators and the jury box were two long tables on each side of the room.

After I sat down on the witness stand, there it was again. I was asked to raise my hand and swear to tell the truth the whole truth…so help me God. As I said those words this time, my thoughts went to all of the people before me who had sat on this same witness stand and probably not done that. They were pressured by the government to say the things that needed to be said to convict Jeff and Ken. Asking us to tell the truth seemed so hypocritical now.

Seated around one table were Ken and Jeff and their attorneys. Seated at the other table there were at least twelve attorneys for the prosecution. Grady tells me as Ken's attorney started questioning me there was a flurry of activity around the prosecution table. Notes were being passed back and forth among the attorneys. When one of those attorneys got up to cross examine me he brought with him two large black binders with my name on the front of each one of them.

My first thought was, *If they are going to cover everything in those books we were going to be here for a while.* Of course, the questions he asked me were for the purpose of discrediting every good thing I said about Ken Lay. I remember getting a laugh from both Ken and Jeff when I was explaining the different committees that I had been on discussing the difference between the management committee and the policy committee. I explained that we had a lot of committees and that it was hard to keep them all straight.

The prosecutor of course pointed out to the courtroom that I had been on the 401(k) administrative committee and started a round of questions on that subject until Ken's attorney objected. He didn't bring up Sherron Watkins at all, but spent a lot of time on the letter from Margaret Ceconi. The most laughable thing he said was that Margaret had to have had a lot of courage to write the letter she had sent to the board and to Ken. I remember thinking, *What a joke!*, and I said that I didn't believe that was courage. After all, she was a terminated employee essentially blackmailing the board and Ken Lay.

The final thing that the prosecuting attorney did to attempt to discredit me, was show that infamous video of me standing in front of the employees back in 1999 again. After the video stopped he encouraged the jury to believe that I was giving the employees investment advice in that employee meeting. Of course I told the courtroom that no one in that room that day back in 1999 took my answer seriously, and by no means did anyone take that answer as investment advice. It was hard to tell what the jury actually thought, and I doubt if it mattered to Ken and Jeff's case at all.

I also got questions about how I felt when Mr. Skilling demoted me. I simply answered that I was very disappointed. I was glad that I did not get emotional. I felt better about not getting into what seemed like trivial issues compared to everything he was facing now. As much as

Jeff's business decisions hurt me, Jeff wasn't being tried for his business decisions, but rather conspiracy and fraud, and I didn't believe he was any guiltier of committing those crimes than Ken was.

After my twenty-five minutes on the stand I was dismissed and Grady and my attorney exited the courtroom and we all went back to his office. He told me that I had done a good job, but more importantly I had done something good. I was glad it went okay, but most of all I was glad it was over.

My attorneys' office was on the opposite end of the 49th floor, down from Ken Lay's new office. After we went back to my attorneys' office to debrief, I walked down the hall to the other end of the floor to see how Rosie had done. She had testified after I left the courtroom.

As I stood at her desk discussing the experience we both had just completed, Ken walked down the hall. He had just returned from the courthouse for the day and told us both we had done a good job. Of course we needed to hear that because the interrogation we had just gone through was not in any way fun.

Later I would pick up a voice message on my cell phone from Linda Lay. She told me in that message that I was strong, believable, had a lot of courage and she so much appreciated what I had just done for Ken. They had not changed at all. Each of them always had been so appreciative and gracious about thanking people for what they did. It was nice to hear all of those kind words, but I was concerned that none of what I had done would make a bit of difference for Ken.

Grady and I left Houston the next day. Throughout the next several weeks I kept track of the trial from Colorado through the *Houston Chronicle* Web site. Ken and I talked several times. He called to share with me how hurt he was to hear the lies that were being told by other Enron employees as they testified for the prosecution against him. The testimonies of both Mark Koenig and Paula Rieker were devastating to him, and he shared how he understood because they had to protect their families. All of the news reports seemed to indicate that Ken was making a huge mistake with his testimony by being combative with the lead prosecutor John Hueston.

Everyone I spoke to in Houston was concerned about the way Ken was coming across in his testimony and cross-examination. He was not coming across to the jury as the kind man we all knew. He was determined, I believe, to make sure the truth was told. He had finally gotten his chance to set the record straight for himself and for Enron.

As I look back on it now I believe Ken was fighting for not only his life, but for the reputation of the great company that he built and for the rest of the employees who had been wrongly accused. He knew he was innocent of the criminal charges he was facing, and he wanted the world to look upon Enron as the company it truly was, and not the one that the media had made of it.

I was absolutely sure in my mind that no matter how Ken came across, a jury couldn't begin to find him guilty of anything criminal.

Yes, we all lost a lot. We lost our jobs. We lost our life savings. We lost friends that we had worked with for years. It seemed like someone should have to pay. When I think about the money I lost it does make me sad. It also makes me angry that I lost my reputation, but that was thanks to the media.

I don't blame Ken or Jeff. We would never have had all of it to begin with had it not been for Enron. Ken and Jeff built Enron. Ken tried to save what he had built. Jeff even offered to come back after he had left and tried to raise money to pay off the Enron creditors. It just wasn't in God's plan for any of that to happen.

The Verdict

In early May of 2006, my sister's youngest son graduated from New York University. I hadn't gone to any of the other kids' graduations and I wanted to go to this one. In fact, most of our family went. The graduation was in Radio City Music Hall. We all went to several plays, ran in Central Park every morning and took the subway everywhere.

We saw Ground Zero and just being there brought back all of the memories of that day in 2001 and how much my life had changed. We ate hot dogs off of the street stand in Union Station and visited Chinatown. We experienced New York like I had never done.

We actually took time to see things instead of flying in, jumping in limos and running to meetings before we had to get back on the plane. It was a fabulous week with my family, one that I could have never experienced if I had been working at Enron.

We were back in Colorado on May 26. We had just eaten breakfast and I was getting ready to go outside to help Grady with something in the yard when the phone rang. I took the time to answer it before I got busy. It was our friend from Romania and he was calling from his office there. I had introduced him to Ken Lay a number of months ago and he was performing some preliminary work for Ken's new company, Envirofuels, in Romania.

When I answered the phone he asked me if I had heard the news about Ken and of course I asked him what about? He went on to tell me that it had just been announced that Ken was convicted on all counts. That was the saddest I had felt since the Enron collapse. Of course Grady and I were both devastated and could not believe that they could find him guilty of a criminal charge.

The remainder of the day I watched the coverage on CNN and Fox News. Much of what was said over the last five years was being repeated again. This time, however, it was being reported with a stronger sense of certainty because of the verdict that had just been given.

Later, I would pick up my cell phone messages and discover that Rosie had left me a message that morning telling me they had all just gone to the courthouse for the verdict. I had asked her to let me know when they went to hear the verdict, and as usual she kept me in the loop.

The rest of that day was a blur. Sadness overwhelmed me all day. What had just happened was unthinkable to me. The great company we had all built was again being called a fraud. Everything we built was bad. I guess the idealist in me wouldn't let me believe that Ken could be found guilty for something he had not done.

The sadness of that day spilled over to the weekend. Not only was I sad about the verdict, but not a single person from my family called to let me know that they realized how sad I would be. It hurt me to think that an event as significant as that in my life would go unnoticed by the people who loved me. They just simply hadn't put the significance on Enron as I had.

The sadness was much worse than what I had experienced throughout the several years leading up to the trial. I think it was because there was so much hope that we all held. Hope that the truth would come out and the truth was Ken was not guilty and Enron was not a bad company.

Grady left for Texas on that next Monday, which was Memorial Day. My mother had told me that she would call to check on me when Grady was gone. Sure enough she called Monday afternoon, but I just could not pick up the phone. She called several more times on Monday night and Tuesday morning before I could talk to her.

Grady explained to me that she loved me a lot even though she had not called that Thursday Ken was convicted. He went on to explain that he thought that it was hard for any of our family to understand the way we felt about Ken Lay. She couldn't possibly understand how that verdict would affect me. He was right. I'm not sure even I could have imagined the hurt I felt. I realized at that point that the hope was gone that the truth would be told about Ken and the wonderful company I spent most of my life working for.

When I finally did speak to my mother I had several days to think about a lot of things. I went back over in my mind the things she had said to me over the last four years. First, she had wanted me to give back all of the money that I made at Enron. I know she was just trying to help me solve the problem I had, but now as I thought about what she said, I could only rationalize that she didn't think I had earned it or even deserved it.

I remembered she had told me that my aunt said I should have known something was wrong because I was making too much money. Neither of them knew that our compensation structure for each executive job was benchmarked with other companies and had to be approved by Towers Perrin and our board of directors.

My mother had also asked me sometime in 2002 that hadn't I wished now I had never been promoted? Now that I thought about all of the things she had said to me I felt like she was telling me she wasn't proud of what I accomplished. In reality she didn't really understand the corporate world I had become a part of.

Even now, with everything we have all had to go through, I would do it all over again. I doubt if anyone who wasn't at Enron could truly appreciate that. We had a special company at Enron and I would bet that a large majority of the employees would agree—even knowing the ending they would do it all again.

The thing that probably hurt me the most was when my mother told me, during a discussion of our faith, that "God puts people in their places." Again, I felt like she was saying I deserved what happened to me. I remembered what our pastor had said one Sunday. He said that God uses whatever He can to bring people to Him and I believed that's what He had done for Grady and I. Did we deserve it—probably, but more importantly, through all of the loss and hurt we realized we needed the Lord. I also realize God doesn't punish—He teaches.

All of these things had been going through my mind since Friday. After I spoke to Grady I decided I should call her back because she would worry about me. So, I called her on Tuesday afternoon to tell her I was doing fine with Grady gone. I also told her how sad I was about Ken's conviction and that no one from my family realized how the verdict would impact me.

I didn't think I was going to explode like I did, but her

response was not something I expected at all. She told me she was surprised I hadn't realized that Ken would be convicted. She went on to tell me that after all, all of her friends believed that Ken was guilty.

When I heard that come out of her mouth I couldn't help myself. I exploded at her, asking why she believed that I would testify for someone who I thought was guilty. I also asked her if in fact her friends had known Ken Lay and had worked closely with him for nearly twenty-three years as I had.

I couldn't understand how my mother could believe her friends over her own daughter. They had not spent their careers building Enron, and didn't even know Ken. I also went over every thing she had said to me that had hurt my feelings since Enron's collapse. Of course, she was surprised that I had been hurt by the things she said and told me she was just trying to fix things for me.

What I've realized since that conversation is how could my mother or her friends think any differently? The press destroyed Ken and everything Enron stood for. They had him convicted from day one. There have been movies, books, news reports, late night jokes and the endless articles and press with guilty, guilty, and guilty. My mother didn't know Ken Lay. She was as influenced by what she heard as anyone else. I couldn't be mad at her for that. Besides, I loved her and I had to forgive her for what she had said to me as God forgives me.

I guess I was the one who should have expected what happened. But he wasn't guilty and Enron was the best place in the world to work. I was there. I knew Ken Lay. I know he was a positive, upbeat person who built an incredible company and treated everyone with respect.

No one can imagine how exciting and motivating Enron was to work for unless you were there. No one can understand Ken's innocence without really knowing him like many of us did. I believe that Ken stepped back in as the CEO of Enron and tried to save his wonderful company not only for himself, but mostly for the employees.

I sent Linda Lay an email that next week after I had some time to digest what had just happened. I told her how sorry both Grady and I were. I told her many of our church family were praying for them. I also shared with her what Grady and I realized during those years since Enron's collapse—how much real, true friends can mean, and that only a handful of our previous friends could truly understand what we all were going through.

On May 29, we received the following email from Linda:

> Dear Cindy and Grady,
>
> Just wanted you to know that Ken and I decided at the last minute to get away and arrived in Snowmass last night. We are hoping to get grounded and regroup in this beautiful place that God created. We will try to give you a call before returning to Houston.
>
> We and our family appreciate all of the support you have given Ken and me over these difficult years and especially during his trial, it has been a great comfort to him and to all of us. We are also thankful and grateful for your kind words, care, and concern but most especially for your prayers and continued prayers. Please forgive me, but I just could not pick

up the telephone to call and share that with you personally.

Enron's bankruptcy and the years since seem so surreal and now after the verdict…even more so. I cannot comprehend the current future that my precious Ken, our loving children and our tender grandchildren will have to face. In fact, I still have not come to grips with the fact that anyone might think that Ken could do anything illegal or that he might ever consider hurting anyone. I and the children have always admired Ken for the choices he made throughout his life and the way in which he lived it. It is supremely unfair for him to be persecuted, branded and punished for crimes he did not commit. But, then again, there is so much tragedy in this world that eventually encounters everyone in it. I have so many unanswered questions, yet I still trust God and know that He will take care of us and you too. We pray for you daily and I am trusting God to restore you to His perfection. Although, "Why" will surely be on my lips when the day comes as I arrive in heaven and face God.

Thank you again with all my heart, you both have been a blessing to us and we treasure you for it. God bless you.

Much Love, Linda

Her email made me stop and think about the first time I knew how strong Ken's faith was. I wasn't sure, but I think it was when we reconnected with him and Linda in 2005. We had renewed faith in the Lord as a result of everything we went through, and were able to talk openly with them about the trials of life and the importance of faith. I believe you have to be in that place before you can see it in someone else. I immediately sent her an email back inviting them to join us for church when they were in town next.

On May 31 we received the following reply from Linda:

> Dear Cindy and Grady,
>
> Thank you so much for your e-mail. We would love to see you and visit your church, but not right now. Our hearts are broken, although Ken and I were in such shock initially that neither of us could feel anything. Once we got to Snowmass and had some privacy, we totally let go and had a down-and-out pity party. Thankfully to God, we woke up this morning to crisp cool air, brilliant sunshine, and turquoise blue sky with somewhat different attitudes. We have stirred up our faith and are trying to get strong for the next battle. Phone calls and conference call meetings have already begun to put the wheels in motion for appeal.
>
> There is so much that is wrong with our criminal justice system that I don't know where to begin and I fear only God can fix it. As far as the jurors are concerned, their comments since the verdict have been quite telling. It is clear that they convicted Ken for Enron's bankruptcy and not for any illegal act that he personally committed because they haven't articulated any crime. The facts that the defense presented were very complicated, but they were real and decisive…if understood. Apparently, they didn't fully understand them, or chose to ignore the facts and believe the

character assassination by the government. The jurors' comments portray their firm belief that the person at the top must be convicted for whatever goes on inside a company even if that person didn't know about any criminal behavior that was going on secretly. They also believe that with so many jobs lost and retirement monies lost in the bankruptcy that the person at the top must pay for that loss by going to prison. Sadly, our hometown newspaper convicted Ken years ago as several writers were relentless with articles in the paper every single day. That clearly helped create a real lynch mob mentality that climaxed in a very, very terrifying way last Thursday. God was no where in the mix.

Our plan is to return to Houston this coming Saturday. We need to be back for a meeting with the woman assigned to Ken from the Bureau of Prisons...that alone is incredibly difficult as I try to get my mind around such a horribly bizarre realization. Somehow we will get through this. We promise to call you soon.

Much Love, Linda

During the next month Grady and I had several telephone conversations with Ken; he was always interested in how we were doing. He left me a voice message the week after the verdict. In his message he told me he wanted to talk to me. He shared how hard the verdict was on the entire family. He ended his message saying that he still had his faith in God and that God had a plan for him.

Ken had gotten a hold of Grady on his cell phone when he was looking for me one day in late June. Grady tells me that he told Ken he was a much better man than he could ever be, and how much he admired the way he handled himself through all of this. Ken, who had always encouraged everyone to do their very best, told Grady that he was sure that he would be able to handle things even better than himself if he was in the same situation. The Lord would help him just like the Lord was helping Ken.

The last time I spoke to Ken Lay was on June 20. He told me that he and Linda would be in Colorado in a couple of weeks and they wanted to have dinner with Grady and I when they were there. He also asked me if I would speak to a few people about writing letters to the judge prior to his sentencing. I told him that Grady and I would be going to Wisconsin for the weekend, and when I returned I would get back to him about the letters. He told me that he would send an article that he thought I would find interesting. The following is the email that Ken sent me with a note, "This is how hard they had to work to convict me."

> Subject: The Enron Case that Almost Wasn't
> Date: Wed, 21 Jun 2006 13:13:40 -500
> From: "Lay, Ken L."
> To: "grady olson"
>
> Dear Cindy,
> As we discussed, you may find the attached article of interest. It just shows how hard the Task Force had to work to come up with an indictment on me.
> We look forward to seeing you and Grady in a few days.
>
> Warmest regards,
> Ken

The Enron Case that Almost Wasn't

By ALEXEI BARRIONUEVO AND KURT EICHENWALD (NYT) 2897 words Published: June 4, 2006

"Guilty."

Judge Simeon T. Lake III's reading of the verdict landed like a bombshell in his federal courtroom in Houston. The first cries came from the second row, where the children of Kenneth L. Lay, the former Enron chairman, lurched forward and began sobbing.

Dressed in a cobalt blue jacket, Linda Lay, Mr. Lay's wife, dropped her head onto his shoulder as the judge continued to read a series of fraud and conspiracy verdicts. Each count was punctuated by one word: "guilty."

When the judge finished, Mr. Lay, 64, had been convicted of 10 crimes—and a man who was once a close ally of President Bush and presided over one of the nation's most influential companies became someone who may spend the rest of his life in prison.

But the journey from the collapse of Enron to Mr. Lay's conviction was anything but predictable. Instead, it was a long and arduous legal journey for federal prosecutors, filled with false leads and evidentiary dry holes. The public widely perceived the criminal case against Mr. Lay to have been a "can't lose" proposition, similar to the parallel case assembled against Enron's former chief executive, Jeffrey K. Skilling. But the legal hurdles on the path to Mr. Lay's conviction were so daunting that some prosecutors privately worried that they would never even be able to charge Mr. Lay with any crimes.

Prosecutors eventually defined and pinned down Mr. Lay's misdeeds by focusing on what amounted to the most basic of childhood transgressions. After analyzing millions of pages of documents, deconstructing complex accounting mechanisms, unwinding complex trading transactions and interviewing scores of witnesses, they found a theme that carried the day: Mr. Lay chose to lie—to his shareholders, his employees and his banks—and those lies were his crimes.

The process of dissecting Mr. Lay's misdeeds also forced prosecutors to pull apart the strange corporate machinery of Enron itself. There, too, prosecutors discovered, the blindingly complex gave way to the maddeningly simple: Enron was not a delicate, innovative engine of profitability; it was a hodgepodge of often impenetrable activities, some of which were designed so their architects could simply steal money.

"I liken it to being like some strange mechanical device that dropped out of the sky, and a group of engineers who had never seen anything like it had to take it apart and figure out what it was," said Samuel W. Buell, who was one of the first prosecutors to investigate Mr. Lay. "But at the end of the day, the machine just ended up being a coffee maker."

Even so, the case against Mr. Lay was never clear-cut, prosecutors say. And a review of their efforts to directly link Mr. Lay to crimes at Enron reveals that at times it seemed that their quarry might remain permanently beyond their reach.

SHORTLY after Enron collapsed in December 2001, the Justice Department assembled a special federal task force to delve into the complexities of the company. One fact emerged quickly, task force members said: there was no obvious case to be made against Mr. Lay. Investigators focused on the use of murky partnerships, particularly a vehicle known as LJM, to manipulate Enron's financial performance. But that inquiry unearthed little evidence of crimes involving Mr. Lay.

"There was this public perception of Ken Lay as the mastermind, but that really didn't bear out," said Leslie R. Caldwell, who headed the task force in its first two years. "We realized very fully early on that Lay was not involved in the decision-making day to day and that we weren't going to be able to prove his involvement in the structuring of transactions like LJM."

Other areas appeared more promising. Corporate filings revealed that Mr. Lay had sold about $100 million worth of his Enron shares, most of them back to the company through a complex transaction involving a corporate line of credit. Almost all of the money from the sales went toward paying down personal bank loans that were secured by the Enron shares. If the task force could prove that Mr. Lay sold the shares because of nonpublic information he had about the company, the theory went, he may have committed insider trading. But it was virtually impossible to prove insider trading for shares sold back to the company, since Enron theoretically had the same information as Mr. Lay.

"The insider-trading characterization of these sales just never seemed sustainable, except on some very broad theory that, when you know things at a company aren't going well, you can't sell," Mr. Buell said. "We needed something more tangible than that."

So prosecutors developed a new theory about Mr. Lay's trades: that he looted Enron by pulling $100 million out of its coffers even as the company's financial situation was deteriorating. Prosecutors were cagey, never signaling to Mr. Lay's defense team that they had abandoned the insider-trading theory and replaced it with a new allegation.

But the task force ultimately decided it could not even build that case. There was no clear evidence that Mr. Lay had actively tried to deceive Enron's board, and he could contend that he had relied on Enron lawyers to approve all of his trades.

Other avenues of investigation also dried up. There had been suspicions that Mr. Lay had tried, perhaps improperly, to use his political influence with the Bush administration to get assistance for his company as it was floundering in late 2001. He had made numerous phone calls to members of the administration at the time; the task force decided to find out what had transpired.

Over a series of days, the task force interviewed multiple government officials, including Alan Greenspan, then the chairman of the Federal Reserve; Donald L. Evans, then the Commerce secretary; and Paul H. O'Neill, then the Treasury secretary. Each had received telephone calls from Mr. Lay in that crucial period, but no evidence of wrongdoing emerged from the discussions.

In the spring of 2003, Ms. Caldwell called a task force meeting in downtown Washington to reorient the group's legal strategy. Instead of unraveling myriad, intricate details from separate transactions, she suggested, it might be wiser to explore the case as a series of intertwined transactions.

The new approach was called "The Picture of Dorian Gray theory," after the Oscar Wilde story about a man who retains his youth and beauty because his portrait, which shows him aging and corrupt, hides his many sins. Prosecutors speculated that they could build a fraud case against Enron by proving that the company publicly portrayed itself as strong and vibrant, even though executives like Mr. Lay knew that it was rotting from the inside.

"It was definitely a shift in investigative strategy," Ms. Caldwell said of the meeting. "We had to focus on the big picture, and not just the individual transactions. But it was just a seed that pointed to a direction. It wasn't as if that immediately led us to decide what we were going to charge."

By the fall of 2003, other pieces were falling into place. Andrew S. Fastow, Enron's former chief financial officer, had been indicted on fraud and other counts and the outlines of criminal cases against Mr. Skilling and Richard A. Causey, the former chief accounting officer, were taking shape. As the task force shifted its attention to securing indictments against Mr. Skilling and Mr. Causey, it put the investigation of Mr. Lay on a back burner.

But on the same day Mr. Skilling was indicted in early 2004, Enron's former treasurer, Ben F. Glisan Jr., appeared before a grand jury in Houston and gave prosecutors a little gift. In addition to providing evidence against Mr. Skilling, he testified that Mr. Lay knew he was lying in 2001 when he provided upbeat statements about Enron's prospects even as the company was plummeting toward bankruptcy proceedings.

"That was a real turning point for a whole variety of reasons," said Andrew Weissmann, a former task force director who questioned Mr. Glisan that day. "Ben Glisan clearly pointed the way to the Lay case. I was relieved."

After months of being spread thin on personnel, the task force was also reinforced with a crew of top-flight lawyers. Mr. Buell began focusing more closely on the Skilling case, and Ms. Caldwell hired Sean M. Berkowitz, a prosecutor from Chicago recommended by United States Attorney Patrick J. Fitzgerald, to assist Mr. Buell. To take charge of the Lay investigation, the task force turned to John C. Hueston, a well-regarded—and aggressive—prosecutor from Southern California. Although hired to work primarily on the Skilling investigation, Mr. Berkowitz soon began trading notes with Mr. Hueston on how to handle both inquiries.

Mr. Hueston, 42, revived the Lay investigation, bringing Mr. Glisan back to the grand jury and questioning numerous other witnesses. "John is a really,

really good investigator," Mr. Weissmann said. "He just dug into this."

Mr. Hueston turned up yet another potential crime as he examined Mr. Lay's personal finances. Although Mr. Lay signed contracts prohibiting use of his personal bank loans to buy stocks on margin in excess of certain amounts, he had done so anyway. To Mr. Hueston, that suggested that Mr. Lay had committed a fraud by violating federal banking laws restricting such transactions.

Other dominoes continued to fall. An F.B.I. agent assembled evidence that Mr. Lay lied to accountants to help Enron avoid a huge write-down. New witnesses, meanwhile, told the grand jury fresh details about other possible lies by Mr. Lay. As the government continued to build its case, Mr. Lay's lawyers tried to stave off indictment. In the summer of 2004, the Justice Department granted Mr. Lay an unusual final appeal to the highest levels of the agency, but that appeal ultimately failed. Around the same time, the task force wrote sealed letters to two federal judges in Houston, saying prosecutors anticipated bringing an indictment against Mr. Lay—soon.

"I always thought that was an act of betrayal, an act of deceit," said Mr. Lay's lead lawyer, Michael W. Ramsey, suggesting that the letters indicated that the review effort was a sham. Mr. Hueston said in an interview that the letters were simply anticipatory and "courtesy notes" for the judges, not promises of an impending indictment.

Mr. Hueston advocated charging Mr. Lay with

making false statements, similar to the charges being brought against Mr. Skilling.

He interviewed securities analysts, seeking to understand what Mr. Lay had conveyed to the marketplace. He was shocked to find that most of them had not bothered to look closely at Enron's securities filings and were taking Enron's statements "virtually at face value."

Mr. Hueston dug deeper into Mr. Lay's finances, dredging up records on everything from his vacation spending, to a $200,000 birthday cruise for his wife, to more than $100,000 spent on liquor in 2001. They studied Mr. Lay's lifestyle, his bank loans and his reliance on Enron credit lines.

They also focused on statements that Mr. Lay made in an online forum in which he told Enron employees that he was buying falling Enron stock without mentioning the far greater number of shares he was selling to the company itself. That omission, prosecutors believed, amounted to securities fraud. And Mr. Lay's statements allowed prosecutors to bring his stock sales to Enron—and the draining of $100 million from the company—into the case, an issue likely to influence a jury's view of his character.

On Dec. 13, 2005, about a month before the trial began, Mr. Lay fired back at the task force, and at Mr. Hueston in particular. In a speech to a Houston business group, Mr. Lay opined that the investigation had taken so long "because it is complicated to find crimes where they do not exist." He named task force members, including Mr. Hueston, and said they had yet to find any cause to indict him. It was the first public flash of the acrimony between the pursued and his pursuer, emotions that would eventually spill over at trial.

When Mr. Lay's trial began, Mr. Ramsey promised that the defense would show that Mr. Lay had sold Enron stock only when the banks required him to do so. Mr. Hueston and Mr. Berkowitz, by that time the director of the task force, said they believed that that statement was the defense's first fatal blunder.

The prosecution team flip-flopped on whether to call some important witnesses. The night before Mr. Fastow was due to take the stand, Andrew Stolper, a junior lawyer on the team, visited Mr. Hueston's office. He was concerned that Mr. Fastow's admitted crimes would damage his credibility before a jury and hurt the government's case.

"Are you sure you want to do this?" Mr. Stolper asked. "We're doing well."

"That train has left the station," Mr. Hueston replied.

In the end, prosecutors said they thought Mr. Fastow's testimony turned out better than they had expected. Mr. Glisan, several jurors said later, was more convincing—and more critical to the case against Mr. Lay. During Mr. Glisan's first day on the stand, he said Enron's financial condition was "weak" when Mr. Skilling resigned in August 2001. Mr. Lay, who until then had seemed unfazed by weeks of testimony, exploded outside the courtroom.

"I have never heard so many lies in one day in my whole life," he seethed to a group of reporters.

As the sleepless nights dragged on during Mr. Lay's trial, task force members eased the tension by organizing jogs around Houston parks and tossing around Nerf footballs and baseballs in a large office room they called "the bullpen." The compact Mr. Hueston, a marathon runner, often urged colleagues agents to join him in push-ups and pull-ups to stay alert late at night.

About a week before Mr. Lay took the stand, he and Mr. Hueston found themselves on a courtroom elevator for the first time during the trial. "John's been eating red meat," Mr. Lay declared without elaboration and in a disarmingly friendly way, according to Mr. Hueston.

Mr. Hueston said that he said nothing in reply.

The night before Mr. Hueston began his cross-examination of Mr. Lay, Mr. Berkowitz went to his co-prosecutor's office and offered him a dose of motivation. "I've been reading that the entire fate of corporate criminal prosecutions rests on this cross," he told Mr. Hueston, only half-jokingly.

The next day, in the closing moments of his direct examination, Mr. Lay allowed his emotions to overwhelm him. He accused Mr. Hueston of interfering with his earlier attempts to repay a $7.5 million loan that Enron had extended to him. "It was not finalized because John Hueston blocked that deal!" he said, his voice rising. When it came time for Mr. Hueston to cross-examine Mr. Lay, the prosecutor accused him of engaging in "character assassination of witnesses."

"Are you considering yourself in that list?" Mr. Lay retorted.

"Mr. Lay, I'm an assistant United States attorney. This is my job," Mr. Hueston responded calmly. "You can call me anything you want. I'm talking about the witnesses here."

As he cross-examined Mr. Lay for four days, Mr. Hueston continually pushed to show that Mr. Lay had essentially stuck his head in the sand by repeatedly ignoring concerns in the fall of 2001 about aggressive accounting and wrongdoing at the company. Mr. Hueston also showed that Mr. Lay continued to assure employees that nothing was wrong at Enron, even as information was dribbling in to him from multiple sources that trouble was brewing. He also homed in on Mr. Lay's personal finances, arguing that Mr. Lay made choices about how to repay his bank loans that repeatedly put his interests ahead of the company he was supposed to be safeguarding.

When Mr. Berkowitz left his office at 3:30 a.m. on May 16, with the trial's final closing argument just five hours away, he looked around and saw more than a half-dozen bedraggled F.B.I. agents, several of whom had been part of the Enron investigation since it began four years earlier.

One agent's young daughter, a toddler, was so angry at her father for his long absence from home that she refused to come to the phone anymore. Still, none of the agents intended to leave the task force's

offices that night. Some of them used a shower in
the basement of the federal courthouse to freshen up
before that last day of the trial.

Days after the jury began deliberating, Mr.
Hueston and Mr. Berkowitz took a five-mile jog.
Later, they settled into chairs on the deck of Big
Woodrow's restaurant on a sweltering Wednesday
night. A waitress eased her way through a rowdy
crowd, delivering a bucket of crawfish and Corona
beers to the prosecutors. As the surrounding crowds
watched overhead televisions, cheering on the Houston Astros baseball team, the two men discussed
their shared ordeal.

"We wanted to tell each other we were proud of
the case we put on, regardless of the verdict," Mr.
Hueston said.

"There was a sense of calm, because we felt we
had done a nice job," Mr. Berkowitz said.

The next day, Mr. Lay and Mr. Skilling were
both convicted of multiple fraud and conspiracy
charges. The jury found that both men carried out
their crimes by misleading investors and employees
about Enron's performance.

In short, they decided that Ken Lay was a liar
and they were going to convict him for that.

As I hung up the phone after that conversation with
Ken I thought, as I always did, how wonderful it was to
talk to him. He was always kind and interested in what
we had going on in our lives even though he had so much
going on in his. If I had known that would be the last
time that I would ever speak with him I would have told

him how much I always enjoyed speaking with him. I would have thanked him for always being there for me and for everything he had done for me and, I would have told him that I loved him and through his faith he was a role model for so many people including me. I am sure he knows all of that now.

God Pardons Lay

On July 3, I emailed Ken Lay copies of letters I received back from two of the people who said they would write them to Judge Lake for Ken's sentencing. The following are those letters:

> **The Honorable Sim Lake**
> **United States District Court**
> **Southern District of Texas**
> **515 Rusk Avenue**
> **Houston, TX 77002**

> Judge Lake:
> I lost a huge part of my life savings due to the collapse of Enron, but I cannot attribute any of that to Kenneth Lay. Enron provided and encouraged a means for employees to diversify retirement portfolio, and many of us chose not to take advantage of that opportunity.
> I flew Enron's company airplanes for over 20 years, starting out with Northern Natural Gas in Omaha, NE, and was witness to the mergers that formed Enron. I was responsible for transporting many of the company executives to all parts of the globe and was fortunate to get to know several of those people. Mr. Lay was among them.

Although we did not become close personal friends, I always found Mr. Lay to be very approachable, friendly and respectful. He was interested in our families and, due to our challenging flight schedule, concerned that we had enough quality time at home. He proved this often by adjusting his schedule and itinerary so that flight crews could be with their families during holidays and special events.

When I was based in Omaha, the company management there made it impossible for me to attend National Guard meetings, a clear violation of Federal Law and company guidelines. Mr. Lay changed that when he became president and CEO. He personally challenged those managers and set them straight on that issue. He went out of his way to ensure that employees could come to him with job-related problems. In fact I have Mr. Lay to thank for my military retirement benefits because without his intercession, I could not have continued serving in the military.

I think that I saw Mr. Lay and witnessed his management style from a unique perspective. I could see that he trusted people. He struggled to keep the company alive when he could have just walked away. If Mr. Lay is incarcerated, it will prove to me that "No good deed goes unpunished."

Sincerely,
James D. Gramke

The Honorable Sim Lake
United States District Court
Southern District of Texas
515 Rusk Avenue
Houston, TX 77002

Your Honor:

Like many other employees and retirees, I too suffered a financial set-back due to the collapse of Enron. I ignored my broker's diversification advice and made the choice to maintain a significant holding in Enron stock. I did so because of the fifteen-year track record that Mr. Lay had while leading a company I had the honor to work for.

While the verdict is in I am perplexed by the following;

Mr. Lay spent sixteen plus years building Enron.

Under his astute leadership he transformed Enron into one of the largest and most enamored energy companies.

Mr. Lay amassed personal fortunes in the hundreds of millions of dollars (which falls in line with other executive compensation for similar successes).

Mr. Lay is an intelligent man, educated and able to understand and recognize risk.

Mr. Lay was, and remains, spiritually led and morally based.

Given this begs one question; Do you really think Mr. Lay unwittingly compromised his faith, family and reputation, in addition to risking all the years of unwavering hard work and personal fortune, in order to make an extra few million dollars? For one second I cannot believe he was ever party to the schemes which contributed to the collapse of Enron.

I am confident there are thousands of us who stand behind Mr. Lay's innocence premised on the man he was and continues to be today. While we have all witnessed imperfect judicial processes in the past, Mr. Lay is at your mercy today. I would ask that you consider a sentence befitting to a man who stands unfairly accused of destroying a company he spent years building.

May God provide you the comfort, wisdom, strength and unwavering judicial leadership in the upcoming weeks as you contemplate the fate of Mr. Lay.

God Bless you for your continued efforts in making our country the greatest in the world!

Joe Nieto

Ken Lay didn't have the opportunity to read either of these letters. He and Linda were on their way to Aspen the day I forwarded them to him.

We spent a pretty low-key Fourth of July with our friends, Jim and Pam Alexander. They had spent the evening at our house for a barbecue but had gone home early. Grady and I didn't even stay up and watch the fireworks that we could see from our deck in Carbondale.

I got up the next morning and started our daily routine of fixing breakfast and cleaning up from the night before. About 8:30 the phone rang and I could tell by the caller ID it was my friend, Sarah Davis. I answered the call, "Sarah, how are you?" The person on the other end of the line was not Sarah, but her daughter, Chelsa.

Sarah had gone out for a walk that morning, and while she was gone a relative called to see if she had heard the news. Chelsa had taken the call, and when her mother returned, shared with her what had happened. Sarah immediately thought of me and called to make sure I was doing all right.

When I heard Chelsa's voice I was surprised that it wasn't Sarah on the other end of the line. Chelsa asked me if I could speak to her mother. I thought it was odd that Sarah would not call herself. When she came on the line I could tell from her voice that she was upset about something. Sarah asked me if I was all right. As she described the conversation later she just wanted to check in and make sure her friend, Cindy, was doing okay.

Of course when she asked if I was doing all right I didn't know what she was talking about because I had not yet heard the news. Sarah tells me that she changed her mission from being a friend to comfort me to the bearer of the bad news. Then she told me—Ken Lay had died. Grady tells me that I screamed, "Oh no!" and started crying. I frankly don't remember anything but feeling numb all over and telling Sarah that I would have to call her back. I had to take it all in and understand what she was telling me.

When I hung up the phone I was shaking and crying and trying to relay to Grady what I had just heard. Immediately, I called Ken's office and Jan Cooley, one of Ken's assistants in the office in Houston, answered the phone. She said they were trying to get more details, but Ken and Linda were in Colorado when he died. They had arrived in Snowmass the night before. Other than that they didn't know much more. I started filling in the blanks on my own since I didn't know what had happened. We were supposed to have dinner with them sometime during their visit. We felt like we needed to do something, but we just didn't know what to do.

Finally, Grady suggested we get in the car and start down the hill to Highway 82 toward Old Snowmass to see if we could find the house the Lays rented. When we had seen Ken and Linda in the past in Colorado we always met them at a restaurant. We weren't sure exactly where they were except that they rented a house in Old Snowmass. I decided to call Rosie and see if she could give us the exact address, which she did. As we got to the highway, Rosie called back to let us know that Linda asked to be alone for a while, so we decided to find the house and go back home until we heard from someone.

I checked with Ken's office periodically that day to make sure there wasn't anything that Grady and I could do. We both felt helpless and wanted to do something, but didn't know what we could do to help. During the day on Wednesday people phoned or emailed wanting more details on what had happened.

Finally, we heard from Liz Lay Vittor, Ken's daughter, and she asked if Grady and I would mind if Reverend and Audrey Lawson, and Howard Jefferson could stay with us. They would be flying in on Saturday morning and would stay Saturday night and leave again on Sunday after the service in Aspen. The rest of that week was a blur.

The Lawsons and Howard flew in with Mark and Natalie Lay, Ken's son and his wife, and Liz's husband

Jose Luis. They arrived on Saturday afternoon and we picked them up at the airport in Rifle as the Aspen airport was closed due to weather. The Lawsons and Howard had never been to Colorado, and kept commenting that they now understood why Ken loved this place so very much.

We stopped for lunch at a great little restaurant on the Frying Pan River in Basalt and then went to the house in Old Snowmass so everyone could visit with Linda. Getting to the house was an experience. When we drove into the driveway we were met by a security guard. The drive was blocked with another car so no one could pass through without stopping to show the guard their ID. Obviously, the press had been more than relentless trying to get any piece of information they could.

When we got to the house Linda and the kids were busy working on the arrangements for not only the Aspen service, but also the Houston service that would take place on Wednesday of the next week. Of course when we arrived Linda took time out to visit with Reverend Lawson, Audrey and Howard. I hadn't spoken to Linda since her email, so I was also anxious to express my sympathies.

The warmth that Ken had always shown us was there in that room. The entire family, amidst their own grief, shared their sincere love for all of us being there. As we left, Linda gave us all a hug. As we embraced she told me how much Ken loved me. She told Grady that he loved him too, but not as much as he loved me. Of course we all laughed, but tears came to my eyes again as flashbacks of his smile came into my mind. I remember feeling again how very much I was going to miss him.

Saturday evening, Grady and I invited our pastor and his family, our friends Jim and Pam Alexander and some other friends from our church to share dinner with our guests. We thought that it would be interesting for all of them to get to know two of Ken's very good friends. We spent most of the evening telling wonderful stories about Ken Lay and what a great man he was.

Reverend Lawson also shared with the group stories about his early days building his church. He built Wheeler Avenue Baptist Church in Houston, which he started as a group meeting in his living room. It now has a congregation of more than 6500 people, and he is one of the most respected people in Houston. In fact, after Ken's service in Houston, he had to leave immediately to fly to New York to speak to a group of Price Waterhouse executives.

During the night on Saturday, Audrey Lawson had trouble breathing because of the altitude. Consequently on Sunday morning she and Reverend Lawson stayed at our home while Grady, Howard and I attended our church. As Howard said, the sermon was just for us. Terry Maner, our pastor, seemed to tailor make the sermon that day for our benefit.

He preached from the Ecclesiastics 7: 1–4 which states,

> A good name is better than fine perfume, and the day of death better than the day of birth. It is better to go to a house of mourning than to go to a house of feasting, for death is the destiny of every man; the living should take this to heart. Sorrow is better than laughter, because a sad face is good for the heart.

The heart of the wise is in the house of mourning,
but the heart of fools is in the house of pleasure.

Howard was extremely interested in the sermon and particularly that specific verse, and he thanked Terry for his words as we left the service to head back to the house to pick up the Lawsons.

Shortly after we got back to the house from our church service we had to head to Aspen for the memorial service. It was another rainy, dreary day, which I guess was appropriate for the occasion. Reverend Lawson was in charge of performing the service and Linda and all of the kids prepared the program that allowed everyone in the family to talk about Ken. Reverend Lawson shared with us before we got in the car how very difficult this was going to be for him, and we all held hands and prayed for God's hand on the service.

The service was in the Aspen Chapel. It is a non-denominational place of worship and a wonderful setting for weddings and funerals. The Chapel is a landmark in Aspen. It sits on a hill as you enter the town with a backdrop of stately mountains. The light drizzle that had been with us all day on Saturday was still falling as we entered the Chapel.

There were reporters trying very hard to get a picture of anyone they thought might be important as we entered the church. In the front of the sanctuary a life-size picture of Ken was displayed in his running shorts with that great big smile that I was going to miss. There were sunflowers everywhere. We were seated at the front next to Reverend Lawson and Audrey.

The Chapel was full of people and I noticed many

familiar faces in the pews. The sadness was evident on everyone's faces.

The service lasted nearly an hour and a half. All of the kids spoke and the twelve grandkids, even though they were not there in person, had some wonderful experiences to add. They had all written things that they were going to miss about their grandfather. These things were shared with everyone by Robin, Linda's daughter from her first marriage, and Liz, Ken's daughter from his first marriage.

I vividly remember several excerpts from the service. Beau, Linda's youngest son, read an email from a friend who had also worked at Enron. The email shared his view that Ken's legacy would be how he upheld his faith through such hard times. I had seen evidence of that in the voice messages, phone conversations and the emails I received from Ken in the days leading up to his death. I too believe that Ken Lay will be remembered as an example of unwavering faith in the Lord.

David, Linda's middle son, spoke of how Ken was treated by the government during the last five years and now, at last he was at peace. That was true as well. The article Ken sent me in the days before he died talked about the lengths the government had gone to not to get the truth, but to get Ken Lay.

Linda's brother talked about how well Ken treated Linda throughout their marriage. How they had grown to love each other, and how grateful their family was that Ken found Linda. I had witnessed this as well. He and Linda always held hands, and the way he spoke to her and about her, you could tell they were very much in love with each other.

Reverend Lawson spoke of how Ken was viewed today, but he compared him with others who were looked down upon during their lifetimes, but left legacies of greatness in death. He spoke of Martin Luther King, Jr. and how he was not well liked in his life but in death became a symbol of hope for many people. Reverend Lawson knew a lot about Martin Luther King, Jr. He marched with Dr. King in the 1960s.

He talked about John F. Kennedy, and how he had failed to get legislation passed during his lifetime, but after his death that legislation went through easily, and today he is considered one of the most respected American presidents ever.

He also spoke of Ken's faith and how strong it was. Some people have said that Ken had come to his faith through the trials he was experiencing with the destruction of Enron, but Reverend Lawson knew that Ken had strong faith all along. Those last few years had served to strengthen the faith that already was there.

Finally, the girls, Liz and Robin, shared what the grandkids loved about their Papia

The one thing I thought was the funniest was Lucas, Liz's son, saying he loved to shake his booty in front of his Papia because it made Ken laugh. The picture that came into my mind again was that big smile of Ken's and his desire to always make everything fun.

Each of them spoke the truth that day. How blessed each one of us was for knowing Ken. We knew the whole truth.

There are two other things that I think illustrate how devoted Ken was to the Lord. The last entry in his journal before his death read, *"We Live by Faith, not by sight,"* (2 Corinthians 5:7).

Also, one of Ken's favorite devotionals was shared with us in the program:

STREAMS IN THE DESERT
– by, L.B. Cowman
June 3

Let us go over to the other side. (Mark 4:35)

Even though we follow Christ's command, we should not expect toescape the storm.

In this passage of Scripture, the disciples were

obeying His command, yet they encountered the fiercest of storms and were in great danger of being drowned. In their distress, they cried out for Christ's assistance.

Christ may delay coming to us during our times of distress, but it is simply so our faith may be tested and strengthened.

His purpose is also that our prayers will be more powerful, our desire for deliverance will be greater, and when deliverance finally comes we will appreciateit more fully.

Gently rebuking His disciples, Christ asked, "Why are you so afraid?

Do you still have no faith?" (v. 40).

In effect, He was saying, "Why didn't you face the storm victoriously and shout to the raging winds and rolling waves, 'You cannot harm us, for Christ, the mightySavior, is on board'?"

Of course, it is much easier to trust God when the sun is shining thanto trust Him when the storm is raging around us.

Yet we will never know our level of genuine faith until it is tested in a fierce storm, and that is why our Savior is on board.

If you are ever to "be strong in the Lord and in his mighty power" (Eph.6:10), your strength will be born during a storm.

With Christ in my vessel, I smile at the storm.

Christ said, "Let us go over to the other side"—not "to the middle of the lake to be drowned."

Daniel Crawford

After the service I ran into Jeff Skilling as we were leaving the church. We hugged and told each other how much we would miss Ken. I felt sorry for everything that had happened to Jeff. He was visibly shaken by the service. I guess that was the only time I had ever seen him that emotional. All of the hurt he had caused me wasn't there anymore. At that moment I forgave him for how he had treated me back in 2001—it just didn't seem that important anymore.

We left the service and Grady and I took the Lawsons and Howard to the airport, and went home to get ready to leave for Houston. It had been an emotionally draining day, and we were planning on leaving early the next morning.

The service in Houston was very similar to the one in Aspen. Reverend Lawson was in charge of saying the prayer at the Houston service, but he took the liberty to share with the audience his thoughts on how the government had treated Ken. The elder George Bush and Barbara were seated near the front of the church, and I almost felt like he was talking directly to them.

He expressed his regret at how Ken had been treated, saying he was an old man and could say what he wanted. He compared what happened to Ken with what happened to James Byrd in Jasper, Texas. Mr. Byrd was the black man who was dragged behind a truck in the late 1990s. He went on to say how well Ken Lay treated him and so many others from the African-American community. When he finished he got a standing ovation from the crowd.

Ken's minister was actually in charge of the service, and he also shared his view on Ken. He talked about not only how strong in his faith Ken was through the very tough years following the Enron bankruptcy, but he shared with the crowd how Ken lived his life during the "good years." He told the men in the audience how exceptional he had treated Linda—holding hands and opening doors, the things husbands rarely do. He got a laugh from them when he told them their wives would probably expect that now as his wife had indicated she would like to see more of that from him.

He shared with the crowd something I saw Ken do many times. Ken always treated every person with respect no matter who you were. I would be in a gathering with

Ken and he would be visiting with the janitor or the food servers rather than with the other CEOs in the room. Ken's minister shared a similar experience.

He was at the courthouse one day during Ken's trial, and an African-American lady mopping the floors tapped him on the shoulder to ask if the man in the suit over there where she was pointing was Ken Lay. He replied, "Yes, ma'am, that is Ken Lay." She went on to say that Ken was the only white man in a suit who had ever spoken to her in her twenty-seven years working there in the courthouse. She went on to tell Ken's minister that Ken had told her she was doing a good job. Again, what I was hearing validated everything I had experienced myself in the years that I had worked so close to Ken. He consistently treated people like he would want to be treated.

It was interesting to see who was there at the service and who was not. Rebecca Mark was there, along with Joe Sutton. Stan Horton was there. John Duncan, who was one of the Enron board members looked shaken, but I would imagine he was there as an obligation—he was one of Ken's friends who had said and done some very hurtful things to him. Of course Drayton McLane and others from the Astros organization were there.

I was surprised how few of the Houston CEOs who Ken had helped were there, and very few of the Enron executive team were there. Of course Mark Frevert was there and I heard Greg Whaley was there. Jeff Skilling didn't attend, but I don't blame him. The media would have been ruthless.

A reception followed the Houston service at the River Oaks Country Club. It was great to reconnect with so many people that I had lost touch with. That's what funerals do. They bring people together and frequently you vow to see each other again. Ken would have been pleased to see that happening.

As Grady and I left the reception we said goodbye to Linda and asked her to call us when she got back to Colorado. She told us she would be in touch. With that, we left and headed back home to Colorado.

Just as Ken had done when he was alive, the Lays wrote several notes expressing their appreciation for picking up the Lawsons and being in Ken's life. Beau wrote a heartfelt note that showed what a truly wonderful person Beau is, and we got one from Linda as well. Ken's good heart was there in the family he left behind.

Linda also wrote us the following email on July 20. It was clear she was dealing with so much pain, and now she was faced with dealing with the government and the lawsuits alone.

> Oh Cindy and Grady,
>
> There is so much pain and sadness inside me and every part of my being aches for my precious Ken. I loved him more than words can say. I count the days until I can have the quiet solitude of the Rocky Mountains and an opportunity to sift through my memories of my life with him.
>
> You will never know how comforting it was to see your sweet faces. I wasn't sure how I was going to take the next breath much less the next step, but seeing you both gave me tremendous courage. It frightens me to think about what wouldn't or couldn't have gotten done without you stepping in to take care of Bill and Audrey Lawson and Howard Jef-

ferson. Your willingness to pick them up, let them share your home, take care of their needs, drive them wherever they needed to go, and deliver them safely back on their way and all under your own emotional duress, was a special gift for which I will be eternally grateful. It meant everything to me and I thank you from the bottom of my heart. You two are angels from heaven sent by God and Ken.

These days are long and intense with lawyers, accountants, coroners, forensic pathologists, sheriffs, press, blah, blah, blah—the aftermath of a five-year nightmare. With Ken gone, one would think that it would finally be over...but not so. I just thank God that Ken is free from all of this. I am blessed to have a strong faith and good friends like you still propping me up.

John Hueston (Enron Task Force prosecutor who was hired to "get" Ken at any cost) is Hell-bent on trying to stop me from getting Ken's criminal cases resolved. It is clear that he is trying to force us to take this beyond him and the Houston court, which means to the 5th Circuit Court of Appeals. He has brought the FBI into the mix and forced Colorado to reopen the investigation hoping to prove that Ken was not the deceased and, failing that, he hoped to prove that Ken either took his life or stopped taking his meds to end his life. He forced Colorado to release of the autopsy records, which I am sure you know went public and is on the Houston Chronicle Web site. That has been difficult for me and the family to bear.

John Hueston has once again tried to block the

Motion that our appellate lawyer wants to file on
Ken's behalf in the criminal cases to vacate Ken's
conviction and dismiss the indictment. Apparently,
if argued, there is some legal precedence that does
not allow an attorney to file the Motion for a dece-
dent in a criminal case and he is arguing that point,
which is forcing it to be done by the administrator of
the estate...who is me. This of course, kept me from
waiting for things to quiet down a bit before I had to
probate Ken's will.

Our family attorney filed Thursday at noon with
the County Clerk, Harris County, Texas, the Appli-
cation for Probate of Will Produced in Court and
for Issuance of Letters Testamentary along with the
original will. This filing will be available to the public, but our hope is that it will go unnoticed. However, as you well know, nothing yet has gone under
the radar screen and I expect it to hit the front page
of the Chronicle when I wake up in the morning.
It will probably appear in total on their website like
Ken's autopsy.

I wish I could drop everything and fly to Aspen,
but I cannot leave Houston until I get more legal
and financial matters further along in the process.
My hope is to spend some part of August at the Old
Snowmass rental house to try and heal. Cindy and
Grady, your loyalty, courage, devotion, love, words
and emotion from the start of Enron's bankruptcy
until now has truly touched my heart. Thanks again,
for being there for and with me when I desperately
needed you and most especially for being so very
good, kind and loving to Ken over the many years

that we all had together. You are amazing human beings and Ken was so fortunate to have had both of you to care so much for him. He loved you and I love you too.

Be well; take care of yourselves and each other. I would love to take you to dinner and I will call you when I know my plans. God bless you both.

Much Love, Linda

P.S. Thank you for the letters to Judge Lake, I plan on reading them carefully over the weekend. Jim Gramke and his wife were wonderful people and I miss seeing them.

The rumors in Aspen were rampant that Ken had killed himself, or that he wasn't even dead yet. The day after Ken died, I spoke to my friend at Continental airlines who had worked for Gordon Bethune before he retired. She told me that she and Gordon had seen each other just the day before and had talked about Ken. Gordon had said that if he was Ken he would have been out of the country by now, but he knew that Ken would never do anything like that because he was such a "straight arrow." I thought about that as I read the paper and listened to people discuss the theories. They didn't know what they were talking about because unfortunately, they didn't know the true Ken Lay.

Something I realized, after the services, was how much Ken had respected Jeff Skilling. Even though many people believed that Enron went down because of Jeff's resignation, I had never heard Ken blame him. I had said some pretty horrible things to Ken about Jeff in the last few years that I now wished I could take back.

After Ken's death and seeing Jeff, I felt like I needed to make amends with him. When I returned from Houston I sent Jeff a note and told him that if he needed me to help him I would.

My friend Mark Frevert was right. He said that the headlines in all of the newspapers should have read "God Pardons Lay." God took Ken away from his enemies in the place that he loved the most after a wonderful day with the person he loved the most. God did what Ken or his attorneys were not able to do. The prosecution may continue to fight, but at the writing of this book Ken Lay died an innocent man by the laws of this justice system and of God's.

The Rest of the Story

In late 2002, my friend, Beth Tilney, started talking about writing a book that would reveal the truth about what really happened within Enron. Nothing positive was being portrayed regarding the great company that we both loved. We felt very sad that not a single source gave Enron credit for anything good.

Beth and Katie Couric had been in college together and were sorority sisters who had stayed in touch. Beth felt her friend, Katie, could give her advice on how she could launch a positive message about Enron and move on with her career. Katie told her that no one really wanted to hear the positive side of the Enron disaster and there would not be a market for that story. Anyway, she reasoned the best thing that Beth could do was get involved in a different position and eventually she could use her new experience to launch a career without having to refer to her Enron days.

As I started to write this book, those words Beth heard from Katie echoed in my mind. I questioned whether what I was writing would ever be read or believed by anyone. But, because so many people encouraged me to sit down and write, I felt compelled to tell my story.

I actually tried to move on to a new career. It seemed, however, that I met a closed door every time I took a path other than this book. I had gotten the perfect job offer from the Colorado Rocky Mountain School, only to have it rescinded after Ken Lay was indicted. The businesses that I tried to help Grady build hadn't worked out, and the concierge business that I believed was the thing that would get me going again was short lived.

In the summer of 2005, one of my friends, Randy Miller, who is a successful business man in Portland, Oregon, and served with me on the PGE/ Enron Foundation board, called to tell me he would be in Vail, Colorado, for a conference in the following few weeks. We planned to meet for lunch in Beaver Creek one afternoon during the week of the conference. Again, I heard from him, "You need to finish your book." I felt like God was telling me this is what He wanted me to do.

I had never really written anything substantial before this point in my life, but it seemed I kept getting the same message from many different people, so, that's exactly what I did. I wrote the story of "my" Enron and my personal journey and lessons I had learned from that incredible experience.

After I finished my story, I allowed myself to finally read the many other books that had been written about Enron. I had vowed not to read these at the time they were released. After all Grady said to me many times, "You don't need to read them—you lived it." Most of the books were written by outsiders who did not work at Enron, and even the books written by Lynn Brewer, an Enron mid-level employee, and Sherron Watkins, Enron's Whistleblower, reflected the same slanted view of what went on at the company that I and many others loved so very much.

After reading those books, quite frankly, I had second

thoughts about how I had actually seen the company, and wondered if maybe I was wrong. I also was concerned that readers of my story would put it down and think, *Nice story but is she ever delusional!* After all, how could all of these other books get it so wrong?

I have always been a glass half full kind of person. I know the difference because Grady, my other half for the past thirty-one years, is a glass half empty kind of guy. For all of those thirty-two years we have been a great team of balance.

I like happy endings, and sometimes I think others believe that I live life in a fairy tale. I see the positive in every thing and every one. I believe that if a person really believes in something, it will happen. So, it might be easy for those that know me to think I am still living in the "Fairy Tale of Enron" as they read my story.

But, my response to all of that is, "I was at Enron for twenty-three years." I lived through its transformation. I was a true insider and I communicated or I was with Ken Lay nearly every day from 1997 until early in 2002. As I have pointed out, not every day of my time at Enron was fun. There were days I was angry and days I was frustrated or sad, but after I step back and look at the entire twenty-three years, and even the last six years following the bankruptcy, I remember most vividly the "good days." I don't dwell on those times that I found difficult to get through. Even during the months that I worked for Stan Horton I developed new friendships, and when I left his area I wrote him a letter thanking him for my growth during the time that I worked for him. I didn't tell him how much he had hurt me or how mad that I got at him, all of that was part of the learning experience.

I didn't hate Enron during the months that I was reporting to Kevin Hannon because he yelled at me everyday telling me I was an idiot. I became his friend.

I didn't blame Enron when Jeff Skilling made decisions that were not good for me. I found a way to add value for the employees.

When Enron filed for bankruptcy I didn't get mad that I had lost so much or fade away. I went to work to find over one thousand of the laid off employees jobs at other companies.

So, for those people who "really" know me, it's not surprising to them that I would tell the Enron story the way I have.

I know there are two "sides" to every story. People either acknowledge that or they go one way or the other. Enron has two sides to its story as well. It was full of great people, but there were a few that were not so great. The culture was tough, but if you let it happen, you grew as a person. The benefits we offered at Enron might have been considered greed or excess but it allowed us to attract top talent from all over the world. The collapse of Enron was bad and many people got hurt, but if you allowed yourself to get beyond the financial hurt there were some very positive things that happened in people's lives after Enron.

Many people blame Enron for losing their retirement, but I doubt if Enron would have reached the $90 share mark under another leadership team like some suggest. Losses incurred by us all are unfairly calculated from that share price unless we give Ken Lay and Jeff Skilling credit for getting us there to begin with.

There are conflicting opinions and accounts of several facts that I doubt will ever be known for sure. Did Ken Lay convince the board to not vote on Rich Kinder for CEO back in 1996 or did the board convince Ken? Did Jeff Skilling quit for personal reasons or did he know something was wrong at Enron? Did Ken Lay regret the decision to promote Jeff to CEO, or did he feel good about that decision in the end? Finally, did Ken Lay really believe he could save Enron, or did he buy himself time so he could get his personal finances in order?

Only Ken Lay and Jeff Skilling know the truth and the answers to those questions. The true answers are locked in their hearts probably forever. We can only answer those questions for ourselves and I have chosen to answer them based on my personal experiences with both of these men.

I have done a lot of soul searching about what I could have done differently. I believe it boils down to two things. Actually, I believe these things can be the best lessons learned from this entire tragedy.

1. If an employee did not display the values that Ken Lay laid out for the Organization, even though they made the company a lot of money, that person should have been removed from Enron.

2. The stock options we all received should have had a much longer vesting period to encourage long-term performance versus short term gain.

In my Human Resource role I was given in late 1999, I could have impacted both of these things much more than I tried to do. For that, I will always feel regret.

But I will never regret the twenty-three years I worked and grew at Enron. I will not regret working with some of the most creative people in the world. I will not regret the experiences that Enron gave us all, or the many employee benefits we offered to all employees. I will never regret working for either Jeff Skilling or Ken Lay. I will not regret loving Enron. All of these things have made me the person I am today and allowed me to find the most positive thing of all—my faith.

Looking Back on the Journey

The saying "hindsight is better than foresight" is certainly accurate for my life. As I look back on all of my life experiences I can clearly see many things that were not evident at the time. There were so many blessings that came my way. Some didn't seem like blessings at the time, but certainly turned out to be in time.

The first blessing was being born into a loving family with parents who encouraged us and loved us very much. You don't get to choose your parents but if I could have, I would have chosen the parents I had. They instilled the moral values that were important in my life. They brought us up with a strong work ethic. We knew we were loved. That solid foundation was so important through out my life.

Then I was blessed with two wonderful siblings. When we were growing up that probably wasn't something I thought about as we had our arguments and my brother, at times, was mean to me. But in time, my brother would be the primary person in my family who would lend his support for what I was going through, and my sister would provide a friendship that a person only hopes to have with a sibling.

I was blessed with a husband who many believed would be the wrong person for me, but turned out in time to be my best friend, my true soul mate and my lover. We would grow to have the kind of relationship that women only dream of.

I was blessed with a fairy tale career at Enron. At the time I thought I was making it all happen myself. I had gotten good at setting goals for every aspect of my life and then achieving them.

In 2001, however, the goals I set for that year included several things that didn't happen because I was simply not in control. Certainly my work related goals had not included Enron's bankruptcy. At the beginning of 2001, I had not planned on finding over one thousand Enron employees jobs in other companies. Our personal goals hadn't included determining what we were going to do without my salary from Enron. Grady had not planned that his company would be struggling to even survive after an acquisition that was supposed to increase profits.

For many years, life seemed perfect. Oh, there were bumps along the way, but nothing that I would consider catastrophic really happened to me. Then in that one year, everything fell apart. What that year taught me is that I am not in control—someone else was definitely in charge of where I was going. That seemed like such a bad thing at the time, but looking back on that now it was truly a blessing.

Since the first day I sat in our church in the Woodlands in 2003 and listened to Dave Andersen preach to me on the teachings of James, I started to understand. It became increasingly clear, as my faith grew, that God was working in my life all along even though I didn't see it. I have also realized that even with God in your life the bad things don't stop happening to you. It's just easier to deal with them because of the help you have from Him.

Finally, I also understand now that you can't be perfect, no matter how hard you try. That is why I need the Lord so badly.

The "bad" things that happen to you aren't a lot of fun. However, without the low places in my life I would not be at this place. I wouldn't have a peace about life. I wouldn't have the strong relationship with my husband. I wouldn't have four dogs to share life with. I wouldn't spend the time and have the incredible relationship with my family that I do. Most importantly, I wouldn't know the Lord.

God truly blessed my life by allowing me to know Ken Lay. The career that I enjoyed at Enron wasn't an accident. It was all a plan so that one day I would be writing this book about a wonderful man who helped lead me to God.

Coming to Aspen many years ago was part of the plan. Not only to get me here to live eventually, but it helped fuel my desire to have that kind of lifestyle that motivated me to achieve success at Enron.

Marrying Grady, although it presented challenges along the way, was a part of the plan. As everything else that I had built my life around crumbled, Grady was there to pick up all of the pieces and share a love that was essential to my recovery. That love would grow stronger than either of us could imagine in only a few years.

Even moving to Omaha those many years ago was definitely God working. The fact that my first boss, at the advertising agency, told me to find something more challenging rather than stay at the agency was a step toward getting me to Omaha. Those things were part of the plan. God was laying the foundation for my career success. I had gotten to know Ken Lay before I ever knew him personally back in Omaha when I was on that strategic committee studying the energy industry mergers.

Nothing was coincidence. The merger of InterNorth and Houston Natural was part of the plan. My career advancements and the challenges I encountered was part of God's plan. The challenges I found when I worked for Stan Horton and Kevin Hannon were blessings that prepared me for the challenges I would have to deal with later as I met with the Labor Department and testified in front of Congress.

My friends at Enron including Mark, Beth, Terrie, Sarah, Bob, Rick, Kevin and the rest of my community relations team were all blessings. Each of them in their own way helped me see something important.

Mark would be there for me always—before and after Enron. Beth showed me the kind of friendship you rarely see in corporate America. Terrie showed me that you can make things happen without treating people badly. Sarah understood as I started my walk with the Lord and was always there to be my friend. Bob would forgive me for the horrible way I had treated him, and actually help me even though I had been so bad to him. He would show me what true forgiveness looks like. Rick would become like family to me and show me how to handle oneself in the midst of adversity. Kevin would reconfirm the importance of my faith by sharing with me his own beliefs. My old community relations team would be there for me any time I asked—true friends always.

Working for Jeff Skilling and the issues I had with him caused me to sell my options and convert my 401(k) before it could be considered as insider trading. The fact that I did not get a bonus to stay at Enron was good for me as I testified in front of Congress.

The fall of Enron, although it created so much loss and pain, was a blessing that allowed Grady and I to experience a more peaceful, content life with our little family of dogs in this incredible place we now call home.

Jake's death, as hard as it was, put our own loss in perspective and caused us to come to church and begin to know the Lord.

So many blessings from God came our way as we were trying to survive the fallout from Grady's company. The refinancing of our property in Houston within a month, the job offer at Colorado Rocky Mountain School, the introduction to the vice president at WestStar through a sale of our bunk beds, and the arrival of our IRS refund sooner than expected were all keys to be able to survive the pressure by Compass Bank.

Having the banker tell us about the other lawsuit they settled allowed us to be able to file our own lawsuit that may ultimately result in the recovery of some of our retirement.

Selling our Houston house for a huge loss was actually a good thing. That allowed us to move forward with life in Colorado and find the church that would provide the kind of support that we truly needed. Moving to Colorado, finding our church and meeting our friends Jim and Pam Alexander are blessings from God and the foundation for our continuing growth in our faith.

Two months after Ken Lay died I lost my two-year-old Great Pyrenees, Tika. We are not really sure how or why she died. She was a blessing for me during a very difficult time in my life, and now she was gone and I was devastated. I literally cried every day after she left us because I missed her so much. I prayed each evening for God to bring her back to me.

In early October 2006, my prayers were answered. A one-and-a-half-year-old Great Pyrenees was advertised as available for adoption at the Aspen Animal Shelter. There were more than twenty people who called about adopting him but he came home with us. Koda is an incredible dog. His previous owners just didn't have the right home for him. He loves our other dogs; he is well trained—doesn't jump on people and has to be invited into the kitchen. He of course will never replace Tika, but he has filled the loss in my heart and has grown to love me like Tika did. I am sure that God again, answered my prayers.

It's hard to see the good in some things that seemed to be all bad at the time. But I now believe that if you look back in your own life, there are blessings in most things that happen.

As our pastor spoke this last Sunday I believed he was speaking right to me again. He was preaching on John 2:1–11. This particular passage is about the first miracle that Jesus performed. He was attending a wedding when they ran out of wine. He turned the water in the stone water jars used for ceremonial washing into wine. When the master of the banquet tasted the wine, he told the bride and bridegroom that unlike other people who bring out the best first, they had in fact saved the best for last.

That's exactly what Jesus does with people's lives. He saves the best for last. I thought I had the best when I worked at Enron and I could buy anything I ever wanted. But I was being taught that addiction to money and success only leaves you with a feeling of wanting more and more—you are never satisfied. With the collapse of Enron, I learned that in fact, the best was yet to come.

This is my story but this book is not about me. It's about how God works in peoples lives. How Jesus saves the best for last. *The Whole Truth...So Help me God* is actually about truth, hope and faith. The truth that God does work in people's lives, the hope that the "bad" things that happen in our lives will actually work out to be blessings, and finally that faith in the Lord comforts you as you live your life.

Epilogue

Through the journey my life has taken me so many things changed; however, the most important change was what I now believe.

- I believe that if you hold tight to the Lord in what ever storm you are going through, you will grow tremendously in your faith.
- I believe that even with a strong faith in the Lord you will go through storms, but that faith comforts you along the way.
- I believe that I can never be perfect, no matter how hard I try, and even though I call myself a Christian I will stumble and the Lord will forgive me and pick me up.
- I believe that the greatest growth in us comes in our darkest hours.
- I believe that the Lord brings you to him with whatever he has to because of his love.
- I believe that God has a plan for each of us and everything works for that good.
- I believe God nudges us along his plan with the people that come into our lives.
- I believe that the rewards in the Kingdom of God are far different from the rewards on earth.

- I believe when your priorities are in the right order life becomes much easier.
- I believe God makes everything beautiful in its time. I believe he saves the best for last.
- I believe that all things are possible with God and everything is a blessing from him.
- I believe that Enron was a great company, and some of the best and brightest worked there.
- I believe that many companies and people projected their own guilt on Enron because it is human nature to point the finger away from yourself.
- I believe in the Justice System of God because with God's judgment the truth will be told.
- I believe in the power of prayer.
- I believe that life with the Lord is what makes us truly rich.

At the writing of this book many convictions related to Enron have been overturned.

All others are currently under appeal. Prosecutorial Misconduct is being used as the basis for some appeals.

The United States Labor Department is investigating me again; after three years from the date of the settlement I originally reached with them in 2004. Maybe it is due to my willingness to help my friends Rick Causey and Ken Lay. Maybe it is because of this book.

History seems to have repeated itself in 2007. As a result of the so-called "sub-prime mortgage crisis," many of the largest financial institutions in the world (including Citigroup, Merrill Lynch and many others) were forced to take enormous losses totaling tens of billions of dollars. Those losses related to their involvement in very large investments in financial instruments associated with the sub-prime mortgages.

As the housing bubble burst, those investments lost significant value. Amazingly, the investments were held in off-balance sheet entities and the financial institutions' investors knew little about them or the risk that remained with the banks.

In addition to incurring huge losses, these banks have now had to consolidate those multi-billion dollar investments on their balance sheets, causing strains on their financial positions. As a result, many banks have been forced to seek outside equity capital from foreign investors, principally from the Middle East and Asia. This entire issue has caused a significant credit crunch which threatens the U.S. economy.

This is a virtual replay of what happened to Enron. Off-balance sheet debt, undisclosed risks resulting in huge losses. The most sophisticated companies in the world seem to have made the same mistakes and followed similar accounting and disclosure practices as we did.

This provides real evidence that so much of what Enron management was accused of was truly standard business practice. The failure of Enron hurt the Houston economy and devastated thousands of people. The sub-prime debacle may result in a world-wide recession and is costing hundreds of thousands of people their homes. There is still so much to learn about these mistakes and, perhaps, a lesson about the conclusions reached regarding Enron.

Finally, for those readers who might say, "Well no wonder she believes, all she has left is her faith." Or other readers who are still not convinced that God has a plan for each of us. A plan that is truly better than we could ever imagine. You should know that not being able to sell our Colorado house in 2002 was another blessing from the Lord. That Colorado property today has appreciated almost enough to make up for the financial loss that we suffered after Enron. Thanks only to the grace of God are we able to live in this truly beautiful place that God has made.

Index

Ken Lay
Jeff Skilling
Rick Causey
Andy Fastow
Mark Frevert
Mark Koenig
Kevin Hannon
Greg Whalley
Beth Tilney
Jim Alexander
Pam Alexander
Joe Sutton
Rebecca Mark
Joe Nieto
Jake Nieto
Dave Andersen
Mark Rae
Terry Maner
Chuck Radda
Melinda Tossoni
Jim Prentice
King Oberg
Senator Waxman
Lynn Brewer
Senator Joe Lieberman

John Boehner
Jeff McMahon
Cliff Baxter
Dave Duncan
Ben Glissan
Rick Buy
Bill Strauss
Linda Lay
Sam Segnar
Casey Olson
Ron Burns
Rick Richard
Jim Rogers
Rod Hayslett
John Katzenback
Steve Kean
Mark Palmer
Lou Pai
Drayton McLane
Joe Sutton
Chuck Watson
Rosalie Flemming
Nancy McNeil
Terrie James
Sarah Davis
Bob Sparger
Leslie Perlman
Rich Kinder
Miki Rath
Cynthia Barrow
Naomi Hall
Steve Rogers

Grady Olson

Sherron Watkins

Robert Jones

Dennis Rader

Dan Ryser

Wayne Thompkins

Gordon Bethune

Jackie Martin

Clyde Drexler

George W. Bush

George and Barbara Bush

Carl Lewis

Troy Aikman

Elizabeth Dole

Henry Kissinger

Oprah Winfrey

Bobbie Power

Scott McNeally

Denny Dent

Margaret Ceconi

Jesse Jackson

Jim Gramke

Paul Newman

John Hueston

Herb Kelleher

Stephen Cooper

Jake

Chelsea

Tika

16B Insider

Tittle Lawsuit

Newby Lawsuit

United States Department of Labor
Delta Gamma
Pizza Hut
Koch Oil Company
InterNorth
Houston Natural Gas
Transwestern
Florida Gas
Enron Capital & Trade
Interstate Pipeline Group
Aspen Racing and Sports Car Club
Quality Transportation Services
Northern Natural Gas
Colorado Rocky Mountain School
Juvenile Diabetes
Search
United Way
Alley Theatre
Cosmopolitan Club
Pepsico
General Electric
Governor's Business Council
Greater Houston Partnership
Committee to Encourage Corporate Philanthropy
FBI
United States Justice Department
Global Galactic Agreement
Compass Bank
BTK Killer
United States Chamber of Commerce
Enron Energy Services
Enron Broadband